"Out of the softening sunset came the airship, and the manner of its moving was beautiful. Few inanimate objects attain beauty in the pursuance of their courses, and yet, to me, at least, the flight of the ship was far lovelier than the swooping of a bird or the jumping of a horse. For it seemed to carry with it a calm dignity and a consciousness of destiny which ranked it among the wonders of time itself."

— From *Even the Birds*, 1934

HINDENBURG
AN ILLUSTRATED HISTORY

Text by Rick Archbold ~ Paintings by Ken Marschall

❧

HISTORICAL CONSULTANTS:
Dennis R. Kromm, Dr. Henry Cord Meyer, John Provan

A WEIDENFELD & NICOLSON/MADISON PRESS BOOK

Published in Great Britain in 1994 by
Weidenfeld & Nicolson
The Orion Publishing Group Ltd
Orion House
5 Upper Saint Martin's Lane
London WC2H 9EA

A catalogue reference is available from the British Library.

ISBN 0 297 81423 0

Produced by
Madison Press Books
40 Madison Avenue
Toronto, Ontario
Canada
M5R 2S1

Printed in Italy

To my parents,

who've helped me fly

high and travel far

Pages 2–3: The *Hindenburg*'s first season found
her soaring above Berlin's Olympic stadium in time
for the opening of the 1936 summer games.

Page 5: The *Hindenburg*'s huge tail fins loom
over ground crew and sightseers at New Jersey's
Lakehurst Naval Air Station as the navy airship
Los Angeles lies moored to her mast in the distance.

Pages 6–7: Navy personnel and hired civilians
strain against the spider lines as the *Hindenburg*
is pulled to earth during a 1936 landing.

Page 9: The *Hindenburg* hovers over the Lakehurst
airfield on May 6, 1937, moments before the fire
that ended the era of the great passenger airships.

CONTENTS

PROLOGUE

Thursday, May 6, 1937

BY MIDAFTERNOON THE CROWD AT NEW JERSEY'S LAKEHURST Naval Air Station was growing impatient. Many had arrived early that morning to meet the *Hindenburg* at the end of her first flight of the 1937 season. But the huge German airship had encountered strong head winds over the Atlantic, delaying her well past her scheduled 6:00 A.M. arrival. The passengers who expected to be boarding that evening for the return trip to Frankfurt began to wonder whether they would take off on time. If not, it would be a rare exception to an already impressive performance record.

In contrast to the rapturous reception given the *Hindenburg* on her maiden flight a year earlier, this time the Americans seemed almost blasé about her arrival. What had once appeared marvelous was now merely routine. The airship's comings and goings were listed in the *New York Times* as matter-of-factly as the sailings of an ocean liner. Most of the reporters on hand were local stringers for the big city papers, which hadn't even bothered to send someone to cover the story. Only the newsreel cameramen and a few still photographers made a press presence. The year before, a whole bank of phones had been insufficient to cope with the crowd of reporters representing practically every major daily in the country. This year a handful would do.

Reaching this point of public acceptance had been a long time coming for the rigid airship—almost forty years. Since the first experimental flights in southern Germany at the turn of the century, these strangely graceful envelopes of buoyant gas had seen many ups and downs and had more than their share of spectacular mishaps. The most successful French-owned airship had exploded in the air. All three American-built rigids had crashed. And of the two passenger-size airships built by the British, one had met disaster on her maiden voyage and the other had managed a single return trip across the Atlantic before being broken up and sold for scrap. Many lives had been lost in the pursuit of the elusive dream of safe, reliable lighter-than-air flight.

Now only the Germans still piloted these serene giants through the world's skies. Somehow they had avoided the disasters of other nations, despite the fact that their ships were inflated with hydrogen. The most buoyant lifting gas known was also highly flammable, potentially explosive. Yet when it came to carrying passengers, German zeppelins had a perfect safety record that stretched all the way back to before World War I.

Just before 4:00 P.M., a newsreel cameraman shouted, "There she is!" Those who had been lolling in the grass scrambled to their feet. The crowd, perhaps a thousand sightseers, relatives and friends, pushed forward toward the fence that kept them from the landing area.

And there indeed she was, coming in low from the north, her vast silvery bulk shifting hue with the changing colors of the troubled spring sky. Any sense of nonchalance instantly vanished. Even if you had seen the *Hindenburg* before, you could not fail to be moved. Her sheer size, her stately, inexorable progress, her elegant, streamlined shape—even the ugly black swastikas emblazoned on her tail fins—simply took your breath away.

The deep drone of the four big diesel motors grew louder as the *Hindenburg* sailed overhead without pausing, her passengers waving gaily from the open promenade windows. Inside the control car the ship's uniformed officers could be glimpsed attending to their tasks. For a moment the airship blotted out the sky. Then she moved on, the hum of her engines growing dimmer and the great shape gradually smaller.

Reporters groaned, spectators murmured restlessly, children loudly asked their parents where the *Hindenburg* was going and why she wasn't landing. The weather wasn't good enough, parents answered. The captain would wait for the approaching thunderstorm to pass, for the wind to die down. Then, in another hour or two, surely no longer than that, the zeppelin would reappear from the sky and float down to the ground so gently that it would seem possible to stop the largest aircraft that had ever flown with a single finger.

THE "FOOLISH COUNT"

"In the long, sun-bathed Brazilian afternoons, when the hum of insects, punctuated by the far-off cry of some bird, lulled me, I would lie in the shade of the verandah and gaze into the fair sky of Brazil, where the birds fly so high and soar with such ease on their great out-stretched wings, where the clouds mount so gaily in the pure light of day, and you have only to raise your eyes to fall in love with space and freedom. So, musing on the exploration of the vast aerial ocean, I, too, devised air-ships and flying machines in my imagination."

— Alberto Santos-Dumont

"My system is the best, the only conceivable one for military purposes and, if airships are possible at all, then mine are possible."

— Count Ferdinand von Zeppelin

THE SMALL BALLOON ROSE EFFORTLESSLY in the intense heat of the midsummer day. One of its passengers, a young man with a clipped mustache and bushy side-whiskers, watched intently as the frontier settlement of St. Paul, Minnesota, grew smaller below him. He had seen such bird's-eye views climbing the Alps across the border from his native town of Konstanz on the Bodensee (Lake Constance) in southern Germany. But never had he experienced this magical sensation of effortlessly defying gravity. The sense of freedom was something entirely new.

At close to seven hundred feet, the balloon jerked gently to a halt. It had reached the limit of the rope tethers that anchored it to the ground.

Abruptly the young man forgot the initial thrill of buoyant flight and began to survey the surrounding landscape with the practiced eye of a German military officer. He had already observed such balloons used to reconnoiter enemy positions in the War Between the States. This one was, in fact, a military balloon until recently in use by the Union army.

From his aerial vantage point he had a commanding view of the Mississippi River. Beyond the river to the west, the valley sloped up toward a ridge of hills. He imagined himself as part of an attacking force advancing toward a defensive position on the slope of the ridge. In a letter written to his father later that day he concluded, "No method is better suited to viewing quickly the terrain of an unknown, enemy-occupied position."

The twenty-five-year-old who wrote these warlike words was Count Ferdinand von Zeppelin. What was the young German aristocrat doing so far from home? Officially he was on a year's leave from his position as a junior officer in the Württemberg army to observe the American Civil War. But after less than two months with the Union army, the count had set off to take a firsthand look at the American frontier—a journey that eventually took him to St. Paul. The date of his first experience of lighter-than-air flight was August 19, 1863.

A number of Zeppelin's biographers would later claim that it was during this first ascent that he formed the idea for the invention that would one day make him famous. Certainly it is tempting to imagine the future

Count Zeppelin (pictured opposite as he looked in 1863) got his first taste of buoyant flight in a tethered balloon similar to those used by the Union army during the American Civil War (left, top and bottom). Zeppelin arrived in St. Paul, Minnesota, following an adventurous canoe trip with

a couple of well-heeled Russians and two native American guides (above). Zeppelin is the one resting a rifle jauntily on his shoulder.

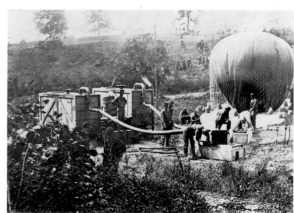

inventor of the rigid airship surveying the landscape from his lofty perch and immediately visualizing the potential for turning this unsteerable balloon into a fully controllable aircraft that could carry passengers and cargo over great distances. But there is no mention in his personal diaries of such forethoughts. Apart from professional interest the balloon ride was simply one more adventure during a year away from the constraints of a junior officer's life. Probably he thought nothing more of the incident for a long time. However, he *had* experienced the thrill of escaping the earth's pull. Perhaps that was the seed that would later germinate into a hardy plant.

Long before Count Zeppelin's first balloon flight, aerial pioneers had sought to solve the problem of dirigibility: to build a steerable aircraft. Lighter-than-air craft had been around since 1783, when two French paper manufacturers, Joseph and Etienne Montgolfier, sent the first hot-air balloon soaring into the skies just south of Lyons, France. The same

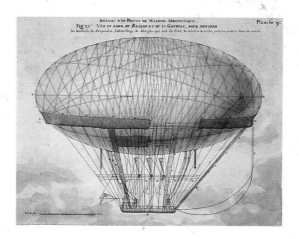

(Opposite) In 1783 the Montgolfier brothers launched the first of their many hot-air balloons. That same year Jean-Baptiste-Marie Meusnier conceived an egg-shaped dirigible (above) with an internal air bladder—or ballonet—to compensate for changes in gas pressure.

year a French army engineer designed a theoretically workable dirigible—an elongated balloon. Unfortunately the engine that would make guided flight practical had not yet been invented. Subsequent dirigible designs called for everything from muscle-powered air oars to harnessed teams of vultures as means of propulsion. Although primitive steam engines existed in 1783, they were only suitable for simple earthbound tasks like pumping water.

A more easily mastered challenge for dirigible designers was the problem of "pressure height," which was discovered by the earliest balloonists using hydrogen instead of hot air for lift. (The first hydrogen balloon, built by a French physicist named Jacques Charles, flew the same year as the Montgolfiers' creation.) To be effective, a hydrogen balloon had to be as gastight as possible. However, the higher it rose and the more the surrounding atmospheric pressure diminished, the more the gas expanded. The highest point a gastight

Balloons pulled by birds, balloons sailed like ships— early dirigible designers envisioned every imaginable means of propulsion. Jean-Pierre Blanchard, who made the first crossing of the English Channel in 1785 (right), found his air oars were useless and chucked them overboard when his balloon began to sink.

Henri Giffard's pioneering dirigible, which made history's first powered flight in 1852, could achieve a top speed of six miles per hour.

envelope could reach without exploding was pressure height. During a flight on July 6, 1784, the Duke of Chartres saved his balloon from bursting by poking a hole through the rubber-sealed silk to allow gas to escape. Subsequent balloons and airships adopted valves that would vent excess lifting gas once pressure height was exceeded.

The first airship that actually worked—up to a point—sprang from the brain of Henri Giffard, the French inventor of the steam injector. He developed a steam engine weighing only 250 pounds—but that didn't count the boiler or the coke required to fire it! It generated an anemic three horsepower, but in September 1852 he used it to fly a 144-foot-long

balloon, sharply pointed at both ends, from the Paris Hippodrome. Not surprisingly, the craft was steerable only in still air. In even the lightest breeze it could manage but a slow circle. As a result, Giffard's invention went nowhere.

The problem that defeated Giffard was the same one that would haunt all the early airships: the weight of any engine powerful enough to buck more than a moderate breeze consumed too much of the "useful lift"—the lifting power that remains when the fixed weight of the airship and its engines is subtracted from the total lifting power of the gas. Only the development of light, efficient internal-combustion engines for automobiles in the final decades of the nineteenth century would make airships truly practical. These engines also ensured the eventual success of the airship's heavier-than-air competitor, the airplane, whose development was still a long way off. In 1863 neither of the Wright brothers had even been born.

ONCE HIS YEAR'S LEAVE WAS UP, COUNT ZEPPELIN DUTIFULLY returned to his regiment. In 1865, while still only a lieutenant, he went to the royal court at Stuttgart as a military aide to King Karl I of Württemberg. Zeppelin's family enjoyed a long and close association with the rulers of this southern German kingdom. His grandfather had served King Karl's grandfather as both a soldier and diplomat during the ticklish Napoleonic period. In the 1870s, when the heir apparent, Prince Wilhelm, turned rebellious and began to talk of refusing to accept the throne, Count Zeppelin became his personal military attaché, given the job of bringing the young man to his senses. He succeeded, and the count and Prince Wilhelm remained friends for life.

Württemberg remained loyal to the Hapsburg Empire during the 1866 war between Austria and Prussia, but Zeppelin accepted the Prussian victory and fought enthusiastically during the Franco-Prussian War of 1870–71. To this conflict he owed one of the more enduring legends about his career.

The day war was declared he volunteered to lead a reconnoitering party into enemy territory to scout the positions of the French army. During this mad dash on horseback into Alsace, he displayed his complete lack of physical fear, his passion for action—and a certain tendency toward rashness. Even after he had gathered the essential intelligence he pushed on, wanting to learn more about enemy movements. On the second night, French cavalry units surprised his party while it was resting briefly at a farm. Zeppelin realized they faced overwhelmingly superior forces. He leapt on a Frenchman's horse and led a desperate retreat. The count became separated from his men, most of whom were captured. Only he escaped back to Germany.

At the time this exploit drew criticism from his superiors, but it earned him a reputation for courage under fire that became part of the heroic image he acquired later in life. He was, however, a far more complicated figure than this story of youthful derring-do suggests.

Zeppelin was very much a man of his class and time—a provincial aristocrat devoted to his military career—yet also something more. As a boy, when most of his contemporaries learned Greek and Latin and read the classics, he was more interested in science and engineering. As an adult he seldom hesitated to question the conventional way of doing things, while never doubting the hierarchical social order that placed him near the top. For example, he returned from the United States impressed with the virtues of its more individualistic citizen army—views that did not endear him to the Prussian military establishment. His great-grandson Albrecht, the current Count von Brandenstein-Zeppelin, relates one example of the count's willingness to buck convention. In the Prussian army an officer never climbed a tree to reconnoiter the landscape himself; he always sent up a subordinate. Count Zeppelin insisted on seeing the lay of the land with his own eyes and wasn't worried about the loss of face this might imply. Such behavior seems only to have endeared him to his men. Whatever his faults, there is little question that he was a remarkably charismatic man who inspired great respect, even devotion, among those who knew and worked with him.

Zeppelin was not afraid to hold fast to an unpopular position or risk ridicule if he believed he was right. Otherwise his first airship would surely never have been built. According to Henry Cord Meyer, in his book *Airshipmen, Businessmen and Politics*, this single-mindedness could have an unpleasant side, leading to "petulant impatience, peevish stubbornness, occasional flashes of anger when crossed, and resistance to accepting advice from those more sophisticated or technically competent." In sum, Count Ferdinand von Zeppelin was a charming, self-confident and intelligent man with a will of iron and a secure social position to back him up. A very potent combination, but hardly the typical résumé for a famous inventor.

Yet somewhere between his balloon ascent in Minnesota in 1863 and March 1874, when he first put down some ideas in his diary under the heading, "Thoughts about an airship," Zeppelin had developed a visionary concept for a dirigible with a rigid framework and multiple gas cells. This came at a moment in history when virtually no airships had been built since Henri Giffard's pioneering but inadequate contraption of 1852.

"The craft must have the dimensions of a large ship," the count wrote. "The gas volume so calculated that the weight of the craft would be supported except for a slight excess. Elevation will then be obtained by starting the engine, which will drive the craft, as it were, towards the upward-inclined wings. Having attained the desired altitude, the wings will tend to flatten out so that the airship remains on a horizontal plane. To descend, the wing surfaces will be flattened out still further or speed will be reduced. . . . The gas compartment should, whenever possible, be divided into cells which can be filled and emptied individually."

Count Zeppelin had solved, at least theoretically, an essential airship design problem: how to make a craft big enough to carry a useful load of passengers and cargo. In the nonrigid designs of his day, there soon came a point when what was essentially an elongated balloon tended to buckle under structural and aerodynamic stresses. Zeppelin realized that a rigid framework would permit a ship of greater size and therefore a much greater volume of lifting gas—as long as a light and strong material could be found for the frame. Since the lifting capacity of an airship increases with the cube of its dimensions, each increase in size would pay a big dividend in lift.

What is remarkable about Zeppelin's diary entry of 1874 and the other notes and sketches that followed is how closely they describe the dirigibles he ultimately built. According to airship historian Douglas Robinson, at one point the count wrote of "a ship of 706,200 cubic feet capacity, with cabins for 20 passengers, together with cargo and mail holds under the hull, which would be a rigid structure made up of rings and longitudinals. (The short-range passenger Zeppelin *Bodensee* of 1919 carried twenty to twenty-four passengers and had this exact gas volume.) There were to be 18 gas cells, and a fabric outer cover."

Zeppelin soon abandoned the wrong-headed idea of keeping the ship aloft by means of lifting surfaces, or wings—the basic principle of heavier-than-air flight. But, as Robinson points out, the "other distinguishing features—the large dimensions, the separate gas cells and fabric outer cover—were unique in Zeppelins, and in almost all other rigid airships, to the very end." On the question of how to power the ship, the young inventor was silent. An adequate internal-combustion engine had not yet been developed.

Where did this gifted amateur gain the expertise to concoct such a farsighted scheme? The answer is unknown. His one year of engineering studies at the University of Tübingen hardly qualified him as a leading aeronautical designer. Thousands of others had taken a brief ride in a balloon. And legions of German soldiers had, like him, witnessed the performance of the French balloons during the siege of Paris in 1870, successfully carrying messages to French troops.

For the next decade the count kept his thoughts about a giant airship to himself while he continued to rise through the ranks of the Prussian-led German imperial army. In 1879 his wife, Isabella, gave birth to their only child, a daughter named Hella. His military career seemed secure. In 1882 he gained command of a full regiment; two years later he achieved the rank of colonel. Thoughts of airships were probably put aside. Then, in 1884, Germany's archrival flew a dirigible called *La France*.

La France's designers were two members of the French army's balloon corps, Captain Charles Renard and his assistant, Captain Arthur Krebs, and the ship was financed by the French government. Under the power of an electric motor (the batteries alone weighed more than half a ton each) the

La France (left and opposite), which first flew in August 1884, was propelled by an electric motor and represented a modest step forward from previous dirigible designs. When Gottlieb Daimler invented the first lightweight internal-combustion engine only two years later, practical powered flight suddenly became possible.

nonrigid airship achieved an aeronautical first: she returned to her starting point *against* the wind. But her top speed was a mere fourteen miles per hour—making her steerable only in light breezes—and her endurance was severely limited by the short life of her heavy batteries.

Early rumors about the new French airship exaggerated her performance and military usefulness, which ultimately proved to be nil. But in the patriotic mind of Count Zeppelin, Germany's traditional enemy had suddenly gained a dangerous advantage. And in his airship—until now conceived as a passenger craft—he saw the means for Germany to gain mastery of the air. Soon he found himself in a more influential position from which to promote this belief. In 1885 he was appointed military attaché to the Württemberg embassy in Berlin. (Despite German unification, Württemberg still retained considerable independence and sent an ambassador to the capital.) Two years later, when the ambassador suddenly died, Zeppelin was appointed in his place. It was then that he chose to act.

He sent a long memorandum to his old friend King Wilhelm of Württemberg, urging a program of airship development for military

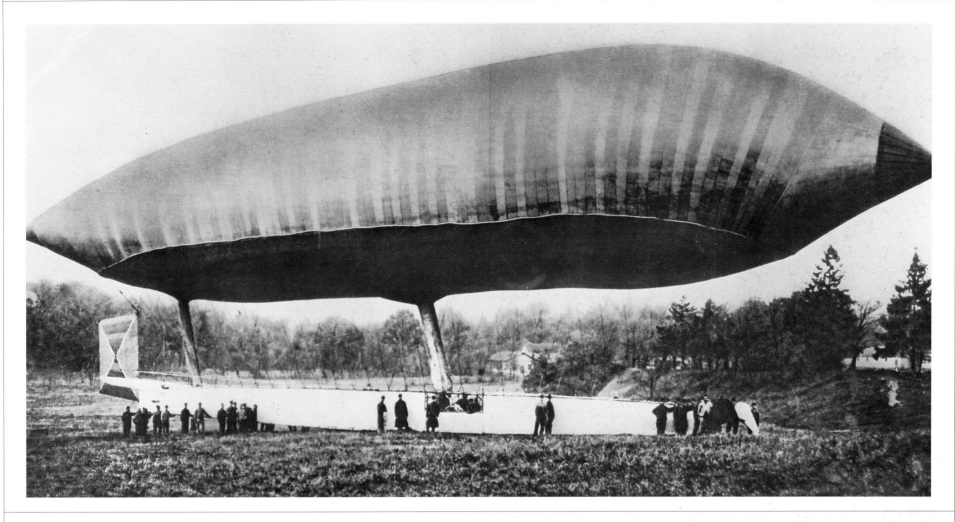

purposes and describing the type of aircraft he had in mind. "It should have a very large carrying capacity," he wrote, "in order to carry personnel, cargo or explosive shells. All three requirements demand a very large gas volume, hence a very large airship." While the memo also mentioned the civilian possibilities of dirigibles, Zeppelin's primary motivation was now military. A rigid airship was needed as a weapon to defend the fatherland.

At this time the count seems to have given no thought to building such an airship himself. In Berlin he had his hands full promoting Württemberg's interests without offending Prussian sensibilities—a task that ultimately proved impossible for someone so staunchly loyal to his region. In particular he objected to the erosion of the autonomy of Württemberg's army and he resented the fact that a Prussian officer was always placed in its command. He said as much in a secret memorandum to Kaiser Wilhelm II in early 1890, soon after resigning his ambassadorial post to return to his first love, military command.

The emperor was not amused, nor were the members of the Prussian general staff, and Zeppelin's return to soldiering was brief. After the annual autumn maneuvers of 1890, he was removed from the command of his cavalry brigade for allegedly failing to adequately carry out the assigned exercise. In the face of this disgrace, the count had no honorable option but to resign from the Württemberg army and retire from military life.

In fact, the count had performed as well as or better than many others during the annual exercises. According to August von Parseval, who later developed the nonrigid Parseval airship for the German military, "it was a great blow to him and a surprise to all those who appreciated his military talents. One can imagine, however, that a man with such independent views, which were not always in agreement with the conventionally accepted maxims, might have been an inconvenient subordinate for the Powers that were in command."

And so, at age fifty-two, at what should have been the peak of his career, Count Ferdinand von Zeppelin found himself without a purpose in life. It was a traumatic experience, even for one so well-placed and so self-possessed. But he was not the sort of man to sit passively in the provinces awaiting his dotage. Since his chosen career had ended so prematurely, he would create a new one. He would design and build the great airship he had until now only dreamed about.

BY 1890 THE DREAM OF DIRIGIBILITY HAD BARELY ADVANCED SINCE *La France*'s first flight of 1884. But that situation was about to change. In 1886 Gottlieb Daimler finally perfected a gasoline engine that drastically reduced the crucial ratio of weight to horsepower. At last the technology existed to make a truly steerable balloon a reality. Over the next fifteen years inventors in France and Germany vied to be the first to build a practical airship. But of these aeronautical visionaries, Count Zeppelin was one of the few who set out to develop a rigid structure for his craft, a task that presented many additional engineering problems, not the least of which was building a framework strong enough to support the airship's cover and carry its engines but light enough to leave ample lift for crew, weapons or cargo.

Not being an engineer himself, the count searched for a talented young professional who shared his optimism. The man he found was Theodor Kober, who had previously worked for a German balloon maker. With the applied science of engineering still in its infancy, and aeronautical engineering not yet out of the cradle, Kober had almost as much to learn as his employer. Luckily his first design never got past the drawing board. Kober had conceived an amazingly impractical "aerial express train," in which a motorized dirigible towed a string of unpowered balloons carrying passengers and cargo. In 1894 a scientific commission, grudgingly appointed by the kaiser at the urging of the king of Württemberg, examined the designs and rejected them outright.

Undeterred, Zeppelin revised the plans and tried again. This time he proposed a single ship with a stronger frame. But again a scientific commission turned him down. The integrity of the framework remained highly dubious, they concluded, and the count's claims for his ship's maximum speed were clearly exaggerated. In all likelihood an inventor who lacked his military background and royal connections would not even have received this second hearing. Nonetheless, the count pressed on.

During the long ordeal of the 1890s Count Zeppelin proved his remarkable strength of character. The well-born former military officer and diplomat became a figure of local ridicule. His aristocratic contemporaries called him the "foolish count." "This was the period in which the count was publicly derided as a lunatic and names were shouted at him from the streets of Stuttgart," wrote biographer Hugo Eckener. More than once, Zeppelin was on the point of abandoning his dream, but he always found a reason to continue. Finally the first small glimmer of hope came

COUNT FERDINAND VON ZEPPELIN

This image of Count Ferdinand von Zeppelin has the quality of an icon, something he had most definitely become by the end of his life. It evokes the steely determination that helped Zeppelin triumph against enormous odds. Undoubtedly he owed much of his strong sense of self to his idyllic childhood, spent on the family estate of Girsberg near Lake Constance, and to his close relationship with both his father and his mother. But even as a boy, he had to overcome adversity. His "best of mothers" died when he was thirteen, and for a time he was determined to become a missionary. Later, as a young military officer, he fell in love with one of his cousins, and was devastated when her mother refused them permission to marry. When at age thirty-one he finally chose a wife, he chose wisely. According to biographer Hugo Eckener, Zeppelin's marriage to Baroness Isabella von Wolff "developed into a true life-companionship and one which stood the hardest tests the future held in store."

in the form of a cautious endorsement from the Union of German Engineers in 1896.

Meanwhile, competing airships in various nations were moving from blueprints to the test stage. In May 1897 a former German pastor named Dr. Karl Woelfert took flight in the first dirigible to employ one of Daimler's new motors, which, unfortunately, ran with an exposed flame. Moments after takeoff it exploded and burned, killing Woelfert and his mechanic. This was an early demonstration of the risks of juxtaposing flammable gasoline with hydrogen, which when mixed with air becomes highly explosive.

If this disaster gave Zeppelin pause, there is no record of it. A few months later, he learned with interest of the first test flight of an airship created by a German timber merchant named David Schwarz. Schwarz had died suddenly the previous January, but his wife saw his project through with the help of industrialist Carl Berg, who was pioneering the manufacture of aluminum. Built of thin sheets of this unprecedentedly light but strong metal riveted to an aluminum frame and filled with hydrogen, this airship was arguably the first true rigid dirigible. Almost as soon as it rose in the air, the awkward craft (it looked like something designed by the Tin Man in *The Wizard of Oz*) developed problems with its forward propellers. The pilot, a military balloonist, panicked, opened the gas valve to let off hydrogen and crashed the ship to the ground, wrecking it beyond repair. The pilot survived uninjured, but the Schwarz airship never flew again.

Zeppelin was later accused of stealing Schwarz's designs, but the only thing he seems to have gained from this mishap was the knowledge that aluminum's combination of strength and lightness made it ideal for building airships. In 1898 he combined forces with aluminum maker Carl Berg to form a joint stock company for airship construction. Several other wealthy businessmen invested, but Zeppelin put up half of the original 800,000 marks of capital from his private fortune. Soon workers were busy building a large floating wooden shed on Lake Constance near the village of Manzell, just west of Friedrichshafen. The count's family castle of Girsberg, where he had spent his boyhood, was not far away.

Before long the aluminum girders for the airship began arriving by train from Carl Berg's factory at Lüdenscheid near the industrial Ruhr Valley. Because it was a prototype, its construction proceeded very much by trial and error. *Luftschiff Zeppelin One* (*LZ 1*) would take two years to build.

Work on the *LZ 1* had barely begun when word reached Manzell that a dandyish young Brazilian millionaire had briefly steered a pint-sized, elongated balloon with a propeller for a few minutes over Paris. Almost certainly the count was unperturbed. This ship was nothing to worry

David Schwarz's light metal airship (left) flew only once, but it gave Count Zeppelin the idea of using aluminum for the rigid framework of the *LZ 1*, pictured below at a late stage of construction.

In 1901 Alberto Santos-Dumont won the Deutsch Prize on his third attempt with the sixth airship he had built. On his second try, the *Santos-Dumont No. 5* had struck the roof of the Trocadero Hotel and exploded, but he managed to leap to a window ledge and was rescued by the Paris fire department. In the years following his triumph he became famous for stunts such as landing on the Champs Elysées for an afternoon drink at his favorite café.

about. And so it proved. The dashing Alberto Santos-Dumont deserves credit for building the first dirigible that could maneuver in more than a light breeze. And he went on to build a series of more successful airships over the next few years, making himself a French idol and an international celebrity. His most famous exploit came in 1901 when he piloted the *Santos-Dumont No. 6* from St. Cloud to the Eiffel Tower and back in thirty minutes, thus winning the Deutsch Prize with its very rich purse of 100,000 francs ($20,000). But his nonrigid ships were never big enough or fast enough to be much more than expensive playthings. Meanwhile, Count Zeppelin's vicissitudes on the shores of Lake Constance were beginning to attract attention.

ON THE AFTERNOON OF OCTOBER 17, 1900, THIRTY-TWO-YEAR-old Dr. Hugo Eckener rose from his studies unusually early. He was finally making real progress on his book about the economics of capitalism, but it could wait. He donned his long gray autumn coat and a soft hat, then left his comfortable house on the outskirts of Friedrichshafen. As he turned his steps west toward Manzell, he automatically sniffed the air and eyed the sky over Lake Constance. (Once a sailor always a sailor—and he had spent the happiest days of his youth piloting small sailboats in the Baltic Sea off his native Flensburg.) The weather was fine for mid-October in southern Germany—clear and sunny with only a slight breeze blowing. It appeared the weather gods were smiling on that eccentric local figure, Count Zeppelin, for the second flight of the *LZ 1*.

On her maiden flight back in early July, the *LZ 1* had dazzled the thousands of spectators who lined the shores of Lake Constance as the 416-foot-long cylinder rose slowly from the water with the diminutive sixty-two-year-old count at the wheel. Military observers on hand for the occasion were less impressed. After only eighteen minutes aloft, technical problems forced the ship to land on the water. During the short flight in calm weather the frame buckled slightly and the ship proved awkward, slow and difficult to maneuver—but she had flown.

The first zeppelin, *LZ 1*, begins her maiden flight on July 2, 1900.

Now the indefatigable former cavalry officer was trying again.

Eckener had not witnessed the first flight. In July, he had taken time away from his book to go on a yachting vacation on his beloved Baltic. But he had been impressed by the newspaper accounts of the *LZ 1*'s ascent, and of her tireless inventor. He wasn't, however, much interested in the pioneer airship. Technology was not his thing. He was off to observe the second flight only because he'd been commissioned to cover it for the *Frankfurter Zeitung*. Occasionally he wrote articles on economics for that prominent German newspaper. Since the editors didn't consider the second flight of the *LZ 1* worth the expense of sending down a regular reporter, they'd asked Eckener to take on the job.

The ordinary citizens of Friedrichshafen were out in force, streaming along the lakeshore. To them Zeppelin was not the "foolish count" as many still called him, but a visionary and a great patriot. Eckener finally found a suitable spot to set up his telescope. He watched as the little steamer *Buchorn* panted its way to the floating hangar and slowly began to tow the ship from her lair. To borrow a phrase from Ernst Lehmann, later to become a zeppelin captain, "it looked like a gigantic caterpillar slowly creeping forward."

Tiny figures now swarmed over the long raft on which the hydrogen-filled caterpillar rested. One of the tiniest was Count Zeppelin himself. Eckener could just make out his great white moustache and the white cap perched jauntily on his head. He looked for all the world like a wealthy yachtsman out for a pleasure sail on the lake. But a great deal of money and prestige rested on this cruise. The capital of the joint stock company was long exhausted, and all the partners had been required to put up further money to complete the ship. Success was imperative.

Across the still water came a series of coughs and splutters as the airship's two sixteen-horsepower Daimler engines came reluctantly to life. Then, all at once, the giant caterpillar became a butterfly, rising gently, gracefully. The crowd of onlookers cheered, temporarily drowning out the insistent thudding of the motors. As the chorus died, the *LZ 1* sailed off toward the middle of the lake. An hour and thirty minutes later, after a

The first flight of the *LZ 1* (above) took place from the Bay of Manzell, which is clearly visible in the modern photograph of Friedrichshafen at left. (It is the second bay beyond the town.) The airship's floating hangar (below) was towed from shore out into the bay and faced into the wind before launching. The inset (opposite) shows the later *LZ 3* passing over the old palace church, which still stands today.

mechanic accidentally put water into one of the fuel tanks, shutting down the motor, the airship landed gently on her raft and was towed slowly back to the shed.

"Certainly the airship proved itself maneuverable," Eckener wrote. "Amid cheers, it rose calmly and majestically into the air. It hovered over the lake, making small turns about its vertical axis. It also turned slightly about its horizontal axis, remaining steady and calm, always at about the same height and above the same place. . . ." That was all the good that could be said, however: "There was no question of the airship flying for any appreciable distance or hovering at various altitudes. One had the feeling that they were very happy to balance up there so nicely, and indeed the fine equilibrium of the airship was the most successful aspect of the whole affair. But under what circumstances were the modest results, which I have described, achieved? Under the best possible conditions—an almost complete calm!"

Eckener went on to question whether the apparent maneuverability of the ship was, in fact, nothing more than the result of slight shifts in the air currents over the lake. He criticized the device for controlling altitude, arguing that a rudderlike apparatus would surely work much

In 1900, Ludwig Dürr was a twenty-two-year-old assistant to the *LZ 1*'s designer, Theodor Kober, but he went on to become the Zeppelin Company's chief designer, responsible for the building of 118 rigid airships. A Swabian who never traveled far from his south German homeland, Dürr was a shy and difficult man, stubborn in his beliefs and reluctant to listen to other people's ideas. But he was fiercely loyal to Count Zeppelin and his vision.

better than the heavy weight that slid along a cable stretched between the forward and aft gondolas. Furthermore, the ship clearly needed more power and better steering. All in all it was an interesting experiment but hardly very promising. Eckener sent off his article and promptly forgot about Count Zeppelin's curious experiments.

The *LZ 1* flew a third time on October 20 for twenty-three minutes, managing to reach a speed of seventeen miles per hour. That, at least, was encouraging. But the rest of the story of the first rigid airship is one of anticlimax. Count Zeppelin's dream had flown, but without a clear destination visible on the horizon. He disbanded the company that had built the ship, assumed the assets himself, had the floating shed towed ashore and told his workers to take the *LZ 1* apart. He let all but three of his employees go—two nightwatchmen to guard the airship's bones and a young engineer named Ludwig Dürr. He had not given up quite yet.

Count Zeppelin seems to have been profoundly depressed by the sad end of his first "success." The ship had flown, but not well enough to attract the financial backing of the German military for a new and improved model. In a letter to a sick friend he wrote, "I, too, have become an invalid: my heart is broken." But he was not the sort of man to stay down for long.

For succor he turned to his best friend in high places, King Wilhelm of Württemberg. Wilhelm had not forgotten Count Zeppelin's guidance during his days as the doubting young crown prince. Now he repaid the older man by organizing a state lottery that brought in 124,000 marks. The Prussians reluctantly anted up a paltry 50,000. That left the count to find more than 200,000 marks himself. He talked Carl Berg into donating the aluminum and Gottlieb Daimler into giving him new engines. Then he persuaded his wife to mortgage part of her family's estate in what is now Latvia.

One learns little of Zeppelin's wife, Isabella von Wolff, in the standard airship histories. There is some suggestion that she actively encouraged her husband to pursue his airship vision when he was forced to retire from the army. And even after more than a decade of great expense with little to show for it, she was willing to draw on her own money to support her husband's obsession. Her great-grandson Albrecht recalls that during this early period, when Zeppelin persisted against all the odds, the local people began to make jokes about the long-suffering countess. "Oh, yes, his poor wife," they would say. "What does she do all day?" "Why, she sits sewing covers for the zeppelin," came the reply.

It was five full years after the final flight of the

The Lebaudy brothers' first airship, nicknamed *Le Jaune* because of the yellow coating on its cloth envelope, was a prime attraction at the Paris Exposition of 1903.

LZ 1 that Count Zeppelin's second airship was completed. In the meantime, and to his great consternation, the French military began to build a series of ships designed by Pierre and Paul Lebaudy. The first of these, the *Lebaudy I*, had flown successfully in 1902, setting endurance records. This was the first true semirigid airship, which like a nonrigid ship, depended on internal pressure to maintain the envelope's shape, but had a rigid keel for added strength. Airship historians consider the *Lebaudy I* to be the first truly practical dirigible.

Finally, the *LZ 2* was ready to fly. But her first launch in November 1905 had to be aborted when a tow rope failed to release, dragging her bow into the water and damaging the steering surfaces. At least on the *LZ 2*'s second attempt, on January 17, 1906, she got off the lake. But at takeoff the crew dropped too much ballast and the ship rose quickly to 1,500 feet. Hit by a strong breeze, the nose pitched up, then came violently down. Moments later the cooling system for the forward engine failed, and it went dead. Then the stern engine broke down. The wind now blew the count and his helpless airship, careening along without power or helm control, northeastward away from the lake. No zeppelin had ever made

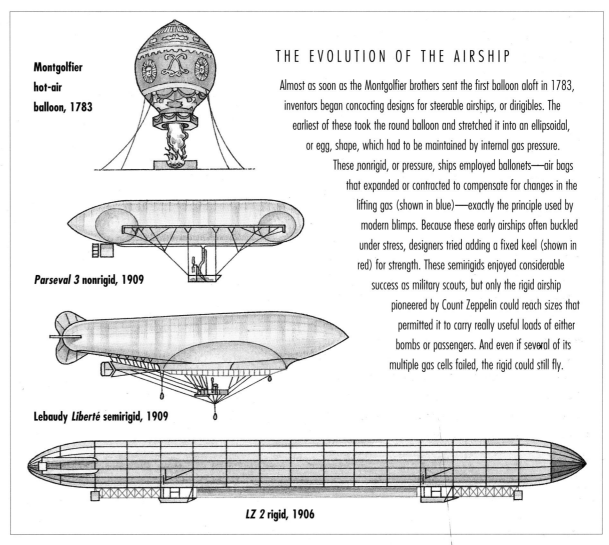

THE EVOLUTION OF THE AIRSHIP

Almost as soon as the Montgolfier brothers sent the first balloon aloft in 1783, inventors began concocting designs for steerable airships, or dirigibles. The earliest of these took the round balloon and stretched it into an ellipsoidal, or egg, shape, which had to be maintained by internal gas pressure. These nonrigid, or pressure, ships employed ballonets—air bags that expanded or contracted to compensate for changes in the lifting gas (shown in blue)—exactly the principle used by modern blimps. Because these early airships often buckled under stress, designers tried adding a fixed keel (shown in red) for strength. These semirigids enjoyed considerable success as military scouts, but only the rigid airship pioneered by Count Zeppelin could reach sizes that permitted it to carry really useful loads of either bombs or passengers. And even if several of its multiple gas cells failed, the rigid could still fly.

Montgolfier hot-air balloon, 1783

Parseval 3 nonrigid, 1909

Lebaudy *Liberté* semirigid, 1909

***LZ 2* rigid, 1906**

a landing on firm ground, but the dauntless airship pioneer managed to bring the ship down in one piece near the town of Kisslegg, about twenty-five miles away, although the stern hit some trees and was damaged. That night the wind did the rest.

"The airship lay in front of us like the skeleton of a giant whale," wrote Hugo Eckener the next day in the *Frankfurter Zeitung*. "Men worked with axes and saws, cutting it to pieces. . . . As the work of destruction proceeded, the old Graf Zeppelin stood upright and calm, occasionally issuing orders. Who can know what it cost the inventor during that sleepless night to make his decision?—to order the destruction of the aircraft to which he had devoted a lifetime."

As for the *LZ 2* herself, Eckener remained sympathetic but critical. "There were moments, particularly at the beginning of the flight, when the airship flew wonderfully well," he commented. She had, in fact, been able to steer against the wind and managed a top speed of twenty-five miles

per hour, a big improvement over the *LZ 1*: "But as soon as the wind or the speed of the airship brought strong air pressure to bear on the hull, distortions must have occurred, preventing the long, rigid transmission systems from the gondola to the propellers and the steering from functioning. In other words, the form of the aircraft is ill-adapted."

According to Eckener, late one afternoon a few weeks after this catastrophe, he was working in his garden when the maid rushed breathlessly out of the house to inform him that Count Zeppelin himself was at the door. "What could the old man want?" he must have muttered irritably to himself. Eckener quickly changed his muddy shoes and entered the drawing room.

The count, who wore morning clothes and carried a silk top hat and yellow gloves, greeted him cordially. Although almost a head shorter than Eckener, his ramrod posture and serene self-possession impressed the younger man immediately. This was the first time they had met at close quarters. Eckener found himself liking the old count, whatever his foibles.

As soon as they sat down, Zeppelin pulled a newspaper from the breast pocket of his morning coat. He said nothing, simply laid it folded on the table. Then he rapped his finger on the exposed article. It was signed simply, "Dr. E."

"You wrote this, Herr Doktor."

"Yes," Eckener replied.

The distinguished visitor thanked him for the sympathetic tone of the piece, but then came directly to the point. "He wished to discuss further with me some inaccurate statements included in my article," Eckener later recalled. "He then explained to me in the course of a long conversation that the only design error in the otherwise successful ship was that she had no stabilizing fins at the stern, no 'empennage,' which an arrow, for instance, must possess if it is to fly straight through the air rather than sideways."

This was the beginning of a relationship that would change Eckener's life. A few days later he accepted the count's invitation to dinner in his rooms at the Deutches Haus Hotel. By the end of that very pleasant evening—during which much wine was drunk and many good Havana cigars smoked—he had somehow become captive of the count's disarming personality, his combination of well-bred charm and an inventor's single-

Count Zeppelin felt sure that the *LZ 2*, with its superior stabilizing surfaces and more powerful motors, would turn out to be a big improvement over the *LZ 1*. Unfortunately his second airship lived to make only one flight.

minded fervor. Eckener offered to help Zeppelin fight "the almost malignant hostility to his ideas among all governmental officials and agencies that were involved in promoting such projects" and to help him "publicize his cause."

For the next few years this relationship was an informal one. Eckener wrote occasional newspaper articles and helped promote the airship project while pursuing his career as an economist and journalist. He planned to leave airships behind—so he told himself. But the more he followed the progress of what were by now almost universally known as zeppelins, the more difficult it became to dismiss them from his life.

With Count Zeppelin's third airship, the *LZ 3*, which first took to the air in October 1906, the inventor finally began to convince the skeptics. Meanwhile his sheer tenacity began to impress the German people. With each successful test flight of the third zeppelin, his stature grew. In 1907 a lengthened *LZ 3* successfully completed an eight-hour voyage. And, at the beginning of July 1908, when the new and improved *LZ 4* made a twelve-hour flight to Switzerland and back, he became a national hero and a world celebrity. Judging from the avalanche of congratulations and honors that attended his seventieth birthday a few days later, he was well on his way to becoming a cult figure.

(Opposite) The *LZ 4* soars above her floating hangar (above left). In the summer of 1908, the *LZ 4* made a forced landing near the village of Echterdingen, where disaster struck (above right).

One month after the Swiss excursion, on August 4, 1908, the *LZ 4* set out on a long-awaited twenty-four-hour endurance flight. If successful, the army promised to buy both the *LZ 3* and the *LZ 4*. The count had good reason to believe that these would be the first two vessels in a military fleet. Finally his airship would be used in the way he had long imagined.

At first everything went well. The count piloted the 530,000-cubic-foot, 446-foot-long gas-filled cylinder placidly along the Rhine Valley to Basel, then north past Strasbourg toward his goal, Mainz. Along the route ships blew their whistles, belfries rang out and guns fired salutes from medieval keeps, while what seemed to be the entire citizenry stood cheering below. It seemed too good to be true—and it was.

Mainz was almost in sight when minor engine trouble forced a landing on the Rhine River near the town of Oppenheim. More big crowds gathered to watch as the repairs were quickly accomplished. But the ship, which had risen past pressure height and had to vent hydrogen before landing, was now too heavy to rise. Zeppelin ordered every piece of excess weight unloaded and left five crew members on the ground. Just after nightfall a passing river steamer towed the *LZ 4* into takeoff. Once again spirits soared. Next stop: Friedrichshafen.

Instead, engine trouble returned, this time serious. At 1:27 A.M., just after passing Mannheim, the forward engine broke down completely. Soon the remaining engine began to lose the battle against the freshening wind. Just south of Stuttgart, Count Zeppelin landed his airship in a sloping field, scattering grazing cows and sheep. The Daimler engine works were nearby, and he hoped their technicians could repair the ruined motor so that the flight could continue. Despite the technical problems, he could console himself with the knowledge that the *LZ 4*'s two successful forced landings, one on water and one on land, demonstrated her adaptability.

As the morning wore on, local soldiers acted as ground crew while a team from Daimler worked on the motor. Soon huge crowds gathered to gaze in wonder at the count's creation. With everything apparently going well, Zeppelin repaired to the nearby town of Echterdingen for lunch.

While the count rested at the local inn a sudden summer storm tore the *LZ 4* from her moorings, threw her upward, then bowled her into a tree. With a loud explosion she erupted in flames and crashed to the ground.

The rest of the story is pure Hollywood, reminiscent of the aftermath of a gunfight scene in a classic western. The crowd parted wordlessly to let the count pass, his usually erect frame bent. Like mourners at a funeral, the men doffed their hats. For once Zeppelin looked all of his seventy years—a broken old man. He gazed at the smoldering wreckage, then turned and left without a word. He had set out with such high hopes. Now he had reached the end of a very long road. This would be his last airship.

But the German people had other ideas. By the time the count's train pulled into Friedrichshafen, the contributions were already pouring in. Count Zeppelin, you must build another airship, the letters said. A bowling club in Baden sent 150 marks; the Mining Association of Essen sent 100,000. A little girl sent seven pfennigs, all her savings. Those who had no money sent gifts—a fine ham, a case of wine. Although most of the money came in fat sums from wealthy and establishment donors, it was as if the whole country had made a collective commitment to the old man's creation. Soon more than six million marks had been gathered. Thanks to what soon became known as "the miracle at Echterdingen," the count's dream had become a national dream.

So, once again, Count Zeppelin began to build.

Meanwhile, airships were becoming increasingly frequent sights in the skies of Europe and America, although none followed Zeppelin's rigid design. In the first decade of the twentieth century, many attempted to imitate the success of Alberto Santos-Dumont, still a far more famous figure than the German count. Relatively few were successful. The first British airship, designed by the ballooning Spencer brothers, flew over London in 1902, and Thomas Baldwin's *California Arrow* impressed the spectators at the St. Louis Exposition of 1904—his was the only airship there to get off the ground. The first Parseval nonrigid, built by Major August von Parseval for the German army, came along in 1906, making the military even less interested in the count's experiments over Lake Constance. And in October 1910 a journalist-adventurer named Walter Wellman set out in his French-built *America* in the first

August von Parseval (right), who began his lighter-than-air career designing kite balloons for the German army, developed a series of nonrigid airships for short-range reconnaissance in close support of ground troops. So successful were these ships that several countries, including England and Russia, purchased Parsevals in the years leading up to World War I.

attempt to fly across the Atlantic. The ship was heavy, and things began to go wrong immediately. One of the two engines broke down, leaving the ship unable to fight the wind. Three days out from Atlantic City, having thrown one broken motor overboard to lighten the ship and facing certain disaster, the crew lowered themselves in a lifeboat and were picked up by a passing steamship. The aeronauts watched as the now lightened *America* floated off to airship heaven.

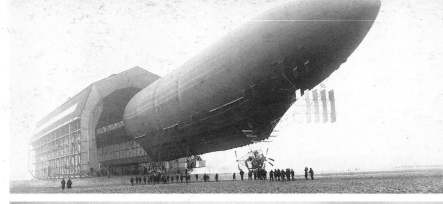

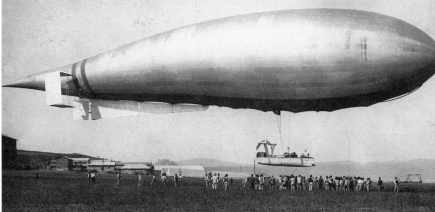

DIRIGIBLES EVERYWHERE

While Count Zeppelin struggled to perfect the rigid airship, inventors in many countries explored a wide range of alternative designs. (Top) The Siemens-Schuckert 393-foot-long semirigid (1912). (Middle) The first Italian semirigid (1908), designed by army engineer Gaetano Crocco. (Above) American Charles Oliver Jones's nonrigid *Boomerang*. (Below) France's *Ville de Paris* (1904), one of the first dirigibles to place stabilizing surfaces at the tail. (Right) The *Clément-Bayard II* over London in October 1910, following the first airship flight from the Continent to London.

By this time Count Zeppelin's dream seemed truly within his grasp. In September 1908, with the miracle money that had poured in after Echterdingen, he founded Luftschiffbau Zeppelin G.m.b.H. (the Zeppelin Company), which exists to this day although it hasn't built an airship since 1938. Soon a system of subsidiaries formed around this core enterprise, including a company for making gas cells lined with goldbeater's skin, the membrane from a cow's intestine, which was the only truly effective means of making the silk bags gastight in the days before synthetics (rubber tended to collect static electricity). But the most crucial subsidiary was Maybach Motorenbau, which finally provided the count with a reliable gasoline engine.

The new business manager of the Zeppelin Company was Alfred Colsman, the son-in-law of aluminum manufacturer Carl Berg. For the first time a hardheaded man of business was in control of the count's day-to-day operations.

One of Colsman's first acts as business manager was his most far-reaching. He brought Hugo Eckener on board as full-time director of public relations. This was a turning point in Eckener's life. Until 1908 he had continued to pursue his writing career. He had taken up a post as a columnist with a Hamburg newspaper and finally published his book about economics.

Alfred Colsman (above) became business manager of the newly formed Zeppelin Company, whose first ship, the *LZ 5*, led a most eventful life. On an endurance flight in late May 1909, she ran into a pear tree during a forced landing at Göppingen (top left), but was able to fly the 93 miles back to Friedrichshafen after makeshift repairs (bottom left). The following spring, after being accepted by the German army as *Z II*, she escaped her ground crew during a gale and crashed at Weilburg with no one on board (top and bottom right).

But somewhere along the road he had given over his heart to airships and he found himself accepting Colsman's offer.

Despite the fact that the *LZ 4* had not passed its required endurance test, the army bowed to popular will and agreed to purchase two zeppelins—a rebuilt *LZ 3* and the *LZ 5*, virtually a copy of the *LZ 4*. The company then completed another ship, the *LZ 6*, which flew successfully, but no more orders were forthcoming. The German army preferred its own nonrigid Parsevals and remained unconvinced that rigid airships could ever achieve more than marginal military utility. It quickly became clear to Colsman that for the new enterprise to survive, it would have to create its own customers. And so he formed a passenger airship company.

The Deutsche Luftschiffahrts-Aktien-Gesellschaft (German Airship Transport Company), or DELAG for short, came into being in November 1909. But its aristocratic founder, Count Zeppelin, never fully accepted the debasement of his invention for lowly commercial purposes. According to Colsman, "In the use of his ships to earn money . . . he saw his ideas being profaned." Nonetheless, he had always known that his airships had more than military potential. In 1910 Zeppelin and the kaiser's brother, Prince Heinrich, traveled to Spitsbergen to scout the possibility for a flight to the North Pole. And he clearly foresaw the day when great passenger-carrying zeppelins would circle the globe.

In an amazingly short time a network of cities all over Germany had agreed to build airship sheds—at their own expense—from which the passenger line could operate. There were no plans at this stage to run a regularly scheduled service between population centers; the airship had not yet achieved anything close to this level of reliability. There were some

Returning from a triumphant flight to Berlin in September 1909, the *LZ 6* flew to Frankfurt to participate in the International Aviation Exposition. From her base in a temporary tent shed, she carried influential passengers over the city and on day trips up and down the Rhine.

33

intercity flights before World War I, but the vast majority were sight-seeing excursions that departed from and returned to a single home base.

Düsseldorf received the honor of originating the first paying passenger flight of the *LZ 7*, christened the *Deutschland*. Unhappily, the only good outcome of this voyage was that no one was killed. On June 28, 1910, with Alfred Colsman as host and a full load of journalists on board, the *Deutschland* took to the air and almost immediately flew into trouble. A persistent problem with early airship operations was the lack of reliable weather forecasts. The *Deutschland* was unexpectedly caught in a violent thunderstorm, which shot her 3,500 feet up in the air, causing large quantities of hydrogen to escape from the emergency valves. Then the suddenly heavier ship plummeted into the forest below. By an incredible stroke of good fortune, there was no fire and the reporters all got off safely. The *Deutschland*, however, was a write-off. The ship was chopped up and the salvageable sections shipped home to Friedrichshafen.

The most important result of this ominous inaugural was the appointment of Hugo Eckener as DELAG flight director. The former small-boat sailor and intellectual would be responsible for hiring and training the

One of many colorful posters that promoted the prewar DELAG, the world's first passenger air service.

flight crews of all the passenger airships and he himself would pilot many of them. When Colsman first proposed the job, Eckener must have been taken aback at the thought of this sudden leap from man of contemplation to man of action. He had participated in numerous airship flights as a passenger and had held the wheel a few times, but this was grossly inadequate training for a chief pilot. Fortunately for history, he learned quickly.

Not without mishap, however. Eckener's first flight as an airship captain was almost his last. On May 16, 1911, a crowd gathered at the Düsseldorf hangar to watch the departure of the brand-new *LZ 8*, the *Deutschland II*. Despite a dangerous, gusty wind blowing across the mouth of the shed, Eckener decided to proceed. How could he disappoint a full load of paying passengers and all these eager witnesses?

"I paid for my weak-kneed decision by damaging the ship so badly she had to be almost completely rebuilt, and thereafter was cured of such impulsive acts," he wrote many years later. As the *Deutschland* was being walked out of the shed, a nasty gust caught the stern and wrenched the ship up and over a windscreen that had been erected to prevent just such an event. The

(Above left) Count Zeppelin looks on as Hugo Eckener (at right) earns his airship pilot's licence. (Above right) Eckener's career as an airship captain began badly when he wrecked the *Deutschland II* at the beginning of a passenger flight from the new hangar at Düsseldorf. Stranded passengers are descending by means of the long ladder.

Deutschland hung thirty feet above the ground with her spine broken. The shocked passengers escaped via fire ladders. By a minor miracle there were no serious injuries, but Eckener had learned his lesson. As Douglas Robinson put it, "never again would [Eckener] take a chance to satisfy the expectations of the public."

No further mishaps marred DELAG's service record that year. In all likelihood the future of passenger airships was saved by what Eckener would call "that marvellous summer of 1911 with its three months of practically unbroken fine weather, a perfect godsend. No longer were flights daily exposed to the threat of weather disasters. For weeks and months our pilots flew in calm safety and began to understand and master the strange new element. Nature, who 'hates man's handiwork,' can at times be kind and gentle. But woe to him who disregards her warnings and grows incautious! It was caution which the *Schwaben* pilots learnt to exercise more and more as public confidence slowly returned. They could not risk losing it again."

Schwaben, the *LZ 10*, was the first successful commercial zeppelin. That summer of 1911 she made almost a hundred flights, with not one serious problem. Her passenger gondola resembled a first-class railroad coach, with mahogany paneling and mother-of-pearl inlays. There was a washroom on board with a basin and toilet. During the flight a tasty cold collation kept away the hunger pangs. The menu included pâté de foie gras, French capon, Westphalian ham and the "best Beluga caviar," accompanied by the traveler's choice of fine French and German wines, French champagne, port, sherry and liqueurs. Nor was there any problem with airsickness. The zeppelin floated through the summer air so steadily that passengers hardly realized they were flying.

Three more passenger zeppelins soon joined the fleet: the *Viktoria Luise*, the *Hansa* and the *Sachsen*. And between 1911 and the outbreak of war in 1914, DELAG carried 34,028 passengers, 10,197 of them fare-paying, and flew more than 100,000 miles. The achievement is all the more impressive when one realizes that planes were still mostly flimsy affairs of limited range and lifting ability. Only fantasy writers foresaw the day when heavier-than-air craft would be able to carry heavy loads over long distances.

On July 8, 1914, when Count Ferdinand von Zeppelin celebrated his seventy-sixth birthday, he was no longer the "foolish count" whose airships drew ridicule from one end of Germany to the other. He was a beloved folk icon, a father figure for the whole German nation and, in the words of Henry Cord Meyer, "its greatest popular hero since Bismarck." Few would have disputed the kaiser's earlier claim that Count Zeppelin was "the greatest German of the twentieth century."

In the summer of 1911 the *Schwaben*, with its elegant passenger gondola (below), carried paying passengers in fine style.

The *Sachsen* (left) and the *Viktoria Luise* float above the Leipzig hangar in June 1913.

IN THE DARK OF THE MOON

"Zeppelin, flieg,
Hilf uns im Krieg,
Fliege nach England,
England wird abgebrannt,
Zeppelin, flieg."
[Fly, Zeppelin! Help us in the war. Fly to England!
England shall be destroyed with fire!]
— German song sung by schoolchildren
in the fall of 1914

"I rated the Zeppelin much lower as a weapon of war
than almost anyone else. I believed that this enormous
bladder of combustible and explosive gas would prove
to be easily destructible."
—Winston S. Churchill,
First Lord of the Admiralty

UNTIL NIGHT FELL, THIRTY-TWO-YEAR-OLD LIEUTENANT HEINRICH MATHY maneuvered the navy zeppelin *L 13* just off the Norfolk coast near Wells-next-the-Sea. Then, under the concealing cloak of darkness, he ordered all engines full ahead and came in over The Wash, crossing land near the town of King's Lynn. Soon he was speeding at fifty miles per hour southward over the English countryside. The moonless, star-filled night was cold and clear—perfect conditions for a bombing run. Even though it was September 8, 1915—a year since the war had begun—below him the lights of towns and villages shone brightly, providing clear beacons on the road to London. Since January zeppelins had raided coastal towns farther north, but contrary to the great expectations back home, none had yet penetrated to the center of the British capital, the heart of the empire.

As Mathy approached Cambridge, sixty miles from his goal, the glow of London's lights became visible on the horizon. "Increase altitude to 2,800 meters," he ordered. At the equivalent of 9,200 feet he should be safe from even the most powerful British artillery. The defenders had little more than ground fire to throw at him. All but a few primitive British airplanes were at the western front, and their pilots were inexperienced at night flying. Moreover, even if a lucky shell hit his airship, it would likely do nothing more than puncture one of his gasbags. And the sailmaker on board the

(Opposite) A wartime zeppelin bids farewell to Friedrichshafen. (Above) Lieutenant Heinrich Mathy, Germany's most famous zeppelin-bomber captain.

L 13 would have any hole quickly repaired. Even if all the hydrogen in one gas cell escaped, the remaining cells held more than enough lifting gas to get him home.

At Mathy's order the elevator man promptly spun the elevator wheel in the control car. The *L 13* took on a slight nose-upward slant and began to rise steadily. The air inside the unheated gondola grew even colder, and crewmen shivered in their fur-lined flying suits. But Heinrich Mathy didn't notice. He was staring intently through his binoculars in search of landmarks.

The heart of the city was partly blacked out, but the zeppelin commander had no trouble finding his way. "Regent's Park could be clearly recognized from the 'Inner Circle' which was lit as in peacetime," he later told a journalist. As the *L 13* came in over the northwest suburbs, various crew members excitedly pointed out possible targets below. But Mathy held off. "There are still better objectives," he told them coolly.

"Only have patience!" Finally, as he neared the center of London, he was ready.

It was getting on toward 11:00 P.M. when Mathy's first bombs fell on the unsuspecting citizens far below. Their first victim was Henry Coombs, who worked for the London Gas Light and Coke Company. Perhaps Coombs, who was standing in a passage just off Theobald's Road, was heading to The Dolphin nearby for a quick pint before closing. Inside the pub a clock stopped at precisely 10:49 P.M. No one inside the drinking establishment was injured. A few minutes later another bomb fell on a block of flats at the end of Portpool Lane.

Mathy could only see that his small bombs were doing some damage. So he ordered the crew to release a 660-pound explosive bomb, the first

Heinrich Mathy's *L 13* was one of the early wartime zeppelins. With a gas capacity of 1,126,000 cubic feet, a top speed of 59.7 miles per hour and an operational ceiling of 11,000 feet, she was one of the first truly satisfactory military rigids.

of this size to be dropped on England. It exploded in a square called Bartholomew Close just after 11:00 P.M., knocking duty fireman Charles Henley out of his duty box, blowing out windows and damaging walls all around the square. As Henley lay stunned on the pavement, he heard children calling for his help. By the light of the flames now licking the surrounding building fronts he could see the bomb crater, "a big hole in the road near to the fire box." It was a miracle he survived.

Far above the human tragedy Mathy was suitably impressed by the visible evidence of the new bomb's destructive power. "The explosive effect

of the 300 kilogram bomb must be very great, since a whole cluster of lights vanished in its crater," he later commented. But his air raid was only approaching its climax.

Searchlight beams now groped the night sky: "From the Zeppelin it looks as if the city had suddenly come to life and was waving its arms around the sky, sending out feelers for the danger that threatens, but our impression is more that they are tentacles seeking to drag us to destruction." At last London's twenty-six defense guns began firing on the aerial attacker. Unperturbed, Mathy dropped several bombs in an area of narrow twisting lanes and large textile warehouses north of St. Paul's Cathedral. By this time British shells were bursting uncomfortably close, so Mathy pushed his ship higher, up to 11,200 feet. Meanwhile his bombs had set off a huge conflagration below. Before turning for home, the *L 13* aimed her last bombs at Liverpool Street Station. Instead they hit two omnibuses, killing or injuring a number of passengers.

As he headed for his home base at Hage, on the northwest coast of Germany, Mathy had good reason to be satisfied with his night's work. Here was convincing proof for his beloved commander, Lieutenant Commander Peter Strasser, that airships could bring the war home to the British. And he would be able to tell his new wife that he had been the first German to bomb London. Before it was too late, he took one last look back. A significant area of the city was in flames.

Mathy's raid would prove to be the single most damaging air attack, either by airplane or airship, of World War I. The *L 13* had inflicted more than £500,000 in property damage and killed a total of twenty-two people while showing London's citizenry that their city was still hopelessly unprepared for aerial warfare. To the thousands of people who rushed out into the streets to observe the spectacle, the slow-moving enemy airship appeared infuriatingly nonchalant and untouchable. "It gave an impression of absolute calm and absence of hurry," one witness commented. Of the three airplanes that managed to take off during the raid, none came close to the *L 13*, and one crashed on landing, killing its pilot.

To many on both sides of the conflict, it appeared that Count Zeppelin's plaything had at last become a fearsome weapon—the first long-range strategic bomber.

NO ONE COULD HAVE GUESSED THESE THINGS ON DECEMBER 7, 1913, six months before the outbreak of World War I, when the small DELAG passenger ship *Sachsen* descended deftly toward the navy airship base at Fuhlsbüttel, near Hamburg. This was not another sightseeing flight for well-heeled tourists, however. Hugo Eckener was delivering the zeppelin to replace the first two navy airships, both lost during training flights. And he would shortly return to put the green crews through their paces. Soon after the war broke out, DELAG's flight director would be appointed chief instructor of the Naval Airship Division.

Though Eckener had grave misgivings about the conflict—he believed it to be a war Germany could not win—his duty was clear: to serve his country. His first impulse was to volunteer as an airship captain, but the navy brass soon talked him out of that idea. He was too valuable to be risked in combat. And, at forty-five, he was getting a little old for the rigors of high-altitude, long-distance flights.

As he had in peacetime, Eckener would play a vital role in the development of the rigid airship. Assuming, of course, that he could hit it off with the recently appointed chief of the Naval Airship Division, Peter Strasser.

No record survives of the first encounter between these two remarkable men, but they formed a strong and lasting bond. "It was Eckener's operating knowledge and Strasser's military spirit that cemented the new organization into one of efficiency," wrote Ernst Lehmann many years later. Lehmann knew both men well. As one of the pioneering DELAG captains, he had learned his craft from Eckener. "I had been his pupil," he later wrote. "He had trained me as a pilot and as an executive." In turn, it was Lehmann who had given Strasser his initial airship training.

Eckener and Strasser seem to have taken to each other instantly. There was no sense of rivalry or one-upmanship. Strasser listened carefully to Eckener's advice and acted on it. The key to successful airship operations

A moment of wartime repose: Count Zeppelin visits with Peter Strasser (right) and Hugo Eckener at the naval airship headquarters at Nordholz.

was accurate weather forecasts, Eckener told him. So Strasser moved immediately to improve weather information and analysis. Unfortunately, most of the storms came from the west, over the Atlantic. It would often be impossible to predict the weather over the North Sea or Britain in advance of a flight.

Like so many of the major figures in the history of airships, Strasser was something of a zealot. He came to the airship division as a former gunnery specialist, but airships soon filled the life of this solitary bachelor. They became, in his mind, the weapon that would win the war for Germany. True to the character of a convert, he had difficulty recognizing the real limitations of what was still an experimental technology. His single-mindedness caused him to repeatedly underestimate the effectiveness of British defenses.

Strasser's men, especially the original corps of airshipmen trained by Eckener in the early days, seem to have loved him without reservation. True, he could be a severe and uncompromising commander. "In a service that emphasized strict discipline, Strasser on duty could be a veritable martinet," writes Douglas Robinson. "Any act of carelessness was soon rewarded with a 'black cigar'—the German Navy term for a first-class dressing down." But between operations he was more of a kindly godfather, taking great interest in the welfare of his men and getting to know them and their families personally. Almost until the end, when Strasser's zealotry degenerated into fanaticism, morale remained high despite heavy losses and increasingly bad odds.

At the war's outset in August 1914 the Naval Airship Division posed little threat to the enemy. It possessed one ship, only one airship base, and no clear operational doctrine beyond Strasser's vague notion of using airships for long-range reconnaissance. And that one ship, the *L 3*, showed no design advance over prewar passenger zeppelins beyond her more powerful motors, nor could she fly above the range of shipboard artillery. In fine weather the *L 3* could perform extended scouting missions over the

English Channel and the North Sea. Unfortunately, ship movements and sea battles took place more often in foul weather than fine. The *L 3* was woefully inadequate for military purposes.

Germany's admirals, however, almost immediately recognized the need for airships as long-range scouting cruisers. They had falsely assumed that the British could be lured early into a decisive battle. Their fleet was therefore top-heavy with battleships and battle cruisers, but desperately short of destroyers and smaller cruisers that could patrol their coastal waters. An airship could be built for a fraction of the cost of a new cruiser and in six weeks instead of two years. Suddenly airships became a priority, but the first fleet of navy airships did not take to the air operationally until early 1915. Until then, the airship war was in the hands of the army.

Unlike the navy, the army began World War I with a small fleet consisting of one Parseval nonrigid, ten rigid airships and several sheds completed or nearing completion. But like the *L 3*, these rigid ships were really souped-up passenger ships, ill-suited for warfare, which helps explain their poor performance in the first six months of the war. These early army zeppelins failed at both reconnaissance behind enemy lines and as medium-range bombers. Since an aerial bomb didn't come into use until the beginning of 1915, they dropped artillery shells instead. By January 1915 Allied artillery and German operational failures (crashes, accidents) left the army with just four ships. Like the navy, they needed better craft. Soon the Zeppelin Company began to provide them.

The sudden demand from both the army and the navy rapidly transformed Count Zeppelin's somewhat poky family business into a big and efficient manufacturing enterprise under government control. New designers came on board, notably Dr. Paul Jaray, an Austrian expert in aerodynamics who soon improved the streamlining of the zeppelin hull, and Dr. Karl Arnstein, who developed the first adequate stress test for these airborne monsters. Meanwhile big new construction sheds were built at

Friedrichshafen and a separate assembly plant was established in the former DELAG shed in Potsdam, just south of Berlin. The plant, which soon moved to nearby Staaken, became an efficient airship factory with a central ring-assembly shed supplying completed framework rings to ships being simultaneously built in two huge construction sheds. At its peak, from 1915 to 1917, the Zeppelin Company was turning out an average of two airships per month—half going to the army and half to the navy.

At first the two airship services went about their separate but mostly routine business. When weather permitted, the navy sent at least one zeppelin out to reconnoiter the North Sea for British surface ships and submarines. The army used its airships for night bombing attacks behind enemy lines—mostly attempts to disrupt supply lines. But both services harbored a more grandiose goal: to bomb the two enemy capitals—Paris and, above all, London. The average German was furious with Britain for entering the war, meddling in what in his view should have been a continental conflict.

First, however, the kaiser had to be persuaded to let go of his nineteenth-century views of combat between Christian nations. Bombing the home city of his cousin, King George V, was not Wilhelm II's idea of gentlemanly conduct. His general staff, faced with the reality that the British

Early in the war the German public held exaggerated expectations of what the zeppelin raiders could do, an attitude reinforced by German propaganda. The cartoon above shows John Bull attempting to tow Great Britain out of bombing range. (Left) The paper seal and match holder both bear the inscription "God shall punish England."

Empire and its allies had literally encircled fortress Germany, urged on him the doctrine of total war, unrestricted attacks on merchant shipping and "strategic" bombing of enemy capitals. But the emperor hesitated.

Finally, early in January 1915, he relented—partially. At Peter Strasser's headquarters at the big new airship base at Nordholz, near the North Sea coast, the news was received with elation: "Air attacks on England approved by the Supreme War Lord. Targets not to be attacked in London but rather docks and military establishments in the lower Thames and on the English coast." The air war against Britain was on.

On the morning of January 19, 1915, three navy zeppelins headed for the English coast. But the *L 6*, with Peter Strasser on board, suffered a

Searchlights catch two zeppelins during a 1915 raid over the English coast in this painting by German artist Zeno Diemer.

broken crankshaft in her port engine and was forced to turn back. It was the first of many occasions when the revered leader of airships would bring bad luck with him. Strasser, a hands-on commander, tried to join one raid per month. Yet whenever he did so, his ship always seemed to run into trouble—either terrible weather or a serious technical failure. The pattern became so noticeable that he soon gained the reputation of being a Jonah.

While the *L 6* headed for home, the *L 3* and *L 4* sailed on, crossing the Channel and approaching the English coast under cover of darkness. Strasser had laid out clear guidelines for any attack on England. The airships would leave their bases by day and approach the English coast as darkness fell. That way they could perform a scouting function during their outward flight. Nighttime raids afforded the best chance of surprise—and of concealment. To maximize the advantages of night attack, the raids were generally confined to the period of the dark of the moon, running from roughly eight days before the new moon until eight days after it. During this time there would be no moonlight to help the enemy gunners when the raiders reached their goals.

Like many zeppelin raiders to follow, the captains of the *L 3* and *L 4* had trouble finding their assigned target—the important dockyards at the mouth of the Humber. Faulty navigation in this late dawn of the aerial age would bedevil airship commanders throughout the war, even after radio direction-finding came into use. For these early raids navigation was entirely by experience, by eye and by instinct. On this first night increasingly nasty weather caused both ships to strike land well south of the point intended. The *L 4* became completely lost and bombed several small villages in the mistaken belief that they were fortified positions. The commander of the *L 3* managed to get his bearings and bomb the small port of Great Yarmouth, but he failed to hit any military targets.

BATTLE STATIONS

German artist Felix Schwormstädt recreated a 1915 bombing raid over England by the army zeppelin *LZ 38*. (Left) The machine gunner in the rear engine gondola peers intently forward in search of enemy fighters while mechanics minister to the 210-horsepower Maybach motor, whose deafening noise makes conversation impossible. Meanwhile, in the cramped control gondola (above), Captain Erich Linnarz holds the speaking tube to the bomb room amidships, waiting for word that the ship is over its target. At such moments the cold in the unheated cabin was forgotten, but even special flying suits (below left) were little help during a winter raid. Coldest and most vulnerable of all were the machine gunners stationed atop the hull (below center and right), one directly above the control gondola and, on later zeppelins, one just aft of the tail. These hardy souls had to worry not only about attacking enemy aircraft but also about the danger of igniting escaping hydrogen with their bullets.

(Above left) A German cartoonist imagines a zeppelin panic in London's Trafalgar Square. (Above right) Army zeppelins bomb the Belgian port of Antwerp in October 1914.

This inauspicious debut ushered in the first and deadliest season of airship attacks on England. As Heinrich Mathy's spectacular raid on London would soon demonstrate, the English were slow to match their defensive capabilities to the new aerial threat. In fact, throughout 1915 the zeppelins' most dangerous adversary was the weather, with technical problems coming a close second. Neither the army nor the navy lost a single ship to enemy fire over England during the year, but the navy's *L 10* went down in flames on September 3, when she was struck by lightning while valving gas during a thunderstorm. Problems with visibility meant that only a small proportion of airships actually found their targets. And once there, inexperience, an inability to identify targets accurately and the primitive nature of bombs and bombsights meant that few of the explosive devices dropped from the skies hit a specific target. The vast majority fell almost randomly.

A deceptive lull followed the inconsequential January 1915 raids. Several attempts to reach England failed because of the contrary winter weather. But with the arrival of spring, the threatened fire storm seemed truly to have arrived. In April, May and June the zeppelins came with frightening regularity. In May London itself became a target for the first time: the kaiser had relaxed his proscription on bombing the capital, but with the proviso that attacks could only be made east of the Tower of London—that is, not on residential areas and historic buildings such as St. Paul's Cathedral, and above all nowhere near Buckingham Palace.

The generally random nature of the destruction made the airship all the more terrifying to the British populace. Most of the damage was to civilian property, and the great majority of casualties were civilians. Inevitably the British soon dubbed the German aircraft "baby killers." But like the German air raids in World War II, the zeppelin attacks seem only to have increased the English will to fight.

After a two-month break in the bombing from early June to early August—the deep summer nights were simply too short for raiding—zeppelin attacks resumed and continued until October and the advent of winter storms. But only with the very last raid of the year, on October 13, did more than one zeppelin manage to raid London on the same night. In fact, the first year of the air war against Britain had achieved relatively little. The casualties, overwhelmingly civilian, amounted to 208 killed and 432 injured. Property damage totaled £815,866—almost two-thirds of which came during Heinrich Mathy's single spectacular raid in September.

Throughout 1915 the zeppelins had bombed Britain virtually unopposed. But this situation would soon change. Although newer and better airships that could climb higher and fly faster were rapidly coming into service, the Germans would never equal the success achieved during this

BRITAIN'S ANSWER TO THE AIR WAR

Contrary to German expectations, the early successes of the zeppelin raiders only strengthened the British resolve to fight. The recruiting poster at left exploited fully the outrage of ordinary citizens at the indiscriminate destruction wrought by the "baby killers," an outrage also expressed in postcards like the one pictured at right. The public warning poster above exhorted Britons to keep their eyes on the skies in search of enemy aircraft.

first year of operations against the island enemy. The British defenses steadily caught up. As the war continued, this first Battle of Britain became a kind of technological chess match: each new improvement on the British side was countered with an airship advance by the Germans.

ERNST LEHMANN, ALREADY AN EXPERIENCED AIRSHIP PILOT, BEGAN the war in command of an army zeppelin. During the siege of Antwerp in early October 1914 he successfully staged a nighttime bombing raid on the Belgian port city, while noting just how inadequate his prewar zeppelin was for such military tasks. Then in January 1915 he and his crew were transferred to the brand-new Z XII, fresh off the Zeppelin Company assembly lines. (The army began the war using a Z plus a Roman numeral to designate each ship it acquired from the Zeppelin Company. However, to avoid the unlucky Z XIII, the army started to give its airships the company's own construction number. The navy, meanwhile, stayed with the designation L plus an Arabic number indicating the sequence in which the ship was ordered from the factory.)

The Z XII, incorporating a number of improvements in airship design and construction, represented the first of many leaps forward during the course of the war. Among her innovations were a more efficient rear propeller that helped give her a maximum speed of fifty-six miles per hour, a more streamlined hull, and a framework of Duralumin, an aluminum alloy that was both lighter and stronger than pure aluminum.

Duralumin would be used in the construction of all future zeppelins.

During an operational lull in the winter of 1915 Lehmann found time to experiment with a device he thought might prove useful in future bombing—the sub-cloud car. This was simply a one-man observation car lowered on a slender cable from an airship flying above the clouds. The idea was for the observer in the tiny streamlined nacelle—too small to be seen by enemy searchlights—to pick out targets while the huge zeppelin remained hidden. In theory, therefore, in the right weather conditions a zeppelin could bomb the enemy without being seen. Many army zeppelins carried this device, but Strasser rejected it for the navy—and quite wisely since it proved of marginal value. Only once did an army airship manage to use it as intended during an actual bombing raid.

In May 1915, with the war on the western front at a virtual stalemate, Lehmann and the crew of the Z XII were transferred to the Polish theater where Field Marshal von Hindenburg's armies were driving back the Russians. Lehmann and his ship were immediately put to work. "Our principal task," he wrote later, "was to harass the retreating foe and disrupt his railway service so that he should not escape the German embrace." While the Sachsen and the LZ 39 operated against Russian forts, Lehmann in the Z XII attacked the crucial trunk line between Warsaw and Vilnius.

When the onset of winter and the lack of reinforcements brought Hindenburg's advance to a halt, Lehmann and his crew were transferred back to the western front—and to a new ship, the LZ 90. (The LZ 90 was

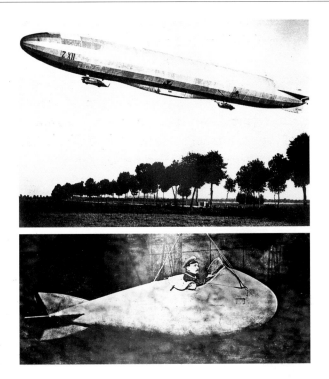

(Left) Ernst Lehmann (front row, third from right) poses with one of his wartime airship crews. To Lehmann's left is his executive officer, Baron Max von Gemmingen, Count Zeppelin's nephew. (Top right) Lehmann's second ship, the Z XII, was a big improvement over prewar zeppelins. (Bottom right) His pet project, the sub-cloud car, turned out to be of limited military use.

actually company number 60, but with *LZ 42* the army began to add thirty to the Zeppelin Company's construction number. The idea was to fool the British into thinking many more airships had been built than was actually the case, but it seems unlikely they were taken in.) The *LZ 90* was faster and larger than any ship Lehmann had captained before. With this state-of-the-art aircraft he and his men would get their first taste of the most glamorous—and dangerous—part of the air war. They would bomb London.

THE YEAR 1916 SAW THE PEAK OF THE AIRSHIP WAR AGAINST England. Three inconclusive army raids on Paris in January brought to an end the brief bombing effort against the French capital, but London remained a prime target for the navy. This was in part because Strasser now had an enthusiastic backer at head office. Vice Admiral Reinhard Scheer, the new commander in chief of the High Seas Fleet, wholeheartedly supported stepped-up airship attacks on England. Navy zeppelins continued regular reconnaissance over the North Sea, but with the advent of better raiding weather in March, they also flew frequent spring bombing missions. Quite often they would be joined by army zeppelins from bases farther south.

The star of these spring raids continued to be Heinrich Mathy, whom the British by now had nominated the "greatest of all airship captains." But Mathy and his fellow commanders found the British defenses markedly improved over 1915. An almost complete blackout became the norm on nights suitable for raiding. There were more searchlights, more and better artillery and above all more airplanes. As a result, the spring raids did little serious damage.

When the airship raids on England resumed in mid-August, an ominous new development characterized the British response. Not only were there more airplanes capable of climbing to combat the attacking zeppelins at their own level, they were equipped with ammunition that could at last do the job—incendiary bullets. Early in the war the British had mistakenly believed that the hydrogen-filled gasbags were shielded by a protective layer of inert nitrogen gas. (The Germans had experimented with this concept but it proved impractical.) The most successful attacks on zeppelins had been by means of bombs dropped from above—on the rare occasions when British planes managed to climb that high before the airship escaped. But these and the standard machine-gun bullets and artillery shells only pierced the gasbags without actually setting fire to the hydrogen inside. With incendiary bullets the zeppelin's aerial ascendancy came to a flaming end.

The turning point came on September 2, 1916. From German navy and army bases sixteen airships took to the air, their chief target London.

FIRST BLOOD

On June 7, 1915, a British airman finally knocked a zeppelin bomber out of the sky. Flight Sub-Lieutenant Reginald Warneford, flying a French-built monoplane, surprised army airship *LZ 37* returning from a bombing mission to Calais. Warneford dropped six bombs onto the ship's hydrogen-filled hull, then watched it explode in flames and crash into a Belgian convent, killing one man and two nuns as well as all but one of the airship's crew. Warneford became the toast of Britain and France, receiving the Victoria Cross and the Croix de Guerre. But only a week after his exploit, he was killed while demonstrating a new airplane at an aerodrome near Paris.

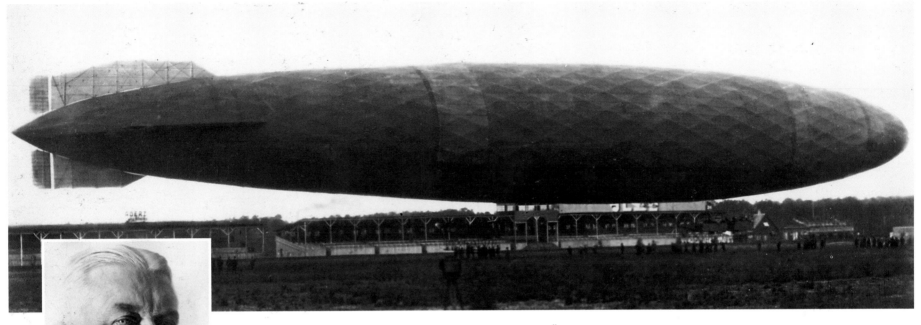

THE SCHÜTTE-LANZ SHIPS

Johann Schütte (left) was Count Zeppelin's most important rival in the development of the rigid airship. In 1909 he joined forces with industrialist Karl Lanz to form the Luftschiffbau Schütte-Lanz, which quickly introduced a number of important innovations in airship design. Notable among these were the streamlined shape (a stark contrast to the early zeppelins' cylindrical hulls), the cruciform tail fins with rudders and elevators attached (these improved stability and steering) and the internal keel (this reduced drag). Unfortunately Schütte initially insisted on using plywood instead of metal for his ships' rigid frameworks, which tended to absorb moisture, weaken and break. During the war, both the army and the navy used these wooden ships, but Strasser never liked them—he derisively referred to their supporters as "glue-potters"—and only a few went into naval service. But by war's end the Zeppelin Company had incorporated most of Johann Schütte's improvements in its own airships.

By now all limits on bombing of the British capital had been removed, beyond the proscription on historic buildings and royal palaces. The cream of the two airship corps would bring a fire storm to the enemy capital, or so Peter Strasser believed.

Ernst Lehmann, now in the brand-new *LZ 98*, flew one of the thirteen airships to reach the target. As he approached the city by way of the River Thames, he could see that London was already under attack: "The entire city lay under a luminous mist dotted everywhere with incessant flickering and flashes of bursting projectiles." As he moved forward he noted that the enemy searchlights seemed more powerful and the ground guns bigger than on his visit the previous spring. The scene before him had an eerie beauty. "We could see many explosions on the ground, evidently from other ships, but they were hidden from view by the haze, bursting shells and searchlight beams. It was like hanging above a lighted stage in a theater with the rest of the house darkened," he later recalled.

This widespread haze would deceive him into believing he was closer to his goal than he actually was. With artillery shells whizzing nearby Lehmann thought he was already over the London dockyards. He released his bombs, then dodged from cloud to cloud to evade the enemy searchlights. In fact, his explosives fell nowhere near the docks. Satisfied at what he believed to be a job well done, he entered a cloud bank, rose to 13,800 feet and headed for home.

Just before Lehmann found his final cloud cover, he was spotted by Second Lieutenant William Leefe Robinson in his single-engine BE2c biplane, the slow-moving night fighter that would prove to be the most effective weapon so far for combatting zeppelin attacks. In vain, Robinson spent fifteen minutes searching for the vanished zeppelin amidst the clouds. Then, in the glare of exploding shells he caught sight of another airship. This one would not get away.

He reached the giant without raising any answering fire—the airship crew had not detected him—then ran the whole length of the ship pumping one whole drum of incendiary ammunition into the hull. Like a whale oblivious to a school of minnows, the airship swam on. Robinson regained his altitude and attacked again, but again he saw no discernible result. "She might have been the Flying Dutchman for all the signs of life I saw," he later commented.

For his third and final attack, Robinson positioned himself just behind the ship, below the huge cross formed by the horizontal and vertical stabilizing fins. Then he emptied a whole drum of ammunition into a small area of the hull, which immediately began to glow pink. The glow quickly spread forward until the entire interior was lit—a later pilot would describe a similar scene as resembling a huge Chinese lantern. Then, suddenly, the tail section burst into flames and the airborne whale began a slow death dive. The falling inferno lit up the countryside for sixty miles around.

Ernst Lehmann was leaning over the maps in the chart room of the *LZ 98* when a call from the bridge told him to look back at London. When Lehmann did so, he saw "a huge ball of fire," perhaps forty miles behind him: "The flaming mass hung in the sky for more than a minute and we could see parts breaking loose and falling faster than the main body. Poor fellows, they had no chance at all when their ship caught fire." (As a weight-saving measure, the wartime airships did not carry parachutes.)

The loss of the *SL 11*, one of the small number of rigid airships built by the Schütte-Lanz company, helped convince the army to abandon the airship as a strategic bomber. Faced with a shortage of men for crews and lacking enough aluminum to build both airships and airplanes, the army high command increasingly favored heavier-than-air craft. And the army airship service had no dynamic leader like Strasser to fight for its survival.

Strasser simply refused to admit that his beloved navy zeppelins were obsolete. That September he sent raid after raid against England. But as more airships fell in flames, his crews became increasingly combat-weary and fatalistic. Even Heinrich Mathy had lost faith. "It is only a question of time before we join the rest," he wrote. "Everyone admits that they feel it. Our nerves are ruined by mistreatment. If anyone should say that he was not haunted by visions of burning airships, then he would be a braggart."

On October 1, 1916, Mathy's *L 31* joined ten other navy zeppelins in yet another raid on London. Due to

The destruction of the *SL 11* on September 3, 1916 (above), the first German airship to be shot down on British soil, made William Leefe Robinson (right) an instant hero. He owed his success to incendiary bullets, a technological advance that finally gave the defenders an edge over their aerial adversaries.

horrible weather—fog, snow and ice—none reached the target. Typically, Mathy came closest. But he was still trying to find the capital when a British plane found the *L 31* and shot her down. There were no survivors.

One of Mathy's fellow captains wrote that "the life and soul of our airship service" died with this great airship commander. But Peter Strasser refused to accept the possibility that the loss was anything more than a fluke, a lucky hit from a British artillery shell. By the year's end, however, even he was forced to concede that the defenders now had the edge in the technological race. "Attack only with cloud cover," he ordered on December 28, 1916, "otherwise turn back." But already he was calculating how to regain the advantage.

AS THE WAR WORE ON, COUNT ZEPPELIN BECAME IN SOME ways a sad and isolated figure. His dream of aerial conflict had come true, but the results fell far short of his expectations. Instead of staying home with his wife at Girsberg, he mostly lived in Friedrichshafen at the Kurgarten Hotel, which he had built, and haunted the nearby zeppelin works. But the Zeppelin Company was no longer under his control, and the men who built and flew the airships that had evolved from his early designs no longer answered to him. When he rode in an airship, as he did in August 1916 on the delivery flight of the new *L 30*, it was only as a distinguished passenger. He made himself something of a nuisance in high circles, begging those in authority to return him to active duty. He seemed unable to sit still, to rest on his laurels, to play with his grandchildren.

But some of the old spark of genius remained. Although he had invented the rigid airship, Zeppelin clearly saw the military potential of heavier-than-air craft built with Duralumin. Soon after war was declared, he founded a company dedicated to building a bomber capable of carrying a 2,200-pound bomb. And he succeeded. In fact, the first Gotha bomber exceeded expectations, and the military, which had initially resisted the old man's latest initiative, suddenly became interested and the company began to develop even larger four- and five-engine Riesen (Giant) bombers. But the count did not live to see any of his bombers go into action.

Despite his age—in July 1916 he turned seventy-eight—the count remained in the pink of health, outwardly the lovable father figure and folk icon. Ernst Lehmann, who visited him at his suite in the Kurgarten in the spring of 1916, found him as energetic and charming as ever. But in late February 1917, while on a visit to Berlin to view an aeronautical exhibition, the count suddenly took ill with serious intestinal problems. After an operation, he caught pneumonia and, following a brief final battle, died on March 8.

(Below) The forward half of the *L 31* crashed into a field near Potters Bar, just north of London, where armed guards were needed to keep the crowds at bay. (Right) The *L 31* and her crew (far right) in happier times. (Heinrich Mathy is at extreme right of back row.)

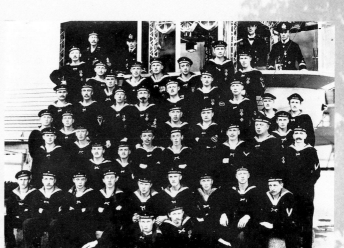

BRITISH AIRSHIPS OF WORLD WAR I

The British built more than two hundred airships during World War I, the vast majority of them nonrigids, or blimps. (The term *blimp* was coined to imitate the hollow sound made by flicking a finger against the airship's gas-filled envelope.) British airships performed effectively as anti-submarine convoy escorts (top left) and in patrolling coastal waters. (Bottom left) The vast majority of blimps built came from the SS (submarine scout) class, identifiable by their distinctive tail-fin configuration. (Right) The first British wartime rigid, *No. 9,* wasn't even completed until late 1916, had to be lightened before the navy would accept her, and ended up flying fewer than two hundred hours, primarily as a training ship. Later rigids did better, but only eight were launched before the war's end.

During the funeral in the Württemberg capital of Stuttgart, church bells pealed solemnly and two zeppelins draped in black dropped flowers as the coffin was slowly lowered into the earth. The whole German nation mourned Count Zeppelin's passing. But they were mourning more than the loss of a great man. The war was not going well, and nowhere was this more apparent than at the headquarters of the Naval Airship Division at Nordholz.

The newly achieved British air superiority forced a hard choice on the leader of airships. Peter Strasser could opt for either faster and better-armed zeppelins or for greater altitude. Both paths held grave risks. Even the fastest airship would provide a huge target for more nimble airplanes. But to rise beyond the range of the best heavier-than-air craft meant to enter unknown precincts. Ever unflinching, Strasser chose altitude over speed.

By April 1917 the first of what the British soon dubbed the height-climbers came into operation. In essence these were stripped-down versions of the previous generation of airships that sacrificed everything—including the last modicum of crew comfort—to save weight and gain height. These new ships did climb to unprecedented altitudes, but thermometers froze, compasses stopped working and, worst of all, the engines gasped and died. New engines had to be designed that gulped more oxygen in the rarified air above 16,000 feet. Soon the height-climbers were regularly operating at altitudes of up to 20,000 feet, "at one stroke rendering obsolete the entire British defense system," according to Douglas Robinson. The British planes could not fly above 13,000 feet.

It took some time, however, for the Germans to learn how to prevent the negative effects of altitude on the human body—lack of oxygen and extreme cold. At first the crews balked at using bottled oxygen—it wasn't manly to require help in breathing. Then impurities in the oxygen left many sick. Liquid air finally solved the problem, but not before a number of airships were lost due to the inability of the crew to function at such great heights. As for the cold, the crews lined their flying suits with newspapers, but frostbite remained common since the cabins were never heated.

Even when all the technical and medical problems were solved, there was one adversary that Strasser never conquered: the weather. Forecasting was chancy enough at the old operating altitudes. In the substratosphere where the gales were often far stronger than below, it was impossible. Furthermore, the height-climbers with their lighter frameworks were more vulnerable to the stresses and strains of extreme air turbulence. Finally, even on the relatively rare occasions when the height-climbers managed to make it to England, they seldom found their targets. The radio direction-finder might give the captain a rough location, but if he couldn't see the ground below, what chance had he of actually hitting something

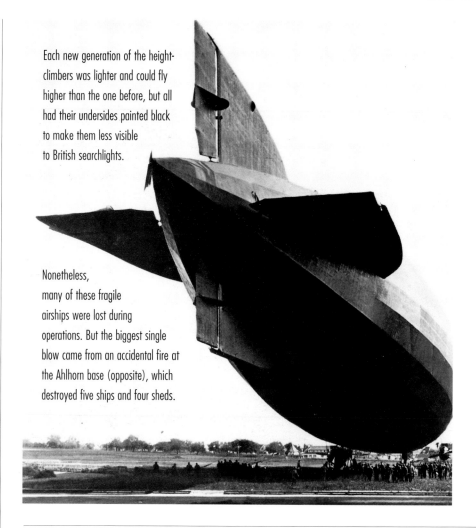

Each new generation of the height-climbers was lighter and could fly higher than the one before, but all had their undersides painted black to make them less visible to British searchlights.

Nonetheless, many of these fragile airships were lost during operations. But the biggest single blow came from an accidental fire at the Ahlhorn base (opposite), which destroyed five ships and four sheds.

useful? In sum, the tactical advantage of height was almost completely offset by the inability of the ships to function effectively at such great altitudes.

But Peter Strasser was not one to admit defeat easily. Through the late spring and summer of 1917 he continued to send squadrons of height-climbers over England and to count more losses in men and airships. As evidence of his weakening judgment, he authorized a raid for mid-June 1917 on the shortest night of the year, during which he lost one of his last senior commanders.

The greatest blow to Strasser's fading hopes of conquest came in the form of a catastrophic accident at the big airship base at Ahlhorn on January 5, 1918, when fire destroyed five zeppelins and four huge new double sheds. Before these losses could be replaced, the war would be all but lost. Yet not even this setback prevented Strasser from launching—and leading—what would prove to be the last airship raid of World War I.

On the afternoon of August 5, 1918, six height-climbers encountered unexpectedly light winds at 16,400 feet as they crossed the Channel. But they

were sighted before they reached the English coast, and three British planes flew seaward to meet them. The lead airplane, piloted by Major Egbert Cadbury (of the chocolate family), with Captain Robert Leckie as his observer, was a DH4 two-seater whose 375-horsepower Rolls-Royce engine enabled it to climb to 22,000 feet, more than enough to take on the incoming "Zepps." Once again the British had caught up with zeppelin technology.

Strasser was aboard the *L 70*, the latest and best of the height-climbers, flying in formation with the *L 53* and the *L 65*. Unlucky to the last, it was the *L 70* that Major Cadbury targeted and on which Leckie brought his single Lewis gun to bear.

It all happened almost too quickly, too easily. As the two British airmen watched in stunned fascination, the huge ship—the state of the zeppelin art—was engulfed by fire and began to fall. The crews of the two nearby airships watched in horror, then turned and ran for home, narrowly escaping attack. None of the other three ships that had approached England that night dropped a single bomb on British soil. It was a sad and ignominious end to a campaign that had begun with such promise.

HUGO ECKENER STARED OUT THE WINDOW OF THE SLOWLY moving train but his eyes did not take in the late autumn landscape of northern Germany. His was the last train permitted to leave Cuxhaven by the newly formed Sailors' Soviet that had taken charge following the November 11, 1918, armistice. Communist-inspired mutinies had erupted through much of the navy—but most of the airship crews had remained loyal to the kaiser. Before departing from the nearby Nordholz airship base, Eckener had been allowed to pack his few belongings. Now he was returning home, a fifty-year-old private citizen. Count Zeppelin was dead. Heinrich Mathy and Peter Strasser and so many young and gallant men were gone. The war was lost. The world into which he had been born had disappeared. Who knew what the new order would bring?

CHAPTER THREE

THE SOARING TWENTIES

"What a strange sight it would have been to another passing aircraft to see a man's head skimming along the top of a cloud-bank at forty knots!"

— Air Commodore E.M. Maitland

"We were not rising; we were poised, and the world was falling away from us as if lowered by hydraulic power. The walls of the fjord leisurely went downward past us. Familiar faces, uplifted toward us, grew indistinct then unrecognizable. From behind the fjord mountains rose up, glaciers and infinite snow fields glistening in the sun. . . . With the dignity of an ocean liner, the ship came around, headed for the mouth of the bay. There we turned northward to maneuver for the meridian of the King's Bay wireless station, which we were to follow to the North Pole."

—Lincoln Ellsworth

ERNST LEHMANN HAD A BRILLIANT IDEA. IN THE NAVY ZEPPELIN *L 72*, now sitting nearly complete in one of the building sheds at Friedrichshafen, he would be the first man to fly the Atlantic. He knew it could be done, and what a boost it would give to the downtrodden fatherland and the beleaguered Zeppelin Company, both trying to put themselves back together following Germany's defeat.

Lehmann, the dashing veteran of the army airship corps, had good reason to be confident. Back in July 1917, while he commanded the army zeppelin *LZ 120*, flying regular patrols far from the war zone over the quiet Baltic, he had tested his ship during a 101-hour endurance flight—more time than ought to be required for an Atlantic crossing. He'd had to dodge a few summer thunderstorms, but otherwise the experiment had gone beautifully. Even more convincing, however, was the evidence provided by the remarkable flight of the *L 59* in November 1917, when she attempted to carry relief supplies to battalions in German East Africa. Fooled by a false radio message from the British indicating that the German forces had surrendered, the *L 59* turned back short of her destination. By the time she arrived back at her Bulgarian base of departure, she had covered a remarkable 4,200 miles—the distance from Friedrichshafen to Chicago—in ninety-five hours, with enough fuel remaining for another sixty-four hours in the air.

By the beginning of 1919 Lehmann had persuaded his old friend and former executive officer Baron von Gemmingen to back the daring flight, apparently over Hugo Eckener's strenuous objections. Following Count Zeppelin's death, his nephew von Gemmingen had taken his place as head of the firm, which at war's end reverted to family control. Eckener,

The as yet unmarked *LZ 126* passes over the Berlin airfield before her delivery to the U.S. Navy.

This poster immortalized the remarkable exploit of navy zeppelin *L 59*, whose flight to Africa in 1917 was, until then, the longest voyage ever accomplished by an airship.

whose postwar role had yet to be defined, hadn't the power to stop the scheme. It was the first, but definitely not the last, time he and his former pupil Lehmann would disagree. Lehmann's intense patriotism seems to have blinded him to the political pitfalls of his idea. Eckener, who always took a more Olympian view, saw the dangers clearly. Even if Lehmann succeeded in slipping undetected over the Atlantic by night, the Allies' outrage at this act of bravado by their freshly defeated enemy would surely be enormous. And who could guarantee that the Americans would welcome this unannounced visit by a former enemy bomber? (In case of a less than friendly reception Lehmann planned to carry enough fuel to make the round trip without touching down.)

As it turned out, once the authorities in Berlin were informed of Lehmann's proposal, they soon quashed it. Now Eckener and the company's longtime business manager, Alfred Colsman, could turn their energies to re-establishing the airship as a commercial vehicle, as a ship of peace. They toyed briefly with plans for an "America ship" big enough to test the feasibility of transatlantic travel, but finally decided that such a project was too risky. In the unsettled society of postwar Germany, with frequent strikes and often chaotic train service, the two men recognized a more certain opportunity: a reliable airship service between Friedrichshafen and Berlin.

Using all the design knowledge and technical gains accumulated over four years of war, they built a new passenger ship, the *LZ 120*, and christened her the *Bodensee* (Lake Constance). She held the same gas volume as the prewar *Sachsen*, but possessed thirty-five percent more useful lift and boasted a top speed of 82.4 miles per hour, faster than any previous airship. She was also the first rigid airship to be fully streamlined. Unlike the perfectly cylindrical early zeppelins, she grew much fatter toward the middle because it had been discovered that this shape greatly reduced air resistance.

Colsman brought the passenger airline company DELAG out of mothballs and Hugo Eckener became its director. The *Bodensee*'s first scheduled flight, with Eckener in command, took place on August 24, 1919. From then until December 5, flights (occasionally with a stop in Munich) occurred daily, in one instance covering the distance from Friedrichshafen to Berlin in just under four hours. The train could take sixteen hours or more. It was a promising beginning, and work began on a sister ship, the *Nordstern* (North Star), that would extend regular passenger service to Stockholm.

But before the 1920 flying season could begin, the Allies suspended DELAG's operations. As part of Germany's war reparations, all her rigid airships—including the *Bodensee* and the *Nordstern*—were to be divvied up among the victorious Allied nations. Under the provisions of the Treaty of Versailles, Germany could no longer build any airships for military purposes and was allowed no commercial airships with a gas volume greater than 1 million cubic feet. Eckener considered 2.5 million cubic feet of volume the minimum for the transatlantic ship he still hoped to build. The extra lift would compensate for the weight of the fuel needed to complete such a long flight.

The existing German airships were divided among France, Italy, Great Britain, Belgium and Japan, where they led short and mostly undistinguished lives. The Americans would have to settle for monetary compensation. Following the armistice, loyal members of the Naval Airship Division had scuttled seven ships in their sheds, leaving too few to go around.

While the Zeppelin Company was reduced to manufacturing aluminum pots and pans and its DELAG subsidiary was left with no ships to fly, a power struggle developed. Baron von Gemmingen was deteriorating steadily from a fatal illness. Meanwhile, Alfred Colsman vied with Eckener, on this occasion backed by Lehmann, for control. Colsman believed airship manufacture would never again be a viable business and sought to diversify production. Eckener was interested only in building zeppelins. When the dust settled (von Gemmingen died in 1924), Eckener had won, combining the roles of chief operating officer and chief

The *Nordstern* (above) and the *Bodensee* were to form the foundation of the postwar resurgence of the passenger zeppelin, but went instead to the Allies as war reparations. The vase at right is an example of the metalware manufactured by the Zeppelin Company after World War I.

executive officer, but Colsman did succeed in creating a much broader manufacturing base. It remained to be seen, however, whether the Zeppelin Company would ever build or fly another airship.

OTHER THAN GERMANY, ONLY BRITAIN COULD CLAIM TO HAVE a rigid airship program at the war's end. Her large wartime airship fleet was comprised mainly of nonrigid pressure ships, or blimps, used for scouting purposes. But even before the war, she had begun experimenting with rigid construction. The first of the British rigids, the *Mayfly*, broke in two before she could take off in September 1911. During the war, the rigid program was a somewhat slipshod affair plagued by bureaucratic delays, false starts, midstream design modifications, political infighting and operational inexperience. Part of the problem was the British obsession with copying German designs instead of developing their own. Each time they did so, whether from a captured ship or stolen plans, they found themselves with an obsolete craft left far behind by the rapid pace of German development. But in the war's immediate aftermath, the British rigid airship did achieve a brief glory.

Everyone in the world of aviation knew it was only a matter of time before some type of aircraft would fly nonstop between Europe and North America. Like airships, airplanes had made huge technological advances during wartime, so either technology was capable of accomplishing the feat. The race was fueled by Lord Northcliffe, owner of London's *Daily Mail* and a big booster of aeronautics. Before the war he had offered a cash prize of £10,000 ($50,000) for the first nonstop crossing in less than twenty-four hours. Now he revived the offer.

Air Commodore Edward Maitland, director of airships for the British air ministry, decided that the craft to win the prize would be the new *R 34*, completed only in March 1919. Before he could act, however, the £10,000 went to two RAF aviators in a twin-engined Vickers–Vimy bomber. On June 15, 1919, Captain John Alcock and Lieutenant Arthur Brown took

sixteen hours and twenty-eight minutes to fly from St. John's, Newfoundland, to Clifden, Ireland. Theirs was a hair-raising passage through incessant fog—sometimes flying upside down—and they nearly didn't make it. The exhausted flyers crossed the coast, then landed nose first in an Irish bog. Maitland was convinced that his airship could do better.

On July 2, 1919, the *R 34* took off from the air station at East Fortune, Scotland, with Maitland on board and Major G. Herbert Scott in command. Just after takeoff she had to ascend above her pressure height in order to clear some Scottish hills, forcing her to vent hydrogen. She thus began her marathon too heavy. To compensate, Major Scott used the elevators to provide dynamic lift, the same kind of lift that keeps an airplane airborne. The *R 34* flew much of the way across the Atlantic at an upward angle that sharply increased air drag, significantly reducing fuel efficiency. To conserve fuel, Scott used only three of his four engines for most of the trip.

Two days after setting out, the *R 34* sighted Newfoundland and ran smack into strong head winds. For another day she fought these while skirting violent thunderstorms as the fuel gauge sank lower and lower. Scott began to consider alternative landing sites. Then his luck turned, the wind became favorable, and he made it to his original destination, Roosevelt Field, Long Island, with 140 gallons of gas to spare—barely enough for two more hours of full-speed flying.

But the *R 34* had made it. The flight lasted a record 108 hours and 12 minutes. (Homebound tail winds helped the *R 34* make it from Long Island to Pulham, England, in 75 hours and 3 minutes, despite a broken

(Left) On the eve of the *R 34*'s Atlantic crossing in July 1919, she shares the double hangar at East Fortune, Scotland, with the smaller *R 29*. (Above) Air Commodore Edward Maitland (in white) poses with some of the *R 34*'s officers following her arrival in Long Island.

GASBAGS FROM COWS' STOMACHS

The British adopted the Zeppelin Company's practice of using goldbeater's skin, the outer membrane from part of the large intestines of cattle, to line each gasbag. (The material derived its name from its use to hold gold being beaten into gold leaf.) Goldbeater's skin had two important advantages over rubber: it did not rip and it did not accumulate static electricity. But it was enormously expensive because of the vast number of skins needed — about 50,000 for a large gas cell —

as well as the careful handling and the amount of labor required.

These photographs show British women at work in the Short Brothers' factory in 1919. (Above left) Each skin was first moistened in brine and carefully scraped clean. (Top) The skins were then stuck together (table at lower right) and glued to linen panels (table at lower left). (Above right) Once a cell was complete, it was partially inflated so that workers wearing soft slippers could patch any holes.

engine.) Maitland was jubilant. And her lone American passenger must have been duly impressed. He was Lieutenant Commander Zachary Lansdowne of the U.S. Navy, destined to become a tragic figure in the rigid airship story.

After the *R 34*'s impressive long-distance demonstration, the U.S. Navy elected to order a big rigid airship from the British. This order— for the then enormous sum of £300,000—saved the *R 38*, the most ambitious British airship yet designed, from cancellation as part of a government economy drive.

At the time of her completion in the spring of 1921, the *R 38* was the largest airship ever built— 699 feet long and with a capacity of more than 2,700,000 cubic feet of hydrogen. Unlike most of the wartime airships, many aspects of her design were British. Unfortunately, however, the chief designer, C.I.R. Campbell, was an amateur when it came to estimating the *R 38*'s ability to withstand aerodynamic stresses. And even though a number of observers raised questions about the new ship's structural soundness, the British decided on an unusually short period of test flights before turning her over to her eager American buyers.

On August 23, 1921, the *R 38* set out on the fourth of these flying tests with seventeen American navy men on board as observers or trainees. Along for the ride were both Campbell and Air Commodore Maitland. Over the city of Hull, the captain, Flight Lieutenant A.H. Wann, ordered the engines brought to full speed and then commenced turning tests. No one seemed to realize that this light-framed British version of a German height-climber simply wasn't made to withstand high-speed turns at low altitudes. First the rudder went to port, then back to starboard, with each turn being put over more sharply.

In the middle of one of these turns the *R 38*'s hull snapped at a point roughly two-thirds of the way back from the bow. The forward section

The mangled remains of Britain's *R 38*, following the crash that killed forty-four men in August 1921.

exploded and fell into the Humber River, killing everyone on it except Flight Lieutenant Wann. The rear third drifted down and landed on a sandbar. From this section only four men escaped with their lives.

The blow to America's fledgling airship program was bad enough—sixteen of the seventeen U.S. Navy trainees perished—but the British loss was devastating. The twenty-eight men who died represented the core of the country's airship world. Britain's remaining airships were either sold or scrapped. A decade later, when the British once again entered the field, Air Commodore Maitland and his seasoned team of airshipmen would be sorely missed.

THE TRAGIC LOSS OF THE *R 38* WAS HUGO ECKENER'S OPPORTUnity, and he seized it. By the summer of 1921, the Zeppelin Company was on the ropes. The aviation control commission set up by the Allies had ordered all German airship sheds dismantled, which would kill any lingering hope of building even small commercial zeppelins for domestic use. However, the Americans still wanted a rigid airship to replace the late *R 38*. And Germany owed them

either an airship or the equivalent in cash under the terms of the Treaty of Versailles. Why shouldn't the Zeppelin Company build them one?

It may sound simple, but given the touchy postwar political situation, it wasn't. Making the deal required all of Eckener's political adroitness and diplomatic sensitivity, the same skills that he would later employ so effectively in promoting transatlantic airship travel. Eckener saw that going through normal channels would tangle him in endless political thickets. Instead he went straight to the American military commission in Berlin. Would the U.S. Navy like a brand-new state-of-the-art zeppelin rather than a cash payment? Of course it would.

With strong backing from the American navy, the other pieces of the deal fell into place. Politicians and bureaucrats squawked—the French were worried, the British were reluctant—but the eager Americans had their way. When the contracts were finally signed, Eckener had saved the Zeppelin Company and its construction sheds in Friedrichshafen—at least for the moment.

The final contract called for a ship that fell short of the 3.5-million-cubic-foot airship the navy originally wanted. (To placate the nervous

The *LZ 126* (*Los Angeles*), the ship that saved the Zeppelin Company and helped launch America's rigid airship program, under construction in the big shed at Friedrichshafen.

Allies, the new zeppelin was limited to a gas capacity of 2.5 million cubic feet and built for "civil purposes.") Nonetheless the *LZ 126* would be the biggest and most modern airship yet built. Construction began in the summer of 1922 for delivery at Lakehurst Naval Air Station in New Jersey the following year.

In 1922 construction assembly began on the first home-built American rigid, the *ZR 1* (to be christened the *Shenandoah*, a Native-American word meaning the Daughter of the Stars). Like the ill-fated *R 38*, the *Shenandoah* was modeled after a German World War I height-climber. But unlike the British, the Americans departed from the original design mainly to add structural strength. And unlike all rigid airships before her, the *Shenandoah* would be inflated with helium.

In the winter of 1922 the Americans had suffered one of the world's worst dirigible disasters to date when the Italian-built *Roma*, a large semirigid recently acquired by the U.S. Army, hit some high-voltage wires during a forced landing and exploded. Thirty-four of the forty-five men on board died. Due to the public outcry that followed, hydrogen was never again used in an American airship.

Helium wouldn't burn, but it had several disadvantages when compared to hydrogen, the lightest of all lighter-than-air gases. First and foremost it provided less lift, only ninety-three percent of the lifting power of hydrogen. It also cost much more. Only recently discovered as a constituent of the natural gas found in a few wells in Texas, helium was extremely expensive to extract and very scarce in supply. When the *Shenandoah* was first inflated, helium cost more than $120 per thousand cubic feet; hydrogen cost $2 or $3. That meant a single fill came to more

Wherever she flew, admiring crowds flocked to see the *Shenandoah*, shown here at her mast at San Diego's North Island Naval Air Station.

than $240,000, an enormous sum in the early 1920s. Over the years the price came down as supplies became more plentiful, but helium would always remain costly compared to its explosive cousin.

The *Shenandoah*'s maiden flight on September 4, 1923, marked several firsts. Not only was she the first rigid airship to use helium, she was the first flown by an American crew (although the German design consultant was in de facto command). And it was the first flight of a rigid from the new air station at Lakehurst, New Jersey. After fifty-five minutes in the air, the *Shenandoah* returned safely to her base. The era of the American rigid airships had begun.

During the *Shenandoah*'s early months in service she went from strength to strength, attracting crowds wherever she flew. At the beginning of October she made the round trip from Lakehurst to St. Louis in forty-four hours. It seemed she was beginning to kindle enthusiasm similar to the zeppelin fever that had gripped prewar Germany.

But it would take more than a few demonstration flights to banish the public's worries about airship safety. On December 18 yet another rigid airship catastrophe made the headlines when the French dirigible *Dixmude* disappeared. The *Dixmude*—the renamed *L 72* that Ernst Lehmann had planned to pilot across the Atlantic—had recently set the long-distance airship record in a 4,500-mile trip around the Mediterranean. Her final radio message was heard four days into an even more ambitious endurance flight. Only the commander's body and a few bits of charred wreckage were ever found, but some Sicilian villagers reported seeing a bright light over the sea at the time of the disappearance. A hydrogen explosion, probably during a lightning strike, seemed the most plausible explanation.

The *Shenandoah*'s next great test, the first transcontinental airship flight, began on October 7, 1924, under the command of her popular young captain Lieutenant Commander Zachary Lansdowne, who had been an observer on the *R 34*'s pioneer Atlantic crossing. Thirty-seven hours after leaving Lakehurst, Lansdowne brought the *Shenandoah* safely to the mooring mast at Fort Worth, Texas.

One of several things this trip set out to prove was the practicality of the mooring mast, a British invention that had been modified and improved by the Americans. With a mooring mast to secure the ship, expensive sheds would not be needed at every airship stopping place. Apart from the huge new hangar at Lakehurst, there were no sheds in North America large enough to shelter the *Shenandoah*. The Germans initially pooh-poohed the mooring-mast idea, but it soon became standard equipment for airship operations and is used by blimps to this day.

Lieutenant Commander Zachary Lansdowne (above) was the *Shenandoah*'s last captain. (Below) His ship passes over Los Angeles on her transcontinental flight in 1924.

On the far more difficult leg from Fort Worth to San Diego, the *Shenandoah* had a couple of close calls. In a mountain pass in southeastern Arizona she was almost blown into a mountainside. Over California a fierce snow squall nearly drove her into the ground. But Lansdowne and his crew prevailed. They arrived in San Diego on October 10, only to see the after gondola damaged when the ship suddenly became too heavy during the landing. It took a week of repairs before the *Shenandoah* was ready to head north to Seattle, then retrace her route to Lakehurst.

Apart from Lansdowne, the most satisfied person on board the *Shenandoah* was surely Rear Admiral William Moffett, chief of aeronautics for the U.S. Navy. After the *R 38* disaster he had stuck by the airship program, using his considerable influence to make sure that the *Shenandoah* was built.

While the *Shenandoah* was still undergoing repairs

This underbelly view of the *Shenandoah* shows her control gondola and four of her engine cars, each containing a 300-horsepower Packard engine.

in San Diego, an even more significant event began on the European side of the Atlantic. Early on the morning of October 13 the new *LZ 126* emerged from the Zeppelin Company construction shed in Friedrichshafen. Water ballast splashed to the ground, and the great hydrogen-filled ship rose gently in the predawn darkness. In the control car Hugo Eckener ordered the engines started. The crowd of onlookers and reporters watched in awe as this huge inflated cigar disappeared into the morning mist and headed toward France and America. Beside Eckener in the control car was Ernst Lehmann, acting as executive officer.

Hugo Eckener had gambled everything on this flight, putting up the assets of the Zeppelin Company as security against the loss of the ship in order to get German government backing. Thanks to Colsman's efforts, these assets had considerable value. The various subsidiaries were now making products ranging from gear systems for cars and trucks to heavy industrial textiles. Many years later Eckener reflected on the importance of the risk he was taking: "It was clear that not only the lives of the participants, but also the fate of the Zeppelin idea, would depend on our success."

On his first aerial crossing of the Atlantic, Eckener knew he was sailing into the unknown. True, the *R 34*, a zeppelin copy, had made a similar flight, but none of his officers or crew had been on board. And that flight had taken place during the summer. No one yet knew what autumn storms over the Atlantic would do to an aircraft made of lightweight Duralumin covered with a thin layer of canvas.

Eckener began by heading to the Azores, well south of the most direct route to Long Island. He wanted to avoid the westerlies then blowing in the North Atlantic. On board he had enough fuel for only eighty hours in the air. If he met strong head winds, he might well run out of gas and find himself free-ballooning back to Europe. However, when he reached the Azores and set a course for New York, he still found himself facing a head wind that cut his speed in half. Based on reports from two American vessels sent out to come to his aid in case of need, Eckener surmised the presence of a low-pressure area south of Newfoundland.

Hugo Eckener and the *LZ 126* made several flights in September 1924, including a visit to Berlin (above), to show off the brand new ship before delivering her to Lakehurst. (Right) The newly christened *Los Angeles* flies over Washington, D.C.

If he kept his course, he would soon exhaust his fuel supply. So he chose to try to sail around the low-pressure system by heading first north, then west. Sure enough, the winds soon slackened. Even better, as he turned toward Boston, a fresh tail wind added to his speed. On a map his zigzag course would have looked like the track of a drunken sailor. But Eckener had guessed correctly, demonstrating the fine art of pressure-pattern flying, taking advantage of high- or low-pressure systems to make the speediest and safest voyage.

The rest of the trip went like a friendly breeze. Just after dawn on October 15 he gave New Yorkers their first of many zeppelin thrills, cruising leisurely over Manhattan. Then he brought the *LZ 126* south to Lakehurst, where he landed her before a huge welcoming crowd.

The *LZ 126*, soon christened the *Los Angeles*, went on to lead a long and distinguished career as a U.S. Navy training ship. Since she had been built to passenger-ship specifications, she already boasted comfortable sleeping compartments for twenty and other amenities unheard of on a military vessel. Seen from afar, her streamlined silver hull enthralled all who saw her. The silvery sheen came from aluminum powder which, for the first time on a German airship, had been added to the dope used to stretch and waterproof the outer cover. When the *Los Angeles* was finally retired from service in 1932, she could look back on a long and unbroken safety record. The *Shenandoah* would not be so lucky.

When the Daughter of the Stars returned from her triumphant

transcontinental tour in late October, Zachary Lansdowne got a chance to shake Hugo Eckener's hand and receive his congratulations. Then he found himself sitting on the sidelines and watching the *Los Angeles* get all the attention. The American navy possessed only enough helium to inflate one airship, but it now owned two big rigids. So, while the two ships sat side by side in the Lakehurst hangar, the lifting gas was pumped out of the *Shenandoah* and into the *Los Angeles*. Until the following spring, the *Los Angeles* roamed the skies while the *Shenandoah* underwent minor modifications. The most important of these reduced the number of emergency valves on her gas cells in an effort to limit the amount of helium leakage, which had been considerable during the transcontinental flight.

Zachary Lansdowne had hoped to pilot the *Shenandoah* to the North Pole. It would have been his crowning achievement. But President Coolidge canceled the 1925 polar flight and instead Lansdowne was instructed to take the *Shenandoah* on an extensive publicity flight to the American midwest. On a similar flight to Minneapolis at the beginning of June 1925, two of the *Los Angeles*'s engines had broken down and she was forced to turn back. Even more serious, her German-made gas cells were leaking badly. So she went into the Lakehurst shed for repairs. There her precious helium was bled back into the *Shenandoah* so that the older ship could complete the flight the *Los Angeles* had been forced to cancel.

Navy supporters of the rigid airship, above all Admiral Moffett, realized that their program depended in part on convincing a still-skeptical public of the airship's practicality and safety. They had wanted the *Los Angeles* to strut her stuff over the American heartland where airships had been seldom seen. When that job fell to the *Shenandoah*, Lansdowne objected strenuously. The summer season of frequent midwestern thunderstorms was too dangerous a time to take an airship on a

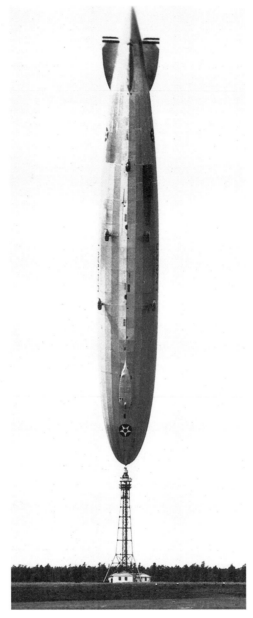

BOTTOMS UP

On the afternoon of August 25, 1927, with the *Los Angeles* floating at the Lakehurst high mast, a strong breeze suddenly lifted her tail into a layer of denser cold air, where it continued to rise even faster. The watch on board tried in vain to compensate by climbing up the steepening keel toward the tail, which reached an angle of about 85 degrees before it finally began to descend. Despite minor damage, the ship was ready to fly the next day, but the incident confirmed Rosendahl's determination to develop a shorter, or stub, mast to forestall such mishaps.

publicity flight where any delay or mishap would undercut the very purpose of the venture. Furthermore, he pointed out, proper landing facilities weren't yet in place.

Lansdowne partly won his point. The flight was delayed until the first week of September, in time to catch the crowds attending the many fall fairs but still a period of potentially violent weather. On the afternoon of September 2, 1925, the *Shenandoah* lifted away from the Lakehurst mast, then headed west into a threatening sky— and into the history books.

LIEUTENANT COMMANDER CHARLES ROSEN-dahl came instantly awake. The crewman sent to rouse him for his watch never had to shake him twice. He sat in his small bunk and looked at his watch: 3:30 A.M.

Rosendahl's bunk was perched next to the keel walkway just aft of the control car. From where he sat, the great spiderweb of polygonal rings and longitudinal girders forming the *Shenandoah*'s Duralumin skeleton stretched into the distance, lit faintly by the string of low-wattage bulbs suspended along the length of the keel.

He slipped on his uniform jacket and rubber-soled shoes, designed for maximum traction, listening to the ship and feeling her motion. The vast bag of helium above his head was quiet. Nothing seemed amiss. He stepped onto the walkway, then moved a few paces forward and climbed down the ladder into the control gondola—the bridge of this ship of the air.

At thirty-three, Rosendahl was already a veteran American airshipman. He had served as junior navigation officer on the *Shenandoah* during her epic transcontinental flight and acted as ground-handling officer during the christening of the *Los Angeles* by Mrs. Calvin Coolidge in November 1924. He'd been aboard the U.S.S. *Patoka* when the *Los Angeles* had successfully moored to her shipboard mast off Puerto Rico the previous May. Moreover, he'd fallen hopelessly in love with these strangely graceful giants. Airships had it over airplanes any day, as far as he was concerned.

When Rosendahl entered the control car it was dark, save for dim lights above the instrument panels and the radium glow of the instrument dials, but he could see Lansdowne and several officers intently watching the night sky through the windows. He walked over to relieve Lieutenant Commander Lewis Hancock, the senior navigation officer. Hancock relinquished his post, but decided not to leave the car. The weather looked worrisome.

During the middle of the previous watch, the ship had altered course to stay clear of a thunderstorm. To the north occasional flashes of lightning now lit the horizon. Although parts of the sky were clear—a muted moon was setting to the west—the wind blew too strongly for the ship's five engines; she was slipping sideways over the hilly Ohio landscape below, but made no forward progress.

At about 4:20 A.M., Rosendahl noted "a thin dark streaky cloud just apparent in the dull moonlight" off the starboard bow. Lieutenant Commander Lansdowne quickly walked over to take a look at this new threat—either it was racing toward them or building up very fast.

"The ship is rising, sir," reported the elevator man.

"Do what you can to check her," responded Lansdowne calmly. He betrayed not a hint of nervousness.

"She's rising fast and I can't check her, sir," the elevator man chimed in moments later. There was tension in his voice. And with good reason. The *Shenandoah* had been captured by a powerful air current that was thrusting her upward at a speed of more than one thousand feet per minute. No airship had ever met such extreme conditions. And worse was to come.

Lansdowne calmly ordered engine speed increased so that the great horizontal elevator surfaces would drive the ship down against the rising air. If possible, he wanted to avoid exceeding the ship's pressure height of roughly 3,600 feet, beyond which precious helium would have to be valved. As the engines took hold, the *Shenandoah*'s downward angle increased. The inclinometer needle headed toward eighteen degrees, dangerously close to a stall, the aerodynamic point when the downward thrust would be lost and the ship would become violently unstable.

"Don't exceed that angle," ordered Lansdowne. Immediately the elevator man eased back on the huge horizontal steering surfaces and the danger passed.

At 3,100 feet the rapid rise slowed for several minutes, and the small crowd in the control car assumed that the worst was over. Despite the watch change, almost everyone had remained on the scene. Instead, the ascent resumed, even faster and more turbulently than before.

"I've got the flippers hard down and she won't check," reported the elevator man.

"Don't worry," Lansdowne replied.

"I've got her hard over, sir, and she won't take it," reported the crewman on the rudders. The giant airship was "now rolling and felt like a raft being tossed about in a mountainous sea," wrote Rosendahl later.

Pressure height passed and still the ship soared upward—at speeds as high as four hundred feet per minute. At this rate the reduced number of automatic valves would never let the helium escape fast enough, and if the bags overexpanded or burst, they could damage the framework. So Lansdowne ordered the manual valves to be opened. But still the *Shenandoah* continued her inexorable rise.

At 6,000 feet a blast of cold air rushed in through the keel hatches and swept through the ship, waking the few men still sleeping in their bunks along the keel. High above them in the hull, some heard noises that sounded like girders breaking and bracing wires snapping. Everyone on board—from the men tending the screaming engines to the man at the elevator wheel—now realized that their ship was in mortal danger.

In the control car Lansdowne understood that the gush of cold meant his ship had passed through the warm air mass that had carried her upwards and that, with so much gas having bled from the cells, she would soon begin to hurtle down again. He didn't wait for the plunge to begin, but quickly ordered the release of water ballast in the hope of slowing the fall.

From a storm-tossed raft, the *Shenandoah* abruptly became a rock in free fall—1,500 feet in a single minute. As the atmospheric pressure increased, the air pressed hard against Rosendahl's eardrums. Then another upward current caught the ship and she began to rise again. Her hull hadn't been built to take this sort of strain.

When this latest ascent ended and the next plunge began, Lansdowne realized he would need to drop emergency ballast—the big fuel tanks amidships. Navigation was pointless, so he dispatched Rosendahl to make sure the crew were standing by and ready to cut free the tanks on his command. Two engines had already broken down, and the three remaining motors wouldn't last much longer. He had to be prepared for the worst.

"To get up into the keel, one had to go up a ladder through a narrow conning tower-like trunk," Rosendahl recounted later. "Just as I stepped upon the rungs of the ladder, the ship took a very sudden upward inclination that seemed to me very much like the beginning of a loop in an airplane. The angle was greater than any I'd ever experienced before in an airship." A few steps more and he heard "the snapping of struts"—the girders that held the control car in place were breaking. Only the heavy cables stretching aft from the control car to the rudder and elevator fins now held the commanding officer and his crew to the hull.

Focusing only on his assigned task—the possibility of the control car breaking free was too awful to contemplate—the young officer began to head aft, toward the fuel tanks. Suddenly he heard "a terrific clashing, metallic din." It was as if two giant hands wanted to twist the *Shenandoah* until she broke. And break she did, at a point roughly one-third of the way back from the bow.

The two severed sections of the hull stayed together for another ninety seconds, held in place by the control cables. When these cables gave way, Rosendahl found himself looking toward the stern "with the unbelievable vision of the rest of the ship floating rapidly away from me and downward into the dull grey light of the breaking dawn." The hull parted with the piercing shriek of metal stressed beyond endurance, "as though a thousand panes of glass had been hurled from on high to pavement beneath."

With this cataclysm the remaining threads of steel holding the control car to the hull parted, and it plunged toward the earth, sending Lieutenant Commander Lansdowne and his crew to sudden death. Lansdowne kept his composure to the last, calmly announcing just before the breakup, "Anyone who wants to leave the car may do so." Only two men took him up on his offer and followed Rosendahl up into the keel.

As the rear section plunged out of Rosendahl's view, it broke again—just aft of the initial break. This hull fragment, with the two forward engine cars still attached, dove downward, taking four men to their deaths.

Meanwhile, the tail section—which had until now been falling at a sharp stern-upward angle owing to the weight of the two forward engine cars—leveled off and slowed, ultimately landing about a third of a mile away from where the control car hit. Before it came to rest, the open end of the hull caught some trees and a narrow piece sheared off, but only one of the four men in this section was hurt. And the remaining eighteen crewmen in the stern survived their wild ride uninjured.

In the soaring bow Rosendahl's initial shock now gave way to fear, then a feeling of intense loneliness. He was by himself—or so he believed—as the 210-foot-long forward section ascended rapidly until the ground below was barely visible. Between him and the forward part of the bow gaped a chasm of open air where the control car support struts had torn away metal and fabric. Perhaps he could climb up into the girders and slash the still-intact gasbags, he thought, but this rough expedient almost guaranteed a crash landing. To do something, anything, he began shouting over the roar of the wind. To his astonishment, voices called back—at least one forward across the chasm and one aft.

He soon discovered that six men besides himself rode in the bow as it

shot up to a ceiling of 10,000 feet. Suddenly the situation seemed less desperate. As part of Rosendahl's basic airship training, he had learned the art of free ballooning. His was an odd-shaped balloon, but the principles still applied. There was no reason, with a crew of six, that he couldn't bring the bow in for a safe, soft landing.

As Rosendahl organized his men for a landing attempt, the ballooning bow sailed in a big, slow circle over the area where the rest of the ship had already crashed. By valving helium and dumping ballast—mainly the remaining gasoline—Rosendahl slowly brought the ship toward earth. When a gust of wind caught him just before touchdown he ordered the remaining ballast dropped to abort the landing—too late, however, to prevent the hull from catching a tree, which ripped the fabric cover open and dumped one of the survivors to the ground. He was badly injured but survived.

The second landing attempt went better: "Gradually we settled, open end leading, and made contact with good old terra firma so gently that not even an egg would have been cracked." As the nose touched, the crewmen there stepped out and secured the ship to the closest mooring points—fenceposts and trees—while the others slashed the helium bags so that the bow would not be carried aloft again.

The wreck of the *Shenandoah* did not cost as many lives as the *Roma*—only fourteen of the forty-three on board died—but it left a far deeper impression. The ship that Admiral Moffett claimed was the strongest in the world had been literally torn apart in a storm. The American rigid airship program was now in serious jeopardy. Only the determination of two remarkable men—Rear Admiral William Moffett and Charles Rosendahl—would save it from an untimely end.

THE NEWS OF THE *SHENANDOAH* DISASTER MUST HAVE BEEN painful for Hugo Eckener. In the wake of his successful delivery of the *Los Angeles* to Lakehurst, he had launched an ambitious campaign to raise money to build an airship big enough for regular transatlantic passenger service. The loss of the first American-built rigid, one closely modeled on a German original, did not help his cause. But it did not deter him.

During 1925 and 1926, Eckener, Lehmann and other senior airship officers traveled all over Germany, giving lectures in support of the Zeppelin-Eckener Fund. Eckener himself gave more than a hundred of these fund-raising talks. "It was the most exhausting work I have ever done in my life," he later commented. Slowly yet surely the money flowed in. There would be no second "miracle at Echterdingen," but the German people still believed in the old count's dream. By the end of 1926, 2.5 million marks—

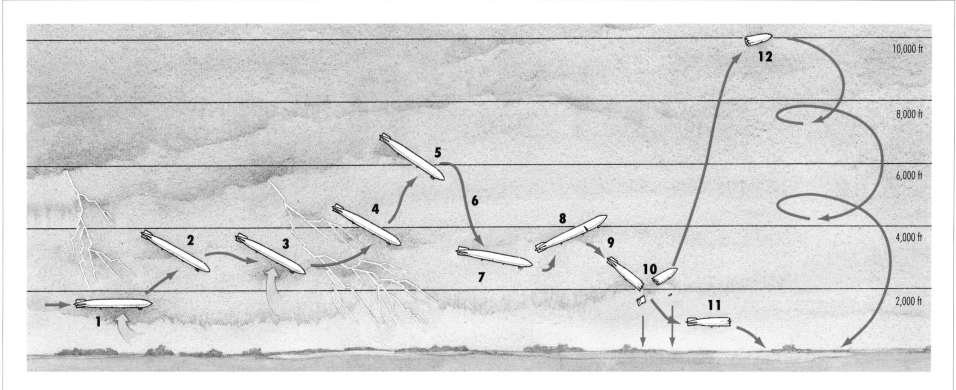

DEATH THROES OF A LEVIATHAN

The diagram above follows the final half hour of the *Shenandoah*'s life on September 3, 1925. **1)** Making no progress against a fierce head wind, the ship suddenly begins a sharp rise. **2)** She levels off for about five minutes but rolls and pitches heavily in severe turbulence. **3)** A second, more violent rise begins.

4) At 3,600 feet the ship exceeds pressure height. Lansdowne orders the crew to vent helium and release water ballast. **5)** The ship pauses, then begins a sickening plunge. **6)** As the ship falls, the crew releases more water ballast. **7)** The third rise begins. Rosendahl leaves the control car. **8)** A terrific gust strikes beneath the bow and wrenches it upward, snapping the hull at frame 125. **9)** The broken ship stays together as it

plunges again. **10)** The strain finally becomes too much, the bow section separates and the control car falls. Moments later, the stern section breaks at frame 110 and this hull fragment, with the two forward engine cars attached, hurtles earthward. **11)** The stern section, with 22 men on board, levels off and floats to earth. **12)** Meanwhile the bow section, carrying Rosendahl and six others, free balloons to a safe landing.

Before news of the *Shenandoah* wreck made newspaper headlines (above), crowds of locals had already gathered at the three crash sites. The remains of the stern section are shown at right. The handful of sheriff's deputies posted as guard couldn't prevent sightseers from looting everything they could carry, from canned food and logbooks to pieces of the gas cells and chunks of girder.

the equivalent of $750,000—had been raised, well less than half of what was needed, but Eckener launched construction anyway. The Allies had relaxed their size restrictions on German airships. Eventually the Weimar government reluctantly agreed to kick in a little over one million marks. The deficit of close to 3.5 million marks was covered by profits from the now-diversified manufacturing business.

WHILE ECKENER BUSIED HIMSELF WITH FUND-RAISING, THE world's interest in airships shifted away from Germany and America and toward the North Pole. This was the era when explorer-adventurers were seeking to reach the last inaccessible places on the planet, when men like Peary, Scott, Nansen and Amundsen gained world fame. To this list was about to be added the unlikely name of an Italian engineer and dirigible builder, Umberto Nobile.

At that time Nobile was the most accomplished airshipman in Italy. As director of the Italian military's airship factory, he had designed or helped design most of his country's fleet of semirigid dirigibles, including the ill-fated *Roma*, whose crash in the United States marked the beginning of the use of helium in American airships.

In the summer of 1925 Roald Amundsen, the first man to sail the Northwest Passage and the discoverer of the South Pole, approached Nobile with a proposition. Would he agree to pilot one of his airships on a flight across the Arctic from Spitsbergen to Alaska? Amundsen had the financial backing of the wealthy American gentleman-adventurer Lincoln Ellsworth, with whom he had unsuccessfully attempted the previous year to make the same flight in two seaplanes.

Umberto Nobile eagerly agreed to participate in Amundsen's project. More reluctantly he agreed that the expedition would take place solely under the Norwegian flag. The ship would be his own *N 1*, purchased by the trip's sponsor, the Norwegian Aero Club, and renamed the *Norge* (Norway). Nobile would be her pilot and his own men would form the core of the crew. Amundsen left virtually all matters aeronautical to the Italian: his area of expertise was arctic exploration and survival; he knew nothing about airships.

In early May 1926 an eclectic crew of Italians, Norwegians, Swedes and one American (Ellsworth) assembled at King's Bay on the west coast of Spitsbergen. Nobile had safely navigated the *Norge* from Rome, via Pulham, England, Oslo and Leningrad—quite an accomplishment in a ship roughly one-quarter the gas volume of the *Shenandoah*. One engine that had failed in transit was replaced while the little airship lodged in a makeshift, roofless hangar that had been built the previous winter.

Italian airshipman Umberto Nobile (above right) joined famed Norwegian explorer Roald Amundsen (above left) in a daring attempt to fly across the polar sea. (Below and bottom) Before taking off from Spitsbergen, the *Norge* was housed in a roofless hangar. (Opposite) An Italian newspaper illustrates a proud moment for the nation as the country's flag is dropped at the Pole, dwarfing the flags of America and Norway.

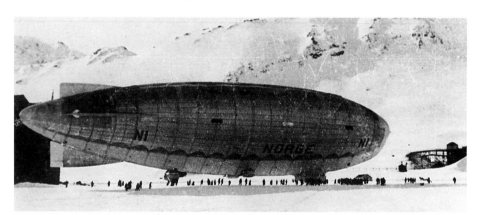

Direzione e Amministrazione Torino, Via IV Marzo, 12

ILLVSTRAZIONE del POPOLO

Anno VI - Numero 21
Domenica 23 maggio 1926

Sedici pagine — Supplemento della «Gazzetta del Popolo» — Centesimi 35

...ica impresa del «Norge» - Mentre la bella aeronave si abbassa sopra la ghiacciata solitudine del Polo, vengono ...ate tra la più viva commozione dell'equipaggio le bandiere della Norvegia, degli Stati Uniti e dell'Italia come segno di questo meraviglioso successo della navigazione aerea *(Disegno di Alfredo Ortelli).*

On May 11, 1926, with the repairs complete and the weather forecasts favorable, the *Norge* lifted off for the unknown. The Amundsen-Ellsworth-Nobile transpolar flight would prove once and for all whether an as yet undiscovered continent lurked in the unvisited reaches of the Arctic Ocean. Fifty-four-year-old Amundsen had announced that this would be his last voyage of exploration. He would retire following the trip, and leave the field to younger men.

In the crowded control car—Nobile had reduced its size to save weight—the eagle-profiled Amundsen sat grandly in a velvet-covered steel-tubed armchair while the hired help—Nobile and his crew—piloted the ship toward the Pole. Nobile's small white dog, Titina, dozed in a corner, seemingly oblivious to the cold. In the unheated chamber of Duralumin with its celluloid windows the men were dressed warmly, but sandwiches froze and the thermoses of tea and coffee soon grew cold.

Before midnight the adventurers encountered heavy fog—Nobile's greatest fear—and the ship began to ice up. The elevator man took the *Norge* up swiftly through the mist. At 3,000 feet she broke back into sunlight and excitement rose. The North Pole was only an hour or two away. Everyone had been awake since dawn, but no one felt tired. At 1:30 A.M. they were there. Amundsen, Ellsworth and Nobile each dropped their nation's flags. The full-size Italian flag, entrusted to Nobile by Mussolini himself, dwarfed the others. Amundsen said nothing amid the general celebration, but he was not pleased.

The *Norge* narrowly missed being the first aircraft to reach the North Pole. Only a few days earlier, Richard Byrd had successfully made the round trip from Spitsbergen in a Fokker airplane. But no one had ever flown beyond this point. As Nobile ordered the engines speeded up and set a course for Point Barrow, Alaska, he knew that the most difficult and important part of the voyage was about to begin. With too few crewmen for regular watches, there would be virtually no rest for anyone until they touched down in Alaska or perished in the attempt.

Soon they were once again flying blind through freezing fog. Every metal surface of the ship was festooned with frost or ice. Then the beauty turned malicious. Chunks of ice slipped off the engine gondolas and whipped through the propellers, which hurled them against the outer fabric covering. The rigger rushed from hole to hole repairing the punctures in the ship's skin. Fortunately, none of these ice bullets pierced a gas envelope. A serious hydrogen leak would have been disastrous.

Onward they sailed through the gray-white twilight, trusting their magnetic compass to guide them toward Alaska. During a brief break in the fog, Nobile relaxed long enough to size up the scene. "We had been in the air for 32 1/2 hours," he later wrote. "The cabin was horribly dirty. The dozens of thermos flasks heaped on the floor, near the little cupboard where we kept the charts and navigation books, presented a particularly sad spectacle: some of them empty, others overturned, others broken. Coffee and tea had been spilt everywhere, and all over the place were the remains of food. In the midst of this mess there stuck out picturesquely Amundsen's enormous feet, with his grass-stuffed shoes, his diver's gaiters and red and white gloves."

Finally, forty-six hours and twenty minutes after leaving King's Bay, the ship's navigator called out, "Land ahead off the port bow!" It was the coast of Alaska. Amundsen, Ellsworth and Nobile had made one of the most remarkable flights in the history of aviation in an airship that many experts had judged far too small for such a mission. And they had proved beyond any doubt that the polar region was one vast frozen sea.

For another day and a half the small airship battled fog, snow and heavy winds, repeatedly losing her way and at one point nearly crashing into the sea. Nobile finally gave up any hope of reaching his intended destination of Nome and brought the *Norge* down in an emergency landing near the tiny settlement of Teller, Alaska.

It was an amazing feat. He and his crew had barely slept since leaving Spitsbergen. More than once Nobile had leapt to relieve a dozing elevator man. On one occasion, when he ordered engine speed increased, there came no response. The tired crewman's brain simply refused to process the order. Yet somehow Nobile had the presence of mind left to bring the airship down for a soft landing on the snow-covered ice of a small Alaskan bay without benefit of lights or landing crew.

Roald Amundsen thanked him profusely. Lincoln Ellsworth offered him the use of his apartment in New York and his villa in Italy. But the warmth and camaraderie were soon forgotten. Even thirty-five years later Nobile was still defending himself against the "calumnies" written and spoken by Roald Amundsen following their joint voyage of discovery. Amundsen had always considered Nobile little more than a mercenary and he deeply resented the credit the Italian now quite justifiably claimed for

At 1:30 A.M. on May 12, 1926, the *Norge* reached the North Pole.

his part in the expedition. Minor events, such as the fact the Italian flag was bigger than the others dropped at the Pole, were exaggerated to make Nobile appear to be a self-aggrandizing egotist. But the biggest blow to Nobile's pride was Amundsen's accusation that during some dangerous moments off Alaska, the Italian had "lost his head completely," and that the ship had only been saved from crashing by the alert actions of the Norwegians on board.

Nobile was not entirely blameless in this quarrel—it was, after all, Amundsen's expedition—but he deserved better from the grand old man of polar exploration who had, in fact, been little more than a passenger during the long flight.

Two years after the flight of the *Norge*, Nobile returned to Spitsbergen in the *Italia*, a newly built sister ship to the *Norge*, at the head of an Italian-funded expedition. In a series of flights he planned to explore some of the 1.5 million square miles of the Arctic as yet unvisited by humans, and with three scientists on board, conduct various scientific experiments.

The second of these exploration flights took Umberto Nobile once again to the Pole. But on May 25, 1928, just·short of Spitsbergen on the return trip, the airship became inexplicably heavy and crashed violently onto an ice floe. Nobile and nine others were thrown from the control car onto the ice along with some of the survival equipment and provisions carried on board. They watched in stunned fascination as their now lightened ship disappeared into the gray fog with six men still on board, never to be seen again. One of the ten castaways was dead, a mechanic had a broken leg, and Nobile had broken his right leg and arm. Chances of survival seemed slim.

However, the emergency radio and an arctic tent were among the items the *Italia* had deposited on the ice pack. Day after day, as the supplies dwindled and the men grew weaker, the radio operator dutifully sent out his distress call. Day after day there was no response. Back at Spitsbergen the captain of the support ship *Città di Milano* knew only that the *Italia*'s radio transmissions had abruptly ceased. He correctly concluded that the ship had crashed, but inexplicably decided that the airship's radio operator had perished and that there was therefore no point in listening for a distress call. The

(Top) Two years after the voyage of the *Norge*, Umberto Nobile returned to Spitsbergen with the semirigid airship *Italia*. (Above) Nobile and his dog, Titina, huddle on the ice after their dramatic Arctic rescue.

sixth day on the ice floe, spirits rose briefly when one of the men shot a polar bear—at least they would not starve. Eventually the survivors tuned in to a radio station in far-off São Paulo, Brazil, which told them that the rescue efforts were concentrating in the wrong place. More depressing, their sextant sightings indicated that winds and currents were carrying them away from help.

Nobile finally permitted three of the able-bodied survivors to strike out for land. Any action seemed preferable to wasting away on the ice. He had privately given up hope of rescue, but insisted that the daily radio transmissions continue. On June 6, after two weeks on the ice, they heard the São Paulo radio station report that a ham operator in Russia had picked up what seemed to be a distress message from the *Italia* crew. The next day the *Città di Milano* finally tuned in. It seemed that rescue was at hand.

In fact, the ordeal dragged on for more than a month while the rescue effort grew to involve ships and planes from six countries. At the news of Nobile's radio message, even Roald Amundsen came out of retirement to help find the man he had vilified. On June 18 he set out from Tromso, Norway, in a borrowed French seaplane. The plane never returned.

Italian planes were the first to find the marooned airshipmen—on June 20—dropping by now desperately needed supplies. Then a daring Swedish flier landed on skis on a nearby floe and took Nobile to safety. The expedition leader was reluctant to leave his men, but the Swede had his orders. Nobile would be much more useful on the base ship helping direct the rescue efforts. The pilot promised to return directly for the others but on the next flight his plane overturned and the Swede joined the castaways on the ice.

What followed made Nobile's nightmare with Amundsen seem like a pleasant dream. Italy's new Fascist air minister, a man named Italo Balbo, who had refused to help fund the *Italia* expedition, now spread the story that a cowardly Nobile had abandoned his men to save himself. Balbo's own newspaper reported that Nobile had not broken his leg during the crash but while running for the rescue plane. On board the *Città di Milano*, Nobile found himself in official disfavor and a virtual prisoner. Nonetheless, he did what he could to egg on the often haphazard rescue efforts while conditions on the ice floe deteriorated. Finally, on July 12, the Russian icebreaker *Krassin* reached the crash site and rescued the five men remaining. (The Swedes had managed one more landing and taken off their own pilot safely.) The *Krassin* also found and rescued two of the three men who had set out to walk to King's Bay. The entire ordeal had lasted forty-nine days.

The loss of the *Italia* marked the end of Umberto Nobile's Italian airship career, but not his days as a pioneering airshipman. The government rigged its commission of inquiry to make sure he took the fall for the disaster, and he resigned in disgrace in 1929. He spent much of the 1930s helping the Russians develop an airship program. During World War II he emigrated temporarily to the United States and only after the defeat of fascism did he return permanently to his homeland, where his name was officially cleared and he finished his professional life as a distinguished professor of aeronautics at the University of Naples.

O N SEPTEMBER 18, 1928, LESS THAN FOUR months after the crash of the *Italia*, the new *LZ 127* was walked out of the big hangar at Friedrichshafen for the first time. The largest airship yet built was ready for her first test flight. Back in July, on what would have been Count Zeppelin's ninetieth birthday, the new ship had been christened the *Graf Zeppelin* by his only daughter, Countess Hella von Brandenstein-Zeppelin. Hugo Eckener, the scholarly journalist turned airship executive, knew the power of a symbol. On this ship's success rested all of his future hopes. As he wrote many years later, "The result would be either victory and fame, or final downfall and the end of a defective concept." But by the time the *Graf Zeppelin* began her record-breaking career, the British seemed poised to surpass everything so far accomplished by the men of Friedrichshafen.

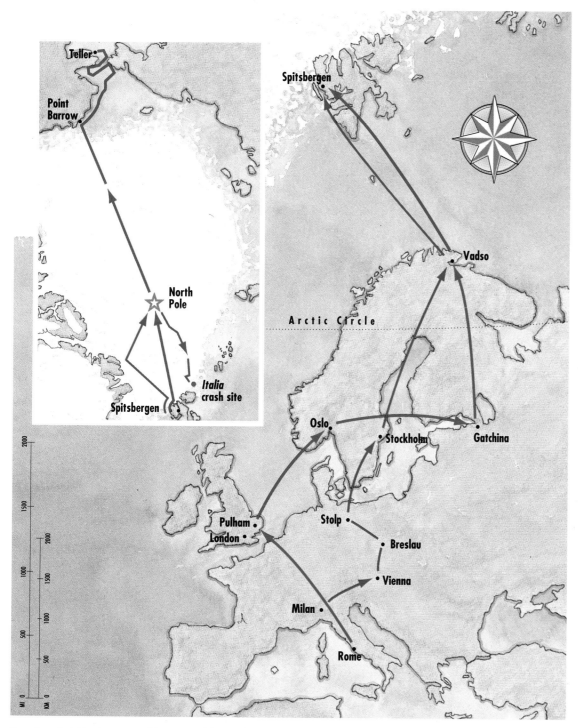

For such small airships the journeys of the *Norge* and the *Italia* from Italy to the Arctic were almost as remarkable as their polar flights. The *Norge's* trip north in the spring of 1926 passed virtually without incident, although the ship had to spend several weeks at Gatchina, near Leningrad, while the facilities at King's Bay were completed. The *Italia* did not have it so easy in 1928. Over Czechoslovakia a severe storm pounded her with hail and blew her badly off course. On landing the upper fin was found to have broken and the propellers to have been pitted by hailstones. But the damage was repaired and she continued on her way. The map inset shows the pioneering voyage of the *Norge* from Spitsbergen to Alaska (red line) and the final flight of the *Italia* (blue line), which ended tragically just short of her home base.

EMPIRE OF AIR

"[The R 101] is as safe as a house—except for the millionth chance."
—Lord Thomson of Cardington

"There is no doubt that but for a combination of circumstances against which the odds would have seemed very long indeed, and but for one last minute error in airmanship, the disaster of R 101 would not have happened."
—Sir Peter G. Masefield

AS DUSK FELL OVER THE ST. LAWRENCE River on July 31, 1930, four men sat casually drinking a pre-dinner sherry in the otherwise deserted dining saloon of the *R 100*. Britain's giant rigid airship was bucking a stiff head wind as she fought her way westward at slightly more than forty miles per hour, but her rise and fall, more gentle than that of an ocean liner at sea, did nothing to disturb the supper that had already been laid on the table at the center of the room. Probably the men talked about the damage—now repaired—to the port and starboard fins suffered a few hours earlier in a sudden squall near the mouth of the Saguenay River. Almost certainly they discussed the small thunderstorm into which they were now heading.

Nevil Norway, a young engineer who had been an important part of the ship's design team, wondered about that storm, which he'd gotten a good look at before leaving the control car: "It stretched across our path as a bank of clouds apparently about fifteen miles long, slightly bronze in

(Above) In the control car of the *R 100,* Major Herbert G. Scott looks down on the passing Canadian countryside. (Opposite) The *R 100* heads east above the Thousand Islands of the St. Lawrence River.

color and raining underneath." The Canadian authorities had advised the *R 100* to turn south to avoid it, but Major Herbert Scott had ordered the ship to plow straight through. The *R 100*, now nearing the end of her first crossing of the Atlantic, had never sailed through a thunderstorm before. And the time saved would be useless, since the ship had already missed her scheduled arrival at St. Hubert Airport near Montreal, disappointing the big crowd gathered to greet her.

But Squadron Leader Ralph Booth, the airship's quite competent captain, had not questioned the major's decision. Scott was, after all, the officer in charge of flying and training for the ambitious British airship program and the country's most experienced dirigible pilot. It was Scott who in 1919 had guided the *R 34* across the ocean to Long Island and back, the first transatlantic passage by an airship, and had later saved the *R 36* from crashing when its upper fin collapsed. He had also developed the high mooring mast pioneered by the British.

The first gust, when it hit, knocked up the nose, then tilted the ship sharply downward as it passed beneath the stern. Scott and Booth immediately put down their sherries and headed back to the control car, attached under the *R 100*'s hull just forward of amidships. Norway and the fourth member of the party, Sir Dennistoun Burney, head of the Vickers subsidiary that built the *R 100*, left the saloon and entered the promenade deck, whose large windows gave them a view of the action.

As they did so, the ship encountered a vertical gust that carried her 1,800 feet upward in a single minute. Those in the control car fought the rise with a sharp down elevator that caused the nose to drop precipitously. At 3,000 feet the *R 100* paused briefly before a second gust shot her upward even faster—Norway later calculated that it was a thousand feet in fifteen seconds or a speed of forty-five miles per hour—while the elevator pushed her nose down even farther. So far the experience was uncomfortably reminiscent of the *Shenandoah*'s initial rise over Ohio.

Soup, meat, vegetables and cakes, along with plates and cutlery, crashed from the table in the saloon and went sliding forward, some items traveling almost the whole way into the bow. In the crew quarters a crewman fell into a can of red dope used in the recent fin repairs, spilling it down the deck, where it began to drip into the control car. Norway, later to become famous as the novelist Nevil Shute, vividly recreated the scene: "The ship was so far nose down that it was necessary to hold on, apparently plunging straight into the ground, in thick cloud and rain, with the altimeter going madly the wrong way, completely out of control. At that moment, in the faint orange light, a torrent of sticky red fluid resembling blood poured down into the control car. Grand Guignol could not have done it better."

Major Scott immediately ordered the lights extinguished to eliminate the chance of igniting the highly flammable mixture. Abruptly, the hair-raising ascent ceased, the ship returned to a level keel, and a few minutes later emerged safely from darkness and heavy rain. The postmortem that followed discovered that a new rip had appeared beneath the starboard fin.

The *R 100* continued more carefully on her way, now avoiding all subsequent storms. At 5:00 A.M. on August 1 she made a gentle approach in calm air to the new mooring mast at St. Hubert. The age of the imperial airships that would link the far-flung capitals of the British Empire had begun. Or so it seemed.

But the nasty scrape over the St. Lawrence carried an ominous message for those who chose to read it: an experimental prototype was being treated like a time-tested aircraft. The *R 100* had never encountered anything like this weather over Britain, yet such violent summer storms are typical over or near continental land masses. Looking back many years later, Norway was scathing about Scott's performance: "In my view, even with the lesser knowledge of those days, Scott should have known better and this decision was a reckless one."

Had the *R 100* been a German zeppelin with Hugo Eckener in command there would have been no question of flying into the storm. The supremely cautious Eckener never took unnecessary risks, and the risks he did take were scrupulously calculated even though he flew with crews far more experienced than any the British could muster. Had one of Eckener's captains behaved as Scott had done, no matter how good his reputation, he would certainly have received a sharp reprimand. Quite possibly he would have been relieved of his job.

THE AMBITIOUS SCHEME TO BUILD A FLEET OF AIRSHIPS FOR imperial commerce took concrete shape in early 1924, immediately after Ramsay MacDonald formed the first Labour government in Britain. The program's chief proponent and guiding light was MacDonald's new secretary of state for air, Christopher Birdwood Thomson, a most unlikely socialist. "A good cricketer and a useful man at golf," in the words of one of his upper-class contemporaries, Thomson was well bred, well read and had had a distinguished military career from which he had retired with the rank of brigadier general soon after World War I. He had long been an idealistic champion of the underdog, and he soon became a great friend and confidant of Ramsay MacDonald himself.

Because Thomson failed to carry his seat during the 1923 election—he never succeeded in gaining elected office—Prime Minister MacDonald installed him in the House of Lords so that he could enter the first Labour cabinet as air minister. He took the title Lord Thomson of Cardington in honor of the Royal Airship Works at Cardington near Bedford. Already, it seems, he had caught the airship bug, although his only previous brush with rigids had hardly been a positive one: in 1916 he had narrowly escaped injury during a zeppelin raid on Bucharest, where he was stationed as the British military attaché. In his new job he became a passionate advocate of lighter-than-air travel and quickly put his personal stamp on the program that had been initiated by his Conservative predecessor, Sir Samuel Hoare.

The Tories had planned to pay the Vickers company to build six ships about the size of the future *Graf Zeppelin*. These ships would provide service to India every two weeks and eventually a weekly service to Australia. Thomson rejected this scheme, arguing that Vickers, a private company, would then possess a complete monopoly on airship construction. A great national endeavor such as this one ought not to be the exclusive domain of private enterprise.

According to Thomson, Britain's fleet of airships would have a more noble purpose: "To give a unity to widely scattered peoples, unattainable hereto; to create a new spirit, or maybe to revive an old spirit which was drooping and to inculcate a conception of the common destiny and the mission of our race." In the wake of World War I, Britannia ruled the waves with increasing difficulty. She was no longer the all-powerful

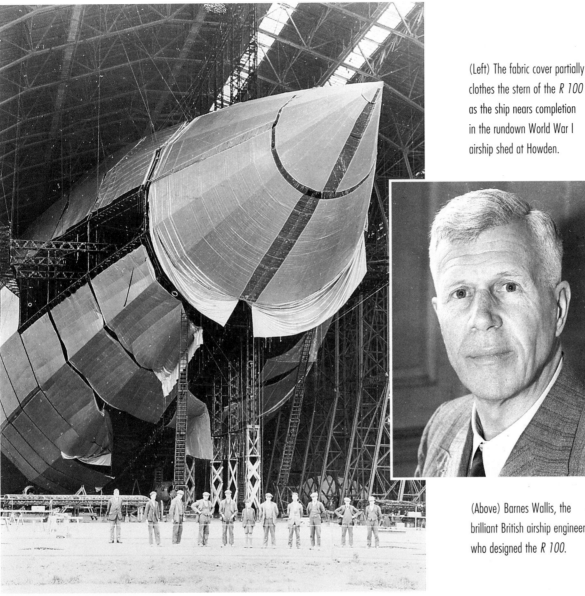

(Left) The fabric cover partially clothes the stern of the *R 100* as the ship nears completion in the rundown World War I airship shed at Howden.

(Above) Barnes Wallis, the brilliant British airship engineer who designed the *R 100*.

crossing—even without the weight of passengers or cargo—and quite a few had failed in the attempt. In an age when ocean liners were still the only reliable way to carry people across large bodies of water, the rigid airship held the promise of comfortable, economical and swift passage to every corner of the globe.

Thomson translated his imperial vision into the following practical terms. Two great airships, each of 5-million-cubic-foot capacity, would simultaneously be built—the *R 100* under contract with Vickers, and the *R 101* by the Royal Airship Works at Cardington. Each ship would be designed to carry one hundred passengers and their baggage plus sixteen tons of cargo nonstop over distances up to 3,500 miles at a top speed of at least seventy miles per hour and a cruising speed of sixty-three miles per hour. From these prototypes would emerge a second generation incorporating the best elements of the competing designs.

This political compromise—the minority Labour government had to placate the Tory opposition—proved extraordinarily ill-advised, but Thomson seems to have genuinely believed that a combination of private and public enterprise would lead to creative cross-fertilization between the two design teams, and that two better ships would result. He hoped for co-operation as well as healthy competition. He got neither.

Thomson failed to take into account several important factors. First and foremost, there were precious few British rigid airship experts following the death of Air Commodore Maitland and so many others in the crash of the *R 38* in 1921. This became apparent to Sir Samuel Hoare when he found himself back in his old job as secretary of state for air upon the fall of the Labour government in November 1924, after only nine months in office. Hoare found that the two teams tended to regard each other with "suspicion and sometimes jealousy." And, "as the construction progressed, what was no doubt intended as friendly competition tended to become a hindering rivalry."

Barnes Wallis, the most experienced British rigid airship designer, belonged to Vickers, where he had been in charge of that company's wartime rigids and the postwar *R 80*, the most advanced British rigid yet

country of Queen Victoria's day. Like his German contemporary Hugo Eckener, Thomson sought to use the airship to help rebuild his country's self-confidence. In Thomson's mind the airship could link the outposts of the empire symbolically as well as practically. This was no mean vision, albeit a doomed one.

It was also a vision that caught the popular imagination, although Britons, who vividly remembered the "baby killers" of World War I, never contracted a serious case of zeppelin fever. In the early 1920s the airship was almost universally hailed as the future of long-distance travel. By 1924 both the British *R 34* and then the German *LZ 126* (the *Los Angeles*) had easily crossed the Atlantic. Meanwhile airplanes could barely make the built. His young subordinate, Nevil Shute Norway, had nothing but praise for the man who created the *R 100*. "To my mind Wallis was the greatest engineer in England at that time and for twenty years afterward," he later wrote. But Wallis had the distinct disadvantage of having to create a ship larger than any German zeppelin under the terms of a fixed-price contract. This meant not enough time or money for a full program of basic research before construction got underway in the World War I airship shed at Howden.

At the Royal Airship Works at Cardington, meanwhile, money was not a problem. While the *R 100* (soon known as the capitalist ship) had to pinch every penny, the designers of the *R 101* (the socialist ship) seemed able to afford to experiment with everything. They even built an entire hull section of the ship for tests, then had it dismantled. And each innovation concocted by the researchers at Cardington was accompanied by blasts of publicity, which then made it hard to discard something paid for by the taxpayers that hadn't really worked out.

According to Lee Payne, in *Lighter than Air*, "it was a little like starting on a skyscraper without ever having built a house." Unlike the Germans, the British lacked a deep tradition of rigid airship construction. Most of their earlier airships had been copies of German designs. Both teams decided to start essentially from first principles and build a truly British rigid twice the size of the *Los Angeles*, until then the biggest zeppelin.

(Above) The blurred vertical bands visible in this photograph are evidence of ripples along the *R 100*'s outer cover. (Below) The *R 101* (left) and the *R 100* sit side by side in their twin sheds at Cardington.

The determination to start from scratch led to some innovative design decisions on both sides. To simplify construction, Wallis and the Vickers team reduced the number of rings and longitudinal girders on the *R 100*, which left extra space between each support. During test flights this caused the outer cover to flap and tear at high speeds. Even after this problem was corrected, the cover was never wholly satisfactory. When the ship was flying fast, the fabric developed an alarming ripple effect.

At the Royal Airship Works one experiment was the use of stainless steel in the *R 101*'s main girders—heavier than Duralumin but definitely stronger. These produced a structurally stronger ship, but at a great cost in weight. More problematical were the dual-purpose gas valves—for both automatic and manual gas release—mounted on the sides of the gas cells. These proved far too sensitive, opening automatically whenever the ship rolled more than three degrees, which it did often. Most innovative of all was the design for the big rings, which dispensed with the wire bracing used in zeppelin construction (thus giving the rings the appearance of huge bicycle wheels) for bulkier unbraced rings, a system adopted in the later big American rigids. These stole space from the gasbags, but were considerably stronger than the German type. They did, however, require an elaborate bridle to prevent the gasbags from surging fore and aft. In zeppelins, the wire bracing acted as a bulkhead that kept the bags in place.

The *R 101*, the coddled government favorite, was the more experimental of the two new ships. But both were remarkably similar in basic aeronautical design, adopting the fat, fully streamlined shape that meant no two rings were of the same diameter—part of the reason they took so long to build. Both attached the control car beneath the hull while passenger spaces and crew quarters were housed within the frame. However, whereas the passenger accommodations for the *R 100* were commodious, those for the *R 101* verged on the luxurious, including a spacious lounge, a big dining room and a promenade with slanted eight-foot-high windows set in the hull. There was even a smoking room, the first ever on an airship, with fireproof floor, walls and ceiling.

In June 1929, with both ships nearing

completion, the Labour party returned to office. Thus Thomson was back at the air ministry for the first flying tests. First out of the hangar and into the air was the *R 101*. But even before her initial flight on October 14, 1929, her builders realized they had designed a ship with a serious flaw: she was far too heavy. When her fixed weight was subtracted from the lift provided by the nearly 5 million cubic feet of hydrogen, she had a mere thirty-five tons of useful lift, far from the sixty-three tons called for in the original contract. Once fuel and ballast, crew and passengers, food and baggage were loaded on board, there would be too little margin of safety for commercial operation over long distances. The *R 101* could fly, but in her current state she would never make it to Karachi, India, where a huge new airship shed, the largest building in the British Empire, awaited.

While the designers weighed every option for increasing the ship's disposable lift, she went through her early trials. Thomson came aboard for her second trial flight on October 18, a trip of 210 miles in seven hours, his first ride in an airship. The only blot on an otherwise successful test came when Major Scott insisted on conducting the landing sequence himself. First he threw the ship out of trim by releasing too much water ballast. Then he overshot the mooring mast, which caused several landing lines to get tangled. But the *R 101* was finally brought home safely.

At the foot of the mooring mast after the flight, Thomson rhapsodized before the assembled gentlemen of the press: "I have rarely had a more pleasant experience. There is a feeling of complete

(Left) Nevil Shute Norway, standing on the stairs at upper left, was one of the Vickers employees who posed for this publicity picture of the *R 100*'s dining saloon, which gave easy access to the promenade decks (top right) that ran along both sides of the ship. (Bottom right) Before the airship's completion, Vickers hosted a tea aboard the *R 100* for government officials and businessmen.

detachment and security. Certainly I have never been so comfortable on any ocean vessel and the motion is comparable to that of a river steamer, only the airship is less noisy. There is room to walk about and to admire the view with always about fifty acres of countryside to be seen. We watched a pack of foxhounds running across country. I signed a good many documents and I found that an airship is a particularly congenial place in which to do work requiring study." He went on to stress what to the eager press and public was not so obvious. "I want to make it perfectly clear as I did when I introduced the program in 1924, that it is all tentative and experimental. So far the experiment has amply justified itself." But had it?

Nevil Shute Norway waxed almost as enthusiastic about the *R 100*'s first flight on December 16, 1929, although he later confessed some unease at the fact that the ship carried only fifty parachutes for the fifty-four people on board. Norway took the precaution of carrying a "very large clasp knife and sharpening it to a fine point and a razor edge." In the event of a crash, he would use it to cut his way through the fabric cover before the ship went up in flames. But his nervousness soon left him: "Rightly or wrongly I felt as safe through all the flights that *R 100* made as on a large ship." Her maiden flight terminated at Cardington, where she officially became government property. When not at the mast she would be

housed in a big shed beside the one for the *R 101*.

The *R 100* was also heavy, delivering a useful lift of fifty-one tons—better than the *R 101* but still well short of the contract specification. And the Vickers ship owed much of her relative lightness to her Rolls-Royce gasoline engines, weighing considerably less than the diesels employed by the *R 101*, which had originally been designed for use in Canadian railway locomotives. Diesels were called for in the original specifications because it was believed that gasoline—more flammable than diesel oil—was unsafe for use in tropical climes. But Barnes Wallis and the *R 100* design team simply ignored this requirement when they realized that the available diesel motors weighed much more per horsepower than gasoline engines. In only one area was the *R 100* clearly superior to the *R 101*: she achieved the impressive top speed of eighty-one miles per hour, compared to the *R 101*'s seventy miles per hour.

The public, however, cared little for weight and other problems. During the summer and fall of 1929, when the *R 101* had floated frequently from the Cardington mast, the roads around the air station went into gridlock. It was estimated that more than a million people made the pilgrimage to see their airship.

At the end of November, a few weeks before the *R 100* arrived on the

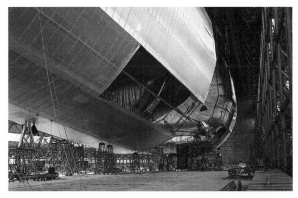

(Above) The newly lengthened *R 101* floats at the Cardington mast in late September 1930. The darker area under her nose is one of the sections of the original cover that was not replaced. The insertion of an extra bay (top and bottom left) added 45 feet of length and slightly over 500,000 cubic feet of gas capacity, enough extra lift to make the flight to India feasible.

scene, the *R 101* had gone back into her shed for a major refit to reduce weight. The simplest move would have been to replace the diesel engines with gasoline. But the government refused to authorize this change. Instead the builders removed every scrap of excess weight, including a number of passenger cabins, and then cut the ship in two, lengthening it by an extra bay and an additional gas cell. In desperation, they also loosened the wire netting that kept the gasbags from surging, thus increasing their capacity.

According to Douglas Robinson, the result was "doubly disastrous." The surging of the gasbags now made the craft statically unstable, causing it to pitch up and down even in calm air and requiring constant correction from the elevators. At least as serious, the expanded netting allowed the surging gasbags to rub against the upper girders, which soon wore holes in the bags and caused multiple leaks. The builders' solution was to put cotton padding on the girders to try to stop the chafing.

Over the summer of 1930, while the *R 101* was being cut apart and lengthened so that she could at last attempt the long-promised flight to India, the *R 100* made her transatlantic trip to Canada. Despite the problems over the St. Lawrence, the trip proved a public-relations triumph. Departing from the specially built new mast at Montreal, she

THE *R 100* IN CANADA

The *R 100*'s visit to Canada in the summer of 1930 caused a sensation. (Below) Hundreds of thousands of Canadians and Americans flocked to St. Hubert Airport just outside Montreal to see the huge ship lying at the mast and to snap up souvenir buttons, photographs and even phonograph records of a new song, "The R-100." The passengers on her publicity flight saw the Parliament Buildings in Ottawa by night, ate breakfast over Niagara Falls, and got breathtaking views of the burgeoning Toronto skyline, including the Bank of Commerce Building (opposite top). On her return from Ontario, the *R 100* passed over Montreal's Beaver Hall Hill, then headquarters of the Bell Telephone Company (opposite bottom).

took a twenty-five-hour flight to Ottawa, Niagara Falls, Toronto and Kingston before enthusiastic crowds. Then she successfully flew home on five engines, one having failed at the end of her publicity flight.

However, when the *R 100* was walked back into her Cardington shed on August 16, 1930, she was not a safe airship. Her outer cover and gas cells had so deteriorated that both would have to be replaced. According to Sir Peter Masefield, author of *To Ride the Storm*, "*R 100* had been a lucky ship to survive the various incidents in the course of its ten flights." She was slated for a complete refit along with the installation of a new bay for extra lift. But the *R 100* would never leave her hangar to fly again.

I N THE MIDDLE OF SEPTEMBER 1930, NEVIL SHUTE NORWAY VISITED Cardington to discuss with two senior officers the modifications Vickers was proposing for the *R 100*. He found the men in question, Squadron Leader Ralph Booth and First Officer George Meager, in a small office in the hangar that housed the now idle airship. Since neither would be flying with the *R 101* on her flight to India, now tentatively scheduled for early October, they had time on their hands. As the men relaxed over a cup of tea, one of the officers pulled out a

square piece of fabric cover and showed it to Norway.

"It was ordinary outer cover, linen fabric, silver doped on a red oxide base," wrote Norway. "On the inner surface two-inch tapes had been stuck on with some adhesive, evidently for strengthening. I didn't know what I was expected to say, and turned it about in my hands, and suddenly my hand went through it. In parts it was friable, like scorched brown paper, so that if you crumpled it in your hand it broke up into flakes. I stared at it in horror, thinking of *R 100*."

"Good God," Norway said. "Where did that come from?"

"All right," Booth replied. 'That's not off our ship. That's off *R 101*."

"But what's happened to it? What made it go like this?" the young engineer demanded.

It turned out that in an effort to strengthen two sections of the outer cover, reinforcing patches had been glued on using a rubber solution. This solution had reacted with the doping agent to cause the fabric to deteriorate.

"I hope they've got all this stuff off the ship," Norway said.

"They say they have," answered Booth.

In fact, this "friability" was only the latest problem with the *R 101*'s original cover. Large sections had rotted and split and most of it had

(Above) Squadron Leader Ralph Booth was the *R 100*'s captain for her successful voyage to Canada and back. (Right) The *R 101*'s lower fin is doped with a red-oxide base.

already been replaced. However, two significant segments of the old cover remained—an area just forward of the fins and a larger section wrapping around the hull just back of the nose. Unlike the parts that had rotted, these areas had been doped in place and had held up much better. So they had been reinforced with cloth strips attached with the rubber adhesive that had caused the fabric deterioration. By the time this new problem was discovered, replacing the sections would have meant canceling the October flight. So the affected areas were simply patched over again, this time using dope as an adhesive. Thus, the reliability of the most vulnerable portion of the *R 101*'s outer cover—the segment around the bow that took the most stress when flying with dynamic lift and bore the brunt of rain or hail—was now an open question.

How on earth had this been allowed to happen? The answer is a combination of publicity, politics and pride—along with a deadly dose of bureaucratic duplicity. Lord Thomson had long made clear his hope to fly to India and back in time for the Imperial Conference of October 1930, as a dramatic demonstration of the airship's potential to forge new links between the distant outposts of the empire. He had been equally clear, however, that he would not do so if the builders of the ship considered the trip premature.

But for years the public had been hearing about the wonders of the Cardington ship with all her made-in-Britain novelties. Ever since the *R 101* made her first trial flight, Lord Thomson had contributed to these exaggerated expectations with his optimistic pronouncements. Then the *R 100* had one-upped her rival with the trip to Canada and back. How could the *R 101*'s builders now admit that their ship, so long in the making and remaking, was not as good as her competitor? And the trip clearly meant an enormous amount to the air minister.

The truth seems to be that the men in charge

THE *GRAF ZEPPELIN* IN ENGLAND

On April 26, 1930, the *Graf Zeppelin* arrived at Cardington (right) to pick up Dr. Hugo Eckener, who had dined the previous evening with Lord Thomson. "It was the most perfect landing I have ever seen," one of the British airshipmen commented. British football fans were less impressed when Captain Lehmann flew low over Wembley Stadium during a Cup Final (below), bringing the game to a temporary standstill.

(Right) Major Herbert Scott (middle) and Lieutenant Colonel Vincent Richmond, the *R 101*'s chief designer, show the ship's control car to Dr. Hugo Eckener (at right).

The elegantly appointed public rooms of the *R 101* included a spacious dining saloon (opposite left). The magnificent main lounge (opposite right) ran the breadth of the ship and was flanked by raised promenades whose 45-degree-angle windows (below bottom right) provided panoramic views. Designers imagined there would be plenty of room in the 30-by-62-foot lounge to enjoy an after-dinner drink or to foxtrot to the melodies of a small dance band (below left). More intimate socializing would take place in the smoking room (below top right), with its fireproof asbestos walls and sheet-aluminum floors.

at Cardington realized the *R 101*'s weaknesses, but chose to discount them. More important, they concealed the full extent of the problems from Lord Thomson. As minister he must be held responsible for the final decision to fly, but his own advisers kept him in the dark as to the risks involved. These men decided there wasn't time to replace the suspect sections of the cover. Instead they would give the revamped ship one twenty-four-hour test flight, then send her on her way.

With the benefit of hindsight, it seems almost impossible to believe that what Sir Peter Masefield calls "virtually a new airship" would set out for India only three days after emerging from her hangar. Even more incredible is the fact that she did so after only *one* test flight—shortened from twenty-four to seventeen hours—and that during that flight she never achieved full cruising speed due to a broken oil cooler. In calm weather the trial flight went well otherwise, but gave no indication whether the padding on the girders would eliminate the problem of gasbag chafing or if the repatched cover sections were sound.

The day before the departure Lord Thomson paid a visit to his old friend at 10 Downing Street, Prime Minister Ramsay MacDonald. MacDonald asked his air minister whether the trip to India was really necessary. Thomson was adamant about going and discounted the element of risk. "He believed in the ship," MacDonald later wrote. "It was his child. He had watched it grow. How could he stay at home whilst it went on its way to attainment?"

Beyond these two men, few knew that the trip held an extra meaning for Thomson, who had been born in Bombay in 1875. Some months earlier the prime minister had asked his friend whether he would consider becoming the next viceroy of India. Thomson was seriously considering the proposition. His first visit in many years to the land of his birth would likely seal his decision.

A T 6:15 P.M. ON THE EVENING OF OCTOBER 4, 1930, A LONG BLUE Daimler rolled across the field of the Cardington Air Station toward the 202-foot-high mooring mast. Locked to the top of the tower the vast, dark shape of the *R 101* swung uneasily in the fitful wind. Along the lower side of the hull, golden light gleamed from the promenade windows and the control car. Already most of the passengers and baggage had ascended the mast

Prime Minister Ramsay MacDonald (left) and his good friend
Christopher Birdwood Thomson.

elevator and crossed the gangplank just beyond the point of the nose.

The Daimler came to a stop at the foot of the tower and out of its back seat unfolded the tall, slightly stooped figure of Lord Thomson of Cardington. He shook hands genially with the group of officials assembled to greet him, their mood likewise cheerful and expectant. Then the group posed for a final photograph that would undoubtedly grace the Sunday papers.

At Cardington the weather seemed to be steadily worsening, but Major Scott gave no thought to postponing the flight. At 6:36 P.M., Flight Lieutenant H. Carmichael Irwin shouted out the order to slip the mast, and the largest airship in the world backed gently away from the tower, then rose slowly upward into the gloomy twilight. As the wind strengthened and a drizzling rain started to fall, she faded into the deepening darkness with forty-two crew and twelve passengers on board. The schedule called for an arrival at Ismailia, Egypt, the midway stopping point, on the evening of October 5. Then on the next morning to Karachi.

After slowly circling the town of Bedford in the traditional departure gesture, the *R 101* sailed into a freshening head wind toward London. To those who saw her pass, she seemed to be flying awfully low. And indeed, she left the mast heavier than planned, needing to drop about four tons of water ballast at the time of takeoff. Even so, she struggled to reach a safe cruising altitude of around one thousand feet. And the turbulent winds caused her to pitch and roll, which meant gas was inevitably leaking from the newfangled valves on her gasbags.

Perhaps Cardington's staff should have thought twice about the plush blue Axminster carpet that covered the passenger lounge floor in order to impress the *R 101*'s future guests. It weighed more than half a ton. Incredible it may seem, but a ship her builders and crew knew needed every ounce of useful lift to make this landmark voyage blithely carried this weighty frill, not to mention an extra nine tons of fuel so as to make the refueling time in Ismailia shorter. That way diesel fumes would not disturb the dignitaries at Lord Thomson's state dinner.

In the control car Flight Lieutenant Irwin and Major Scott—as usual assuming the role of commodore—knew the weather was deteriorating, but they pressed on, even though they were also experiencing engine trouble. Soon after takeoff, the oil pressure to Engine No. 5 dropped sharply, and it had to be shut down for repairs.

The *R 101* circles St. Paul's Cathedral on a flight over London. (Overleaf) A few hardy souls brave wind and rain to watch the *R 101* leave the English coast.

Meanwhile, oblivious to these concerns, the twelve distinguished passengers assembled in the dining lounge at the linen-draped tables laden with fine china and silver cutlery had already finished the hot soup course and were tucking into a delicious cold supper. The motion of the ship was noticeable but gentle, like being rocked in a cradle.

Those who braved the rain to catch a glimpse of the *R 101* as she lumbered low over London could see she was fighting the wind. Though her big diesel engines throbbed powerfully, she pitched and rolled noticeably as she made painfully slow headway. Over the capital, Engine No. 5 came briefly back on line for a few minutes. But the pressure-gauge problem recurred, and it was shut down again for further work.

As the ship headed southeastward over Kent, she received from Cardington the most ominous weather report so far: "Trough of low pressure along coasts of British Isles, moving East. Ridge of high pressure over Southern France." For the next twelve hours along her projected course, the *R 101* would encounter winds of up to fifty miles per hour with low cloud and frequent rain. She was already fighting weather unlike any she had ever experienced, and it was going to get worse. According to Masefield, "had this forecast come through three hours before, the start would almost certainly have been postponed."

At this critical juncture Scott and Irwin had a difficult decision to make. The prudent course was to turn back to Cardington and restart the trip the next morning. But to Scott, who had sailed the *R 100* straight into a thunderstorm over the St. Lawrence when he could without any loss of face have steered around it, this would have seemed cowardly. Nor could there be any thought of slowing down to see how the ship handled such nasty conditions. The minister's arrival on time for his dinner in Egypt was already in serious doubt. With only four engines operational, it took the *R 101* until 9:35 P.M. to reach the English coast just east of Hastings, three hours since slipping off the tower at Cardington. She would need fairer weather and all five engines to have any hope of meeting her schedule.

As the ship passed the coastal cliffs and headed across the Channel, watchers below could see the figures of passengers through the lighted windows. And despite the fact that the ship was now flying near its pressure height of 1,200 feet, dance music could be heard over the dull drone of the motors. The appearance of gaiety and nonchalance contrasted starkly with the

wild wind and rain that soon swallowed up the ship as she made her way toward France.

Just before 11:00 P.M., at mid-Channel, the engineers finally fixed the pressure gauge on Engine No. 5 and cranked it up to full cruising power. Now all the motors were running and the airspeed reached a respectable sixty-three miles per hour. (Due to the head wind, however, her ground speed was roughly half this.) The *R 101* had never traveled through the air this fast. More important, she had never placed this much aerodynamic pressure on the large section of repatched cover at the bow, already weakened by the soaking rain.

The passengers stayed up to watch the lights of the French coast appear through the rain and clouds. A few smoked a final cigar in the smoking room, then turned in. By midnight almost everyone had retired to their cabins, and most of the very tired crew were also catching a few well-earned winks. In the control car the navigator set a course for Paris and then went to bed for a nap. Major Scott almost certainly retired, with instructions to be awakened in the event of any problems.

Despite the foul weather the ship was performing well as she made her slow progress southeastward over the French countryside. With the watch change at 2:00 A.M., an exhausted Flight Lieutenant Irwin, who had been up for eighteen hours, probably left the ship in the charge of Second Officer Maurice Steff and Chief Coxswain George "Sky" Hunt, one of the most experienced airshipmen on board. But no one can know for sure exactly who was in command in the control car during the next few fateful minutes.

The *R 101* labored painfully forward at little more than twenty miles per hour over the ground against a gusty, rising wind now almost dead on the nose. Apart from the duty watch, almost everyone on board was fast asleep. Harry Leech, an engineer from the Cardington design team, sat alone in the smoking room enjoying a last cigarette before bed. And Michael Rope, one of the ship's designers, was prowling toward the bow, looking for problems. Otherwise all was quiet. The ship had performed well in difficult conditions and there seemed to be no cause for concern. Soon the worst of the weather would be over. The sunny Mediterranean beckoned.

Leech was dozing fitfully on a smoking room settee when the ship suddenly dropped away from under him. Every loose item, including himself, flew toward the forward bulkhead. No more than a minute later the ship resumed an even keel, and he began picking up glasses and a soda water siphon that had fallen to the floor.

At almost the same moment as the ship righted itself, Sky Hunt passed by the switch room, just inside the hull above the control car on his way aft toward the crew quarters. As he did so, he called out, "We're down, lads," jolting Chief Electrician Arthur Disley out of a half sleep. Moments later, the ship dove again—and crashed into a French hillside.

Only one person observed the last moments of the *R 101*. He was Georges Alfred Rabouille, a poacher setting rabbit snares on a low ridge near the hamlet of Allonne, just south of Beauvais. "The airship was in distress when I saw her first, seemingly having a hard fight of it in the violent winds," Rabouille later recalled. "And though her engines were running, she was steadily losing height as she was coming over. Suddenly she dipped, and then seemed to straighten out, and then she sank slowly to the earth, her nose pointing downwards. There was a tremendous explosion. A burst of flame swept the envelope. The whole ship was in flames. I was only a hundred yards away and the heat was awful. I lost my head and I ran as hard as I could away from that place."

Harry Leech was not even shaken when the ship hit, so gentle was its impact. Then the door to the smoking room burst open to reveal a wall of flame, and the upper deck collapsed around him. He began to choke from the fumes, although so far the fire had not reached him. Screams and moans came from the crew quarters and the passenger deck. Leech tore a settee from the wall and used it to punch through the asbestos partition. He then found his way out the starboard side of the ship to safety.

Joseph Binks and A.V. Bell, in the after engine car, had almost given up hope when the flames that surrounded them were doused by a deluge of water ballast from a broken tank overhead. Holding wet handkerchiefs over their faces, they left the car and ran through the still-burning skeleton and out the port side, at last rolling gratefully in the long, wet grass. Then they began shouting, "Hello, hello—anybody out? Where are you?"

Their shouts were answered by only four others, among them Leech and Disley. By the time rescue parties reached the scene, most of the forty-eight bodies inside the wreck had been burned beyond identification, including that of Lord Thomson.

What had happened? Just before 2:07 A.M. the *R 101* was flying along normally on the route to Paris. A mere two minutes later it crashed. Examination of the wreck showed the framework intact, so a structural failure could not account for the disaster. The most convincing theory, which comes from Sir Peter Masefield, fingers the repatched section of cover near the bow as the culprit.

The key to Masefield's case is the strange appearance of Sky Hunt moving aft toward the crew quarters by the time the ship briefly leveled off—no more than a minute after the initial plunge began. For the chief coxswain to have reached the switch room by this juncture, he had to have left the control car *before* the ship began its dive. In advance of any obvious trouble, Hunt knew something was gravely wrong.

(Right and below) On the morning of October 5, 1930, all that remained of the *R 101* was a smashed skeleton splayed across a hillside near Beauvais, France. (Bottom) French firemen carry a charred body from the wreck. Few of the corpses recovered from the airship were identifiable.

Masefield's conclusion? Perhaps as little as a minute before the fatal sequence began, Michael Rope, on his tour of inspection, had discovered a tear in the outer cover near the bow—the suspect repatched section. He realized instantly that the already rain-soaked and now exposed forward gasbags would be the next to go. Immediately he reported back to the control car and Hunt rushed off to alert the crew that the ship was in trouble. As he did so, one or two forward cells began to deflate and the bow to plunge.

Now the men in the control car made a fatal error. While the height coxswain fought to bring the ship back to level by applying full up elevator, the officer in charge ordered the engines slowed to ease the stress on the damaged forward part of the ship. (Survivors from two different engine cars remembered receiving slow-engine orders before the crash.) First the ship leveled off—at full cruising speed, the elevators could more than compensate for the loss of gas in the forward cells. But as the engines slowed, the elevators lost their effect and the final plunge commenced. Just perhaps, had the *R 101* maintained her speed, she could have risen out of danger, even with her two forward gasbags completely deflated, then turned and flown home to Cardington with the help of a following wind. But such a scenario seems unlikely, given the fact that she was flying heavy and depending on dynamic lift before the accident happened.

Masefield's theory highlights the critical gap between aspirations and experience that was the root cause of the *R 101* tragedy. Hugo Eckener would

never have embarked on a 5,500-mile voyage in a ship that had not completed a full endurance test nor been flown at full cruising speed. He would almost certainly have postponed such a trip when the weather turned ominous.

No DISASTER SINCE THE LOSS OF THE *TITANIC* IN 1912 had so shocked the British public. Thousands upon thousands filed slowly past the forty-eight flag-draped coffins that lay in state at Westminster Abbey on October 10, 1930. A million people watched the funeral cortege in "the greatest peace-time pageant since the coronation of George V in 1910," according to Henry Cord Meyer. Walking behind the coffins was Dr. Hugo Eckener with a small band of representatives from the Zeppelin Company.

The British government soon canceled plans for two even larger rigids, the *R 102* and *R 103*, which might well have out-*Hindenburg*ed the *Hindenburg* before that German ship even reached the drawing board. In 1931 the *R 100* was broken up; no British rigid airship has since taken to the skies. The future of these aerial giants, if they were to have a future at all, now lay in the hands of the Germans and the Americans.

(Above right) On October 7, 1930, forty-eight Union Jack-draped coffins lay in state in London's Westminster Hall. (Right inset) Among the scorched items salvaged from the wreck was a pocket watch stopped at the moment of the crash, 2:09 A.M. (Left inset) Also recovered was the partly burned Royal Air Force ensign that flew from the *R 101*'s tail. It was mounted above a memorial plaque in the parish church of St. Mary, Cardington, not far from where the airship sheds (left) still stand today.

CHAPTER FIVE

GLOBETROTTER

"She was to be an airship in which one would not merely fly, but would also be able to voyage."
—Hugo Eckener

"The Graf Zeppelin is more than just machinery, canvas and aluminum. It has a soul."
—Lady Grace Drummond Hay

NOT LONG AFTER THE CRASH OF THE *R 101*, Hugo Eckener agreed to write a foreword to the first English-language biography of Count Ferdinand von Zeppelin. He took advantage of the opportunity to defend the count's invention. "In my view," Eckener wrote, "the smoking wreckage of the R 101 furnished us with no argument against the utility of the zeppelin." The fault lay not with the basic concept of the rigid airship design, he argued, but with the many innovations in the *R 101*'s construction.

By October 1930 Hugo Eckener's words on the topic of air travel carried great weight, for he had built and flown what was already the most successful airship in history, the *Graf Zeppelin*. Two years earlier, in the fall of 1928, while *R 100* and the *R 101* were still taking shape in their sheds, the Zeppelin Company launched the *LZ 127*. A few weeks later, after a series of successful test flights (including a 34.5-hour endurance run) proved the new *Graf* airworthy, she set off for

...Zeppelin Eckener Fund badge. (Above) On July 8, 1928, Countess Hel... on Brandenstein-Zeppelin christens the new ship on what would have been her father's ninetieth birthday. (Opposite) Over the Atlantic in 1930, the *Graf Zeppelin* encounters the sailing vessel *Archibald Douglas*.

New York. The flight was cleverly timed to coincide with Columbus Day celebrations in the United States. Eckener wanted maximum publicity to help him establish a regular transatlantic commercial airship service as soon as possible.

Once again the usually prudent Eckener proved he also knew how to gamble when the stakes seemed worth it. Although the *Graf Zeppelin* had passed a far more rigorous series of tests than would the ill-fated *R 101*, she was nonetheless an experimental ship, and at the time, the largest airship ever to have flown. Yet on only her seventh flight, she was heading across the Atlantic with a full complement of twenty passengers.

Her chief designer, Ludwig Dürr, who had had a hand in the design of all the zeppelins built so far, had squeezed every cubic inch of volume he could into the new aircraft because Eckener needed every possible ounce of lift to prove that a big airship could become a reliable long-range passenger carrier. The result, an elongated and somewhat less shapely version of the highly streamlined *Los Angeles*, was the biggest ship that could be built in the largest of the three remaining construction sheds at Friedrichshafen. When the *Graf Zeppelin* was first walked out of the hangar in September 1928, the top of her hull cleared the arch of the hangar doorway by just two feet. Even so, she was much smaller than Eckener would have liked. The *Graf*'s 3,037,000 cubic feet of hydrogen capacity

THE MAGELLAN OF THE AIR

The commander of the *Graf Zeppelin*, Hugo Eckener, seems to have impressed everyone who met him. Although he was slightly under six feet in height, he seemed taller. His bright blue eyes—one set a little higher than the other in his time-worn face—his commanding voice, and the self-confident dignity of his manner combined to produce a man of great magnetism. Eckener could be impatient and brusque when he felt his time was being wasted, and he spared neither officers nor crew when he felt they deserved criticism. But he was also quick to praise and inspired unstinting loyalty in those who served under him. He was a cultivated man, who seldom swore and never told an off-color story. A lover of literature and music, Eckener could quote at will from Goethe, Schiller and Shakespeare and claimed to be able to whistle from memory every theme from Beethoven's nine symphonies.

would soon be well outclassed by the roughly 5 million cubic feet of lifting gas pumped into both the *R 100* and the *R 101*.

Actually, the *Graf* had two sets of gas cells, one for lifting gas, the other for fuel—nearly a million cubic feet of blau gas. This was a gas resembling propane that Dürr hoped would replace gasoline as food for the ship's five Maybach motors. Since blau gas weighed almost exactly as much as air, its consumption during a long flight would not make the ship lighter, thus forcing the crew to valve hydrogen. This novel arrangement proved completely satisfactory and remained in place throughout the long and happy life of the ship.

At 775 feet the *Graf* was only two feet shorter than the lengthened *R 101*, but unlike the British ships, the new zeppelin's bridge area and passenger spaces shared a large gondola tucked into the curve just aft of the bow. This left more room in the hull for hydrogen and fuel while taking full advantage of the maximum height available in the construction shed. Although the lack of streamlining and the big gondola somewhat hampered the *Graf*'s speed, she cruised at seventy-three miles per hour and could reach a top speed of eighty miles per hour—figures that compared quite favorably with the two more aerodynamically efficient British ships.

Because Eckener was determined that the paying passengers would travel in the greatest comfort possible, he insisted, over Dürr's initial objections, that there be a kitchen on board so that hot meals could be prepared. The small dining room—16.5 feet by 16.5 feet—with its large windows along two sides, doubled as the passenger lounge and was located in the middle of the gondola to take advantage of its maximum width. Immediately aft of this were ten two-passenger cabins lining a central corridor so that each had its own window. The crew slept inside the hull along the aft portion of the triangular lower keel that formed a walkway from bow to stern. Ballast and cargo were also stored along the lower keel's length. A novel axial keel passing through the center-line, or axis, of the ship added strength to the framework and gave access to the hydrogen gasbags above and the blau gasbags below. All in all, it was an efficient design that made the most of everything the Germans had learned over more than twenty-five years of building rigid airships.

This was a good thing, as the *Graf*'s first Atlantic crossing would prove.

N THE CONTROL GONDOLA OF THE *GRAF ZEPPELIN*, HUGO ECKENER could not shake the feeling of tension. Thus far the trip to Lakehurst had gone even better than he had hoped, given the gloomy weather forecasts preceding the takeoff. Because of them he had chosen the southern route—down the Rhone Valley, through the Straits of Gibraltar and westward to Madeira. But throughout this warm, humid

(Inset) Passengers board
the *Graf Zeppelin* before
embarking on a
sightseeing trip over the
German countryside.

first night of the voyage, as the ship passed well south of the Azores, ever-more-violent lightning flashes lit the northern horizon.

In the stuffy crew quarters, First Officer Ernst Lehmann could not sleep. He, too, could feel that the new ship was about to face its first real test. As the morning of the second day dawned and the ship neared mid-ocean, that test lay clearly before Eckener's eyes: "Towards six in the morning we saw lying ahead of us a blue-black wall of cloud of very threatening aspect. It was advancing towards us at great speed from the northwest."

For some reason the usually cautious Eckener did not slow down. It was as if he wanted to test his new ship to the limit. He did call for his best elevator man to replace the less experienced fellow then standing at the wheel, but not in time. When the forward-moving ship met the onrushing front, the nose plunged sharply down. Then, moments later, a vertical gust struck with great force.

Lieutenant Commander Charles Rosendahl, representing the U.S. Navy during the *Graf*'s maiden crossing, had come into the control car when he saw the storm front approaching. The man who had free-ballooned the severed nose section of the *Shenandoah* safely back to earth wanted to see how Hugo Eckener, the master airship mariner, would handle the nasty-looking turbulence. To Rosendahl's horror, the inexperienced crewman at the elevator overcorrected for the initial downward plunge. So the bow was still rising when the vertical gust hit. Rosendahl shouted, an officer leapt to take over the elevator wheel, and Eckener grabbed for a girder to keep from losing his balance as the nose shot upward. Books and instruments fell to the floor of the control room, and pots and pans crashed in the kitchen. A crack of thunder exploded nearby. The *Graf* was less than a month old. Had the end come so soon?

The twenty passengers were just tucking into breakfast when the squall front hit. "Coffee, tea, butter, sausages, marmalade formed a glutinous mess and overspread the unlucky ones sitting with their backs to the stern," wrote Lady Grace Drummond Hay, the only female passenger on

board. "Breathless moments passed, leaving not a few blanched faces, and the thought—we were facing death." Then the *Graf* regained her equilibrium. Lady Drummond Hay laughed, turned to fellow journalist Karl von Wiegand, and said, "Karl, would you mind checking my cabin to see that my typewriter doesn't fall on the floor?" This broke the tension. A few others joined in the laughter and soon the passengers were busy helping the stewards clean up the mess.

When the *Graf Zeppelin* returned to an even keel, Hugo Eckener began

(Left) Breakfast went flying when the *Graf* ran into a squall front during her first Atlantic crossing. (Above) Hearst correspondents Lady Grace Drummond Hay and Karl von Wiegand.

to congratulate himself. His ship had handily survived turbulence he judged to be as bad as the Atlantic could offer. But his euphoria was premature. A few minutes later, as the airship rolled and pitched along at half speed through a torrential downpour, the chief machinist arrived in the control car, out of breath and panting. The cotton fabric covering the port horizontal stabilizer fin had torn away, he reported. Eckener immediately ordered the engines slowed further. If the torn and trailing fabric fouled the elevators or rudders, the ship could lose maneuverability. And with the starboard stabilizing fin now taking most of the horizontal load, at full speed it, too, might give way. But could the damage be repaired in mid-ocean?

Eckener quickly called for volunteers to assess the tear and attempt repairs. He said nothing when one of the men who stepped forward was

Repairs often had to be made during flight. Over the southern Atlantic in 1933, the soon-to-be-famous German photographer Alfred Eisenstaedt captured a crewman being lowered down the *Graf*'s side to tend to some damaged fabric.

his twenty-six-year-old son, Knut. Clinging to the exposed tail section in the driving rain and wind over the boiling Atlantic would be dangerous and difficult—like working on a scaffolding in a hurricane. But Knut was old enough to make his own decisions.

With typical self-awareness, Eckener did not let pride stand in the way of common sense. He asked Rosendahl to radio the U.S. Navy and request that a fast ship be sent to their position. If the fin could not be adequately fixed, he would still be able to drop enough ballast to keep the *Graf Zeppelin* airborne for the three days it would take a rescue vessel to reach them. He hoped it was only a precaution. Then he went aft to tell the passengers what had happened.

As the perilous work on the damaged fin proceeded, the slow-moving ship sank steadily toward the ocean. By the time Eckener returned to the control cabin, the *Graf* was only minutes away from crashing into the sea. He knew that a sudden increase in speed could blow someone off the tail, yet it was already too late to send a crewman aft to warn the repair party. He hesitated a moment, then ordered the engine revolutions increased.

Fortunately, Knut and the others had seen the ocean drawing closer and had climbed back inside the hull by the time the ship surged forward. When she regained sufficient altitude, Eckener slowed the engines once more and the men again crept out to continue the work of cutting or securing loose fabric. This start-and-stop process was repeated over and over again until the repairs were completed. There remained a gaping hole in the fin, but the ship could fly.

A relieved Eckener informed Rosendahl that he could call off the rescue ship, and the *Graf* proceeded forward at three-quarter speed—and

No one ever forgot a voyage on the ship with a soul. The excellent meals in the *Graf Zeppelin*'s dining room (above) were prepared in a small but efficient galley (below left), and were served by the chief steward (below middle) and his uniformed staff. Passengers had separate toilet and washroom facilities (below right), situated aft of the ten two-berth cabins.

(Top) In 1935, the year this timetable and fare schedule was issued, the *Graf Zeppelin* made sixteen round trips to Brazil. (Middle) Gummed paper labels like this one were affixed to all checked luggage. (Above) The *Graf* also carried many passengers on shorter flights in Europe. This passenger ticket is from an overnight trip between Münster and Friedrichshafen in June 1930.

(Above) Between meals the dining room became a lounge where passengers could read, play cards or simply contemplate the view out the large windows. When Ernst Lehmann was on board he would often bring out his accordion and serenade the voyagers with some of his favorite folk songs. (Above right) The passengers slept in bunk beds that could be converted into a comfortable couch during the day.

INSIDE THE
GRAF ZEPPELIN

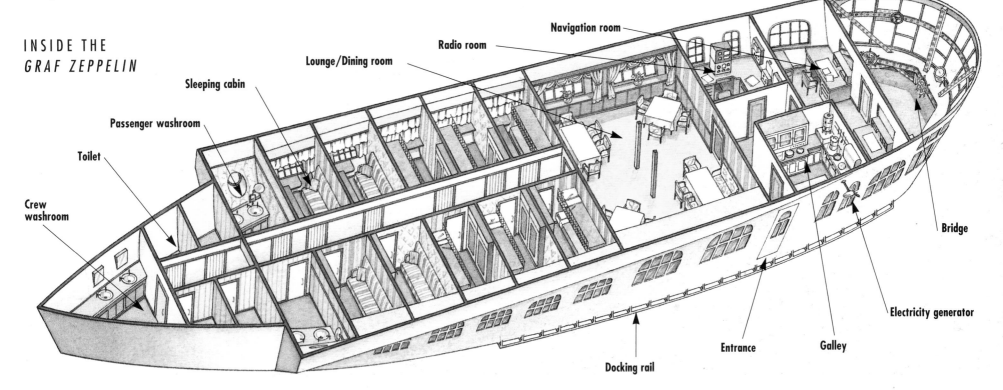

Navigation room

Radio room

Lounge/Dining room

Sleeping cabin

Passenger washroom

Toilet

Crew washroom

Bridge

Electricity generator

Entrance

Galley

Docking rail

toward a second test. As the ship approached Bermuda another storm front lay before Eckener, as did another difficult decision. If he tried to fly around the storm he risked running out of fuel. And to do so would establish the *Graf Zeppelin* as a ship too frail for rough weather. But would the damaged fin hold? Another calculated risk, another gamble worth taking. He ordered the helmsman to steer straight through. For an hour the *Graf* seesawed her way through fierce squalls and heavy rain. When the ship emerged into clear weather, an inspection disclosed only one small new rip in the fin.

In the time between Rosendahl's two radio messages, Americans had waited in an agony of suspense over the fate of the *Graf Zeppelin*. The wind-powered electric generators didn't work

The *Graf*'s midatlantic misadventure in October 1928 guaranteed that the New York ticker-tape parade that greeted Eckener and his crew the day after their arrival would be unusually enthusiastic.

august inmates of the United States Supreme Court were not immune to the excitement. Former president and now chief justice William Howard Taft read the message slipped him by one of the court pageboys and then leaned over to whisper in the ear of Justice Oliver Wendell Holmes, "The *Graf*'s here!"

The *Graf*'s trip northward became a huge victory celebration. Eckener sailed on to circle New York City, where midafternoon business came to a standstill. The next afternoon, after a trip that had lasted 111 hours and 44 minutes and traversed 6,168 miles, Dr. Eckener and most of his crew took part in an ecstatic New York ticker-tape parade. There would be other such welcomes in the future, but none would ever match this one for size and excitement.

when the ship flew slowly, so the ship's radio was silent while the repairs were being made. Grim newspaper headlines reported that the *Graf* was feared lost with all on board, that yet another tragedy had joined the long line of airship disasters. Then, as if by magic, the airship reported that all was well.

By the time the *Graf* finally crossed the American coastline near Cape Charles, Maryland, her mid-ocean travails had assured her a tumultuous welcome. And the canny Eckener took full advantage of the public-relations opportunity. He was already twenty-four hours behind schedule, so a few hours more would not make much difference. Instead of heading straight up the coast for Lakehurst, he sailed inland along Chesapeake Bay and took a triumphant turn over Baltimore and Washington. When the ship passed above the White House, President Coolidge broke away from an official reception to rush out on the lawn. He and the hundreds of thousands of Washingtonians who watched her pass could clearly see the hole in the damaged fin, which only added to the *Graf*'s heroic mystique. According to J. Gordon Vaeth, whose book *Graf Zeppelin* provides the most colorful account of this airship's remarkable career, even the

Looking back a decade later, Ernst Lehmann compared the welcome for the *Graf Zeppelin* with the 1924 arrival of the *LZ 126*: "The emotion that gripped America was very much different from that of years before. Then it was really only German Americans who feted us; the rest of America welcomed the American naval airship [*Los Angeles*], and regarded the conquering of the Atlantic as a technical demonstration and a sporting proposition. This time, however, they stretched out a friendly hand, honoring, in the enemy of yesterday, the friend of today.... The masses of people went mad with enthusiasm; factory sirens were blowing, locomotive and steam whistles shrilled out; the automobiles blew their horns, and a veritable storm of confetti and paper streamers fell from the windows of the skyscrapers."

The next day Eckener, Lehmann and the other officers traveled to Washington for an audience with President Coolidge. "A strange and contagious enthusiasm was rapidly taking possession of the American public," writes Gordon Vaeth. "It was a fascination, sometimes wild and uncontrolled, for the *Graf Zeppelin* and for everything and everybody connected with it. . . . Souvenirs from the *Graf*, especially pieces of the fabric from the fin, were in great demand and brought fantastic prices."

By the time the tumult died, the first transatlantic commercial airline seemed within Eckener's grasp. Before leaving the United States he began to try to raise working capital to found a passenger airline consisting of four airships even bigger than the soon-to-be launched *R 100* and *R 101*. He and Lehmann met with bankers and financiers in New York, then traveled to Akron, Ohio, to talk with Paul Litchfield, president of Goodyear-Zeppelin, which was bidding to build a big rigid airship for the United States Navy. The Americans were interested, but Eckener returned to Germany without any firm commitments for the $15 million he needed. Until this sum could be secured, he would have to keep the new ship in the public eye. And to do this, he needed operating capital.

Even the high prices the *Graf* could charge were not enough to make the ship commercially viable. With a crew of forty-three, not to mention the more than a hundred ground crew needed during landing and takeoff and the many more for maintaining the ship between flights, a single airship was a very expensive proposition. Despite Eckener's considerable powers of persuasion—including a pleasure flight to the eastern Mediterranean for government officials in the spring of 1929—the cash-poor Berlin authorities refused to contribute any more money to keep this symbol of resurgent national pride in the air. Eckener quickly realized he would have to find less conventional sources of revenue.

The aft end of the *Graf*'s passenger gondola looms large in this view of the airship, moored outside of the Goodyear company's huge airship hangar at Akron, Ohio.

Eckener had not yet found the final solution to his financial needs when, in the spring of 1929, the boldest gamble of his career began to form in his mind: the *Graf* would be the first aircraft to fly around the world. And not in Jules Verne's fictional eighty days, but in less than two weeks of flying time. If anything could convince the doubters that the future of airship travel had arrived, surely this was it. But how to finance a flight he estimated would cost a whopping $250,000?

The answer to this question turned out have two parts: journalists and stamp collectors. When William Randolph Hearst caught wind of Eckener's grand scheme, he immediately offered $150,000 for the exclusive rights to cover the flight. Eckener reluctantly countered that he could not exclude the German press from the world tour. In the end the two settled on a sum of $100,000 for world English-language rights. German newspapers offered another $12,500. Now Eckener had nearly half of what he needed.

Stamp collectors, who coveted any piece of mail carried on board the *Graf*, provided the rest. The world flight would be a collector's dream. The prospect of a single postcard franked in Friedrichshafen, Tokyo, Los Angeles and Lakehurst made philatelists salivate. And the Zeppelin Company received a hefty surcharge over standard postal rates for each of the thousands of cards and letters carried. By August 1929, when the world flight was about to begin, it was already in the black, although only two of the twenty passengers actually paid the $2,500 price for a round-the-world ticket.

Choosing a suitable route was Eckener's other major challenge. Two basic choices confronted him, each with serious disadvantages. The safer route, which would take the *Graf* mostly over water, where weather is more predictable than over land and weather reports (from ships) more easily obtainable than over the vast, uninhabited reaches of northern Asia, was also by far the longer. This course began by following the path the *R 101* planned to take to India the following year—through the Mediterranean to Egypt, then down the Persian Gulf to the Indian Ocean—before crossing the China Sea to Japan. But a nearly 9,000-mile route stretched the range of the *Graf* to an unacceptable limit. Any prolonged head wind would exhaust the ship's fuel and leave her drifting powerless over the China Sea.

The shortest practicable way from Friedrichshafen to Tokyo ran just over six thousand miles overland across Europe and Asia, north of the great mountain chains that include the Himalayas. It passed along the southern portion of the Soviet Union to Lake Baikal just north of Mongolia, then down the valley of the Amur River into Manchuria. But the steep mountains that flanked the Amur worried Eckener. If cloud or fog moved in and he lost his bearings, he might easily crash the ship.

Finally Eckener settled on an even more northerly route across central Russia and Siberia to Yakutsk, then over the Stanovoi Mountains to the Sea of Okhotsk. The little-known Stanovoi range, marked on Eckener's atlas at only 6,500 feet, did not appear to pose a serious challenge. Once crossed, he would have clear sailing south to Tokyo. He concluded that this was the safest route and, at only 7,000 miles, should provide ample fuel insurance. But it entailed flying over vast stretches of Siberian wilderness where there could be no hope of help in case of a forced landing.

The round-the-world flight of the *Graf Zeppelin* surely ranks as the high point in the forty-year story of the rigid airship. At the head of a stellar cast stood the already world-famous Dr. Hugo Eckener, the gruff, commanding presence whose grasp of weather had become so legendary as to seem almost shamanistic. The officers and crew under his command represented between them almost the whole past and future of the zeppelin. As usual, Eckener's second in command was Ernst Lehmann, whose career as a zeppelin pilot stretched back to the DELAG days before World War I. Lehmann was surely already eyeing the chair occupied by the man everyone now called "der Alte," for at sixty-one, Eckener was indeed nearing the age when most men retire.

Joining Lehmann, now forty-three, was a team of airship veterans in their late thirties or early forties. Most, like watch officer Hans von Schiller and navigator Max Pruss, had flown in zeppelins during the war. (As the captain of the *L 55*, von Schiller had reached the unprecedented altitude of 24,928 feet, the highest a rigid airship would ever fly.) Navigation officer Anton Wittemann, a former sea captain, had begun his flying days with the prewar DELAG. Taking a regular watch at the *Graf's* elevator wheel was Albert Sammt, whose first airship flight had been on the *Viktoria Luise* in 1912. He would later become the captain of the last zeppelin, the *LZ 130*.

Twenty-seven-year-old Heinrich Bauer must have felt at least a little intimidated at being admitted to this elite echelon. He belonged to a new generation being groomed for the fleet of big airships that seemed just around the corner. Bauer, who had joined the Zeppelin Company only two years earlier, stood one of the three elevator watches, a sure signal that he was slated for quick advancement. As far as Eckener was concerned, mastery of the elevator was the essential art of airship flying.

The twenty passengers on the round-the-world flight included the arctic explorer and pioneer aviator Sir Hubert Wilkins and the two Hearst journalists, Lady Grace Drummond Hay and Karl von Wiegand, by now great boosters of airship travel, three German newspaper correspondents, two reporters from Japan and one from France. Commander Charles Rosendahl, captain of the *Los Angeles*, was once again on board,

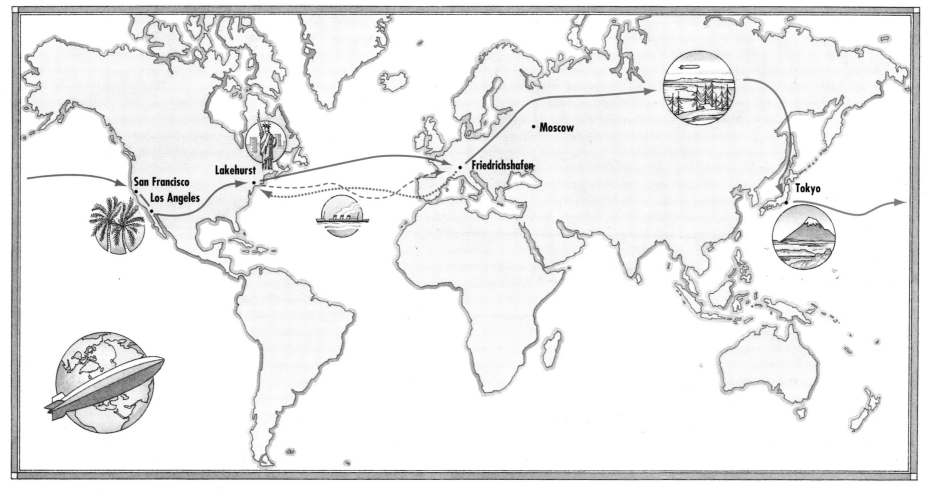

The *Graf Zeppelin*'s round-the-world flight in August 1929 began with a trip from Friedrichshafen to Lakehurst (dotted line), allowing William Randolph Hearst to claim that the voyage started from American soil.

as a representative of the U.S. Navy. The German government had its representative, as did the Russian and the Japanese.

Before dawn on August 15, 1929, the *Graf Zeppelin* lifted up from Friedrichshafen to begin her epochal voyage. Actually, this was a second beginning for the trip. If you asked the Americans, this pioneering attempt at global circumnavigation had begun one week earlier in Lakehurst. It was a harmless compromise to satisfy the trip's chief backer, Mr. Hearst. And Eckener had used this extra flight from Friedrichshafen to New Jersey and back again to give the ship and its recently refurbished engines a thorough workout. So there would be two world flights: one from Lakehurst to Lakehurst for American consumption, and the other from Friedrichshafen to Friedrichshafen for the Europeans.

The first day unfolded magnificently except for a brief and unpleasant contretemps between Dr. Eckener and Comrade Karklin. The Russian government representative insisted angrily that the *Graf* must pass over Moscow; Eckener bluntly informed him that the weather reports pointed

to tail winds farther north and he bypassed the Soviet capital. The orderly farmscape of Germany soon gave way to the vast plains and forests of eastern Europe. Hour after hour the passengers sat gazing from the windows of the lounge. Like strangers at the beginning of a long ocean voyage, they were still a trifle shy. So Ernst Lehmann lightened the mood by unpacking his accordion and serenading them with excerpts from *Die Meistersinger*, Wagner's happiest opera.

Early on the morning of the second day, the Ural Mountains stretched below them. The *Graf* crossed this low mountain range—little more than heavily forested hills—with ease and in so doing crossed from Europe into Asia, from old Mother Russia into Siberia, from the known into the unknown. Everyone knew a symbolic watershed had been overflown.

The trackless immensity set against the forced intimacy of the airship seems to have loosened the passengers' reserve and created a convivial atmosphere as the *Graf* drove effortlessly eastward. The food was good, the wine flowed, and after dinner—with Eckener and senior officers sprinkled among the different tables—the passengers relaxed to the sound of the portable phonograph one of the passengers had brought on board. At one table Hubert Wilkins recounted tales of his explorations. At another Commander Rosendahl listened entranced as Lieutenant Commander Fujiyoshi of the Japanese navy described his amazing escape from a semi-rigid caught in a gale and running low on fuel. (He managed to hover his ship just above a tiny flat outcrop of a rocky island until the crew could jump to safety. Fujiyoshi leapt last, then watched his ship sail off, crash into a cliff and explode.) People autographed each other's menus as souvenirs. Some played cards or read or wrote. And the faint tattoo of Karl von Wiegand's typewriter drifted forward from the passenger quarters.

The romance of the situation impressed even the crusty captain: "The whole region gave the impression of a dreadful waste, uninhabitable for man or beast. . . . In grotesque contrast to all the deadly silence, the airship sailed, its cabins lighted, its care-free occupants dining and enjoying themselves; and yet, if for some reason it had been necessary to land in these swamps, escape from those black-green waters would not have been possible." The unheated cabins seemed particularly cold that night.

Rosendahl, however, had come prepared. He slept snugly in an eiderdown sleeping bag.

Young Heinrich Bauer never forgot the scene that met his eyes at the dawning of the third day: "In the first rays of the morning sun the marshland lay below us, water with little solid terrain. How endlessly small we were at that moment and what pride filled us to be able to contemplate a land that no human eye had seen before."

That afternoon the sky grew dark and ominous as the *Graf* caught up to a trough of low pressure. Now Eckener would discover what kind of nastiness the interior of the Asian continent could throw at him. Rosendahl, who had been through much worse, noted that Eckener's seasoned crew handled the turbulence with ease. After maybe ten minutes of ups and downs, the *Graf* reached the clearer and warmer air on the other side. Far from any large body of water, the dry air masses of the Siberian outback posed no threat to the sturdy aircraft. With increased confidence, she flew onward.

The only doubt left in Eckener's mind was the pass through the Stanovoi Mountains, which the airship entered late on the morning of the fourth day. Only this obstacle now lay between her and Tokyo. Were the

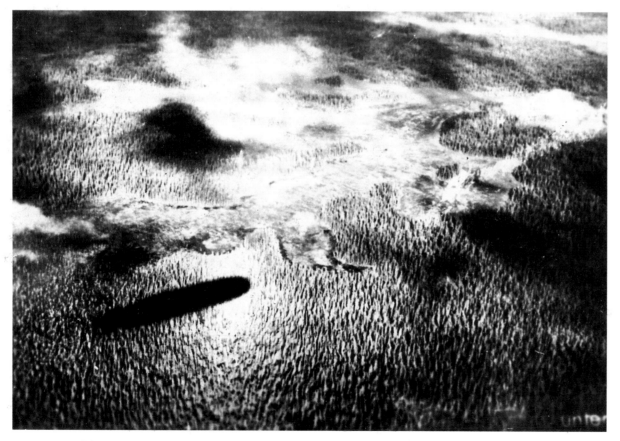

(Left) The *Graf Zeppelin* casts its signature shadow over the Siberian wilderness. (Above) Specially designed pouches, weighted with sand, were used to drop mail over destinations where the airship didn't actually land. (Below) An envelope that circumnavigated the globe from Lakehurst to Lakehurst.

atlases right, or would the crest of the pass be higher than 6,500 feet? If so, he would have to valve hydrogen, doubly precious on such a long flight. Should the ship later become weighted down by rain, he would need every ounce of lift.

With his fingers crossed, Eckener piloted the airship between the steep walls of the mountain pass that snaked slowly upward. Toward noon the crest hove into view, but a gusty wind made navigation in the narrow valley even more perilous. The altimeter passed 5,500 feet, then 6,000, and still the ship climbed. Then, with 150 feet to spare, the *Graf Zeppelin* passed over the highest point and began her descent to the sea.

The passengers certainly found the experience exciting, but Rosendahl wondered if the hairsbreadth passage had been entirely necessary. "At times I am inclined to think that crafty old Dr. Eckener did it purposely to keep us from thinking the flight had been entirely too easy."

Surfing on the edge of a typhoon over the Sea of Okhotsk, Eckener raced toward Tokyo, where he arrived on the evening of August 19, four and a half days after leaving Friedrichshafen. As water ballast splashed groundward to slow the ship's descent, a young German woman in the huge crowd of welcomers—some said they numbered a quarter of a mil-

lion—called out, "Here comes water from Lake Constance." It made the local boys on board feel right at home.

While fresh fuel and hydrogen were pumped into the huge gasbags and the ship got a thorough going-over, the zeppeliners had their first taste of Japanese hospitality. By now Eckener was a veteran of official welcomes and formal dinners. As he would later remark, "When a man achieves fame and success, what he needs most is a cast-iron stomach." In their heavy blue uniforms, the officers and crew suffered terribly in a Tokyo heat wave that saw temperatures rise to more than one hundred degrees Fahrenheit in the shade.

One of the *Graf*'s engine mounts was damaged when the ship was being undocked from the Tokyo shed, briefly delaying her departure. Otherwise the rest of the trip unfolded almost without incident. Catching up with a second typhoon that had swept across Japan the previous day, Eckener covered the more than 5,000 miles to the U.S. coast in only sixty-eight hours, sailing majestically through the entrance to San Francisco Bay while backlit by a magnificent Pacific sunset. This dramatic entrance was quite deliberate. As Eckener explained, "When for the first time in history an airship crosses the Pacific Ocean from the Orient to the United States, it must enter the Golden Gate out of the setting sun."

Remembrances of the world flight. (Right) A Japanese landscape viewed from the *Graf*. (Far right) Japanese tourists flocking to visit the airship. (Bottom left) A tea tin cover depicts the *Graf* over New York, Berlin and Tokyo. (Bottom right) A souvenir world flight book and card game. (Left) A menu cover from the Tokyo-Los Angeles leg of the voyage.

With the sun setting behind her,
the *Graf Zeppelin* flies above
San Francisco Bay after a landmark
crossing of the Pacific.

The only genuine close call came during the *Graf*'s departure from Los Angeles on the evening of August 26. A typical temperature inversion—the kind that later accounted for the city's famous smog—hung over the airfield. Worse, the ship had become heavy—apparently the hot southern California sun had caused the hydrogen in the gasbags to overexpand and vent automatically. Eckener took the drastic action of lightening the ship as much as possible. He left behind as many crew members as he could spare, every extra ton of fuel, and much of his water ballast. Finally the ship was light enough to fly.

"All engines flank speed," Eckener ordered, as the *Graf* rose slowly. He would drive the ship to a higher altitude aerodynamically, more like an airplane taking off than the usual zeppelin lift-off. Once in the cooler and more dense upper air, his hydrogen would have more lift. The big ship began to pick up speed, but suddenly her slow rise ceased with the after engine car only fifteen feet above the ground, the nose somewhat higher. She had hit the layer of warmer air and was now barreling directly toward a row of high-tension electricity wires at the edge of the field.

"Full up elevator," Eckener ordered.

The first effect of this order was to bring the tail down, plowing a furrow in the earth. At last the ship began to rise, but still not enough to clear the line of red lights that marked the tops of the poles holding the wires. Slowly the ship gained height. Faster and faster the high-voltage wires drew nearer. At the last moment the nose lifted above the danger, but Eckener could tell that the trailing fin would almost certainly snag. Coolly he waited until the center of his ship had passed over the wires and then ordered down elevator. The tail slowly lifted clear. He was home free.

Six days and one New York ticker-tape parade later, the *Graf* touched down in Friedrichshafen. To the delight of the American press, the flying time from Lakehurst to Lakehurst had been twelve hours less than from Friedrichshafen to Friedrichshafen—just under three hundred hours, a little more than twelve days. The *Graf Zeppelin* had circled the globe in less time than it then took to make the sea voyage from Tokyo to San Francisco. The "Magellan of the Air," as newspapers now began to call Hugo Eckener, had good reason to believe that his commercial airship line was just around the corner. The American economy was

The *Graf*'s first stop after Tokyo was at Mines Field, Los Angeles (left), where the ground service personnel were identified by specially designed buttons (above). The ship returned to Lakehurst on August 29 (top right) and arrived home in Friedrichshafen on September 4 (right).

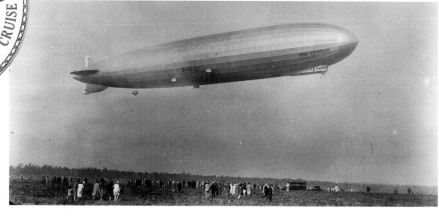

booming and wealthy investors were at last lining up behind the scheme.

Then came the stock-market crash of October 1929, and with it the end for any early inauguration of regular airship travel between Europe and North America. In order to keep the dream alive, Eckener knew he would need to find new ways to keep the *Graf Zeppelin* in the public consciousness. That fall he staged a number of highly successful short flights in Europe, the most popular being trips over Switzerland. But while these "circus flights" raised enough revenue to keep the ship in operation and her crew employed, something much longer term was needed until the world economy recovered and he could again contemplate bigger ships. And so he set his sights on establishing a passenger service to South America.

In those days there existed no fast transportation link between Europe and the sizable German communities in Brazil and Argentina. Unlike the well-served steamer route between Europe and America, which fast ships could travel in less than five days, the southern route took two long weeks. A wealthy businessman who needed to travel to and from Europe would pay a healthy premium to cut those two weeks down to three days.

On May 18, 1930, the *Graf* departed Friedrichshafen on the 5,500-mile flight by way of Seville to Recife, a seaport on the easternmost point of Brazil. The governor of the state of Pernambuco had agreed to build a landing field with stub mast and hydrogen production facilities just outside the city. Eckener fully intended, however, that Rio de Janeiro, the biggest and most important city in Brazil, would ultimately become the terminus of the South American service. The distance to Recife posed no problem for the *Graf*, which had easily managed the 7,000-mile-long first leg of its round-the-world flight. The main imponderables remained tropical heat and tropical storms.

Eckener and his crew found that the worst tropical storm paled beside a North Atlantic squall front. Helped along by the favoring trades, the first flight took only sixty-two hours from Seville (then planned as an airship port). Once the South American service got going, the *Graf* would average only seventy hours from Friedrichshafen to Recife, eighty hours on the return trip. As for the heat, the moderating effects of the ocean minimized any problems while flying. But at Recife, lifting gas could only be replenished during the cooler hours between sunset and sunrise. In fact, the only real problem on this first South American voyage was a shortage of water, which, as the ship neared her destination, forced the passengers to wash with cologne. On subsequent flights more water was carried.

Pushed south from Recife by helpful tail winds, the *Graf Zeppelin* arrived over Rio de Janeiro by night. Seen from an airship, one of the world's most beautiful metropolises seemed like a magical city of dreams: the dark shape of Sugar Loaf Mountain, the giant floodlit statue of

SUPPLEMENT TO THE AIRPOST JOURNAL · OCTOBER 1934

LZ LUFTSCHIFFBAU ZEPPELIN
HAPAG HAMBURG-AMERIKA LINIE

The Hamburg-America Line acted as ticket agents for the *Graf Zeppelin*'s increasingly successful passenger service to South America (above), which terminated at the city of Recife (left), where the gentle weather conditions made a hangar unnecessary.

Christ perched atop the 2,300-foot-high Corcovado, the twinkling lights defining the vast dark contour of Guanabara Bay. The next day the whole town shut down in celebration of the occasion—it was as if Carnival had come eight months early. But the huge crowd that had waited all night at the Campo dos Alfonsos caught only a brief glimpse of this apparition from another world. As the sun rose the hydrogen expanded, forcing Eckener to take off after only seventy-two minutes on the ground.

Regular flights to Recife and Rio began the following year. But Eckener was not yet finished showing the world what the *Graf* could do. For some time he'd cherished the notion of realizing Count Zeppelin's prewar plan of flying to the Arctic, and in late July 1931, the *Graf Zeppelin* set off on her mission of polar exploration. In addition to the latest in arctic survival gear and more than 9,000 pounds of food, the airship carried a distinguished international company of scientists and more than 50,000 pieces of mail. Once again philatelists provided a major share of the funds needed for the expedition, lured by the promise of an exchange of mail with a Russian icebreaker in the polar sea.

A BOARD THE RUSSIAN ICEBREAKER *MALYGIN*, UMBERTO NOBILE anxiously searched the early evening sky for some sign of the *Graf Zeppelin*. If any man knew the perils of arctic exploration by airship, it was he. But he noted with satisfaction that the weather was dead calm, perfect for the first landing by an airship on the polar sea. The high black cliffs of Quiet Sound, Hooker Island, Franz Josef Land were reflected in the still waters. Behind him was the tiny scientific station, the northernmost meteorological outpost on the planet. Toward the mouth of the deep inlet, where his gaze rested, the water was flecked with white ice floes. As long as the wind stayed down nothing should prevent the promised rendezvous with history.

Of course, Nobile would much rather have been flying on the *Graf* than meeting her on the water. Despite the crash of the *Italia* and his long ordeal, he had not lost his zeal for arctic exploration. In fact, he had agreed to participate in the voyage of the *Malygin* before he knew about the rendezvous with the *Graf*. He was on board as a guest of the Soviet government, which wanted his advice on building a fleet of semirigid dirigibles similar to his own designs.

In this season of the midnight sun it was still broad daylight when, in Nobile's words, the *Graf*'s "great silvery bulk loomed on the horizon," at the mouth of the bay. A half hour later Eckener set her gently down on the glassy surface as if he did this sort of thing every day of the week. First the air-filled rubber pontoon under the main gondola

splashed down, then the pontoon under the aft engine car. Nobile was not the only one who admired the landing—Eckener made the difficult seem so easy—or gaped in awe at the appearance of this amazing apparition out of the arctic sky. The *Graf*'s massive profile, silhouetted against the stark black cliffs of the sound, seemed like the invention of a science-fiction novelist. Beside her the icebreaker looked like a

dwarf and the small boat sent out to greet her a pygmy.

As the boat from the icebreaker drew closer, Nobile could see Eckener leaning out the gondola window. There was no mistaking the deeply lined face with the trademark goatee, made famous by a thousand newspaper photos and newsreel pictures. They had expected to be invited on board for tea and a chance to inspect the ship, but Eckener was in a hurry. "Quickly! Quickly!" he called to them. The wind was starting to rise and the *Graf* had already begun drifting toward the small ice floes at the mouth of the bay.

As the mailbags were exchanged there was only time to shake the hands extended through the gondola windows and exchange quick greetings. Then it was all over.

On July 27, 1931, the *Graf Zeppelin* makes an arctic rendezvous with the Russian icebreaker *Malygin* to exchange mail.

(Bottom left) A gondola-eye view of Novaya Zemlya. (Top left) The *Graf Zeppelin* alights on the Arctic Ocean as the *Malygin* stands by. (Right) Hugo Eckener spent most of the voyage lodged in his favorite wicker armchair in the ship's bridge, in this instance completely oblivious to a newsreel cameraman.

A few splashes marked the emptying of the canvas dip buckets used, like sandbags on land, for temporary ballast. Then the *Graf* rose softly, silently, serenely from the surface. Her engines roared to life, and she flew away to the north toward regions only Nobile and a few others had even seen.

AS THE *GRAF* SAILED ON OVER THE HUNDREDS OF ISLANDS THAT comprise Franz Josef Land, the explorers snapped aerial photographs that would allow them to correct the inaccurate maps of this northern archipelago. Later they sailed through calm air and occasional belts of fog to Severnaya Zemlya, the eastern limit of their journey. There they settled once and for all a longstanding cartographical debate by discovering that it comprised two islands, not one. The route home took them over the north cape of the inaccessible Taymyr Peninsula, where they spotted an unknown mountain range, then over Novaya Zemlya. From there it was an easy trip to

Leningrad, Berlin and then home. The *Graf Zeppelin*'s "Arktisfahrt" had lasted seven days and traversed 8,142 miles.

Once again the *Graf* had made aviation history. Unfortunately she was the last zeppelin to venture into polar climes.

By now the *Graf Zeppelin* had achieved an almost mystical reputation. Wherever she went she caused a sensation. It is probably safe to say that she was the most famous single aircraft ever flown—including the modern-day Concorde. Long after the last zeppelin had been destroyed, Hugo Eckener attempted to explain the amazing impact of this elongated, silver-doped balloon filled with explosive gas: "I have always felt that such effects as were produced by the Zeppelin airship were traceable to a large degree to aesthetic feelings. The mass of the mighty airship hull, which seemed matched by its lightness and grace, and whose beauty of form was modulated in delicate shades of color, never failed to make a strong impression on people's minds. It was not, as generally described, 'a silver bird soaring in majestic flight', but rather a fabulous silvery fish, floating quietly in the ocean of air and captivating the eye just like a fantastic, exotic fish seen in an aquarium. And this fairy-like apparition, which seemed to melt into the silvery blue background of sky, when it appeared far away, lighted by the sun, seemed to be coming from another world and to be returning there like a dream. . . ."

A S THE WORLD REELED FROM THE DEEPENING DEPRESSION, the *Graf Zeppelin* sailed serenely back and forth across the Atlantic. In addition to the polar flight, 1931 saw three scheduled commercial runs between Friedrichshafen and Brazil. In 1932 and 1933 the number increased to nine, with several flights extending as far as Rio de Janeiro. The route became such a success that in 1933 Eckener persuaded the Brazilian government to start construction of a hangar just south of Rio that would make possible regular flights to the Brazilian capital. It would be completed in 1935.

But the political winds blew less favorably than the southern trades. In January 1933 the doddering German president, Paul von Hindenburg, made Adolf Hitler chancellor, and the Nazi reign began. On the *Graf's* final South American flight of 1933 she continued on to the United States, where she made an appearance at the Chicago World's Fair before returning by way of Lakehurst to Friedrichshafen. It was three years since the famous airship had last appeared in the United States, and many were shocked to see the black Nazi swastika emblazoned boldly on one side of her tail fins. Aware of this problem, Eckener went out of his way to circle Chicago clockwise so that only the right side of the fin, which bore the black, white and red German flag, was visible.

Eckener was no friend of the new regime, and he had bravely resisted its coming. A political philosophy founded on fear and hate was anathema to him. While Hitler's star was on the rise, Eckener had curtly turned down a Nazi request to use the Friedrichshafen hangar for a mass rally at which the Führer himself would be the featured speaker. Then he agreed to make a national radio address in support of the embattled Chancellor Brüning. Because he was the most famous German of his day, his words carried great weight, and those who heard him speak say that his mastery of the German language put the high-pitched oratory of Hitler to shame. "Danger rises from our unrest," he intoned. "We are preparing, by our lack of unity and by our bitter political differences, a fertile field for the growth of every kind of demagoguery."

A movement arose to persuade Eckener to run for president. And, just maybe, his enormous popularity and his decisiveness might have enabled him to stem the Nazi tide. His friend Willy von Meister, the Zeppelin Company's representative in the United States, believed that Eckener "would have risked civil war in preference to giving dictatorial powers to Hitler." But would such steadfastness have been enough to stem the Nazi tide? It is one of those tantalizing what-ifs of history.

Nice of you to ask, Eckener told the politicians, but my work is yet unfinished. I have more skies to fly, more airships to build. Ironically, however, it was the Nazis who permitted him to complete his work. Eckener still lacked the capital to build a truly adequate ship for transatlantic commerce—one in which at least fifty passengers could travel in speed, safety and luxury. In 1934 the new Nazi propaganda minister, Dr. Joseph Goebbels, contributed 2.2 million marks toward the new airship.

Hermann Goering, the air minister, whose low opinion of the "gasbags" was well known, now moved to regain his turf. He contributed 9 million marks to assure the airship's completion and in early 1935 arranged for the Deutsche Zeppelin-Reederei (German Zeppelin Transport Company) to be formed. The state-supported airline Lufthansa contributed half the $2.2 million capital and the Zeppelin Company contributed the *Graf Zeppelin*. As Eckener wrote, "the Zeppelin enterprise was now at last guaranteed, but it was at the price of its independence."

One has to wonder whether Eckener ever regretted this accommodation with a regime he clearly loathed. It was a choice between a pact with the devil and no deal at all. But were even his beloved airships really worth this moral compromise? He seems to have salved his conscience somewhat by frankly voicing his low opinion of his new masters—and not just within earshot of his tolerant crew, few of whom actually joined the Nazi party. Perhaps no other man in Germany could have said what he did and kept his job—or his life. He even went so far as to mock the Hitler salute when talking to some foreign journalists who asked him whether he would disregard it. "When I get up in the morning, I don't say 'Heil Hitler,' to my wife, but rather 'Good morning,'" he told them. However, he was probably lucky to be out of the country on June 30, 1934, during the Night of the Long Knives, when many opposition figures were either shot or arrested. At the time Eckener was in the *Graf* en route to Buenos Aires, where he hoped to generate enthusiasm for an airship base in the Argentinian capital. It never materialized.

Thus Eckener continued to pilot his otherworldly skyfish over the very troubled world in which he lived. Meanwhile, in a huge new construction shed at Friedrichshafen the airship of his dreams was already taking shape.

CHAPTER SIX

UNLUCKY PIONEERS

"In working out the development of a new project, in gathering experience in the only way possible, human advance seems to come only through trial and error, through grief and agony, and even through loss of life. . . . Such is the price of pioneering, recorded in man's endeavors throughout the ages."
—Charles E. Rosendahl

"Here is the goal of man's dream for many, many generations. Not the airplane, not the hydroscope, man has dreamed of a huge graceful ship that lifted gently into the air and soared with ease. It is come, it is completely successful, it is breathtakingly beautiful."
—Akron Beacon Journal

L IEUTENANT COMMANDER HERBERT V. Wiley wondered whether the captain was making the right decision, but he kept his thoughts to himself. The executive officer of the U.S.S. *Akron*, the largest dirigible in the world, had quickly learned that his new skipper, Commander Frank McCord, liked to make his own decisions. Still, if Wiley had been in charge, he would not have turned the big airship out to sea, but back overland in an attempt to circle around the approaching spring storm.

At 10:00 P.M. the ship's navigator had reported that they were crossing the New Jersey coast near Asbury Park. In fact they were forty-five miles to the south, but no clear landmarks had been sighted, and they had

(Above) Commander Frank McCord, the *Akron's* last captain. (Opposite) The *Akron* pays a visit to the giant Goodyear air dock where she was built.

been unable to make drift measurements—to check the speed at which the ship was straying from its intended course—because fog and low cloud obscured the ground. Their true course was anybody's guess. Now, as they proceeded eastward over the Atlantic the air remained relatively free of turbulence but lightning seemed to be coming from everywhere. The night of April 3, 1933, was a wild one and getting wilder.

"Commander. Go up and have a look at the weather map," McCord ordered. He wanted the latest information before deciding his next move.

Wiley climbed up into the radio room. Severe static had prevented the radio operator from receiving a third of the report but the incomplete information indicated a low pressure area centered over Washington, D.C. Wiley assumed this was the storm center. He had no inkling that a vast storm band, not a single storm, was rapidly moving toward them—the worst to hit the New Jersey coast in years. He quickly climbed back down into the control car and reported the weather picture to Commander McCord.

The captain promptly decided to reverse course back toward the New Jersey shore. It was now about an hour before midnight, but when the airship reached the coast an hour later, he found no break in the weather. So he decided to turn back to sea again and simply ride out the storm. With any luck the worst of the disturbance would pass to the northeast and in the morning the *Akron* could get down to the routine chore of calibrating radio direction-

finding stations along the New England coastline. With both Rear Admiral William Moffett, chief of the navy's Bureau of Aeronautics, and Commander Frederick Berry, the commandant of the Lakehurst Naval Air Station, on board, there was no way McCord wanted to return to base without completing his mission.

For awhile it looked as if McCord might be getting lucky. Lightning still flashed in the distance and the ship passed through frequent cloudbursts, but the air remained eerily calm. Then, at fifteen minutes past midnight, the *Akron* entered fierce turbulence. This time the lightning flashed close by. Thunder crashed in the ears of the men in the control car, and the ship began pitching violently. Suddenly the floor fell away beneath Wiley's feet. The elevator man struggled at the wheel and Wiley rushed over to help him hold the ship level as it plunged. McCord rang the engine telegraphs to full speed. It was clear to the men in command that despite all their efforts, they had flown smack into the center of the storm.

"Shall I drop ballast, sir?" Wiley asked.

"Yes, immediately," replied McCord.

The increased airspeed combined with the release of several tons of water ballast finally halted the ship's fall at seven hundred feet, after a plunge of nearly a thousand feet. Now the lightened *Akron* began to rise rapidly. Thanks to the skillful application of the elevators, however, she was soon back under control and leveled off near her previous altitude. But for only a few moments. Then the bottom dropped out again.

Without waiting to ask Commander McCord's permission, Wiley signaled landing stations. Five long squawks sounded throughout the ship,

REAR ADMIRAL WILLIAM A. MOFFETT

From his 1921 appointment as chief of the Bureau of Aeronautics, Admiral Moffett fought consistently against those who regarded the rigid airship as an exercise in military futility. He was not an unquestioning booster, but saw a potential role for airships as part of an integrated air fleet that would include flying boats and carrier-launched airplanes.

calling all the crew to emergency duty. Wiley knew the *Akron* was in grave danger, but until the alarm sounded, most members of the crew, off watch and sleeping, remained oblivious to the trouble. They had all been through rough air before.

Boatswain's Mate Second Class Richard "Lucky" Deal was dozing fitfully in his bunk well aft of the control car when the second wave of turbulence hit. He had earned the nickname "Lucky" because a last-minute substitution had caused him to miss the *Shenandoah*'s final flight. Groggily he glanced up at No. 7 gas cell and saw it billowing violently. He snapped fully awake at the realization that the ship must be in danger. As he got to his feet, the *Akron* gave a violent sideways lurch. Above him, two longitudinal girders cracked and parted.

In the control car the elevator man had been applying up-elevator in a futile attempt to fly against the powerful downdraft. The ship was falling with her nose pitched sharply upward, and the angle was steadily increasing. Lieutenant George Calnan, watching the altimeter from his station at the ballast controls, called out eight hundred feet. Seconds later came the violent lurch felt by Deal. To Herbert Wiley, it felt as if an exceptionally violent gust had brought the ship to a sudden halt in midair. It then leveled off somewhat.

Almost instantly the rudder man reported that he'd lost helm control. Wiley could quickly see why: the control cable to the lower rudder was gone. Moments later the upper rudder control was also carried away. Now the bow again shot upward and the slant of the floor beneath Wiley's feet increased to a forty-five-degree angle, forcing him to cling to a girder for support. The cabin began to bump and heave in a way he'd never experienced before.

"Three hundred feet," called out Calnan.

"Stand by for crash!" Wiley shouted. He could now see the whitecapped surface coming fast through the fog.

Moments later the control car jolted heavily into the ocean and began sinking with a heavy list to starboard. The inrushing sea pushed Wiley out a port-side window, where he found himself under the ship and under water. He swam for his life.

By the time Wiley reached the surface his lungs had all but given out. Gasping for air and fighting the choppy seas, he saw the *Akron* lit by a lightning flash. About two hundred feet of the bow jutted high out of the water; the rest of the hull lay half-submerged, broken in several places but in one piece. In the next flash he saw men swimming and heard their desperate cries for help. Since the ship carried no life preservers and there had been no time to deploy the single life raft, his only hope was to find something floating to hang onto. First he tried to reach the wreck, but it drifted away from him. Then he swam until, exhausted, he found a board. A few faint cries came from his drowning comrades, then ceased. As he held on and waited for rescue he thought of his three young children, who had lost their mother three years earlier. Would they be orphans before morning?

O F THE SEVENTY-SIX MEN ON BOARD THE *Akron* that night, only four were pulled alive from the icy Atlantic off the New Jersey coast. The German motorship *Phoebus* saw the airship's lights as it went down and steamed directly to the scene, but in the dark and wind the search was fiendishly difficult. Three men were discovered clinging to a floating gas tank and Lieutenant Commander Wiley was rescued still hanging onto his floating plank. One of the four, the ship's chief radioman, died on board the ship. That left only three survivors, one of them the twice-lucky Richard Deal.

The full scope of what had happened—until then the worst aviation

In the days following the *Akron* crash, the wreck, including the port tail fin (right), was found and partly salvaged. The lower tail fin was discovered some distance from the main wreck, supporting the

theory that the crash was caused when this fin hit the water. Among the bodies recovered was that of Admiral Moffett (upper inset). Only three men ultimately survived (lower inset), Herbert Wiley (seated), Moody Erwin and Richard Deal.

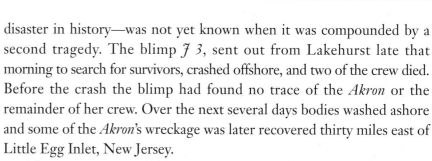

disaster in history—was not yet known when it was compounded by a second tragedy. The blimp *J 3*, sent out from Lakehurst late that morning to search for survivors, crashed offshore, and two of the crew died. Before the crash the blimp had found no trace of the *Akron* or the remainder of her crew. Over the next several days bodies washed ashore and some of the *Akron*'s wreckage was later recovered thirty miles east of Little Egg Inlet, New Jersey.

The ensuing inquiry blamed Captain McCord for "having committed an error of judgement in not setting such courses as would have kept him in the safe semicircle (to the west) of the storm, thereby avoiding the severe conditions finally encountered." But given the long and violent storm front that finally caught up to him, this verdict seems unfair. Once McCord found himself in the thick of it, he handled his ship competently. With hindsight we can see that his only hope of saving the *Akron* would have been to keep her more level as she fell toward the ocean on her second plunge. For the final sharp gust that preceded the crash was not a gust at all, but the shock of the lower tail fin hitting the water.

Later, when Wiley had a chance to reflect on what had happened, he realized that he had felt no wind blowing in the open control car windows as would normally be the case when a gust hit. Furthermore, as he told the inquiry, "After the rudder control broke, I was awaiting the shock of the stern hitting the water. That shock never came." He concluded that the initial, violent lurch was caused by the impact of the lower tail fin hitting the sea, *not* by a blast of wind. Most airship historians have gone along with Wiley's conclusion.

But how could the tail have been so low when, seconds before the "gust" hit, the altimeter read eight hundred feet? Part of the answer can be found in the instrument the *Akron* used to gauge her altitude, which actually measured the diminishing atmospheric pressure as height increased. When the ship entered the center of the storm it also entered a region of exceptionally low atmospheric pressure. This caused the altimeter to deliver

THE LAST MOMENTS OF THE *AKRON*

1) Falling at a sharp nose-upward angle, the *Akron*'s lower fin hits the water. **2)** Her forward progress halted, the nose falls briefly.
3) The nose rises again reaching a 45-degree angle. **4)** The nose is the last part of the ship to crash into the water.

The *Akron* at Lakehurst Naval Air Station on November 2, 1931, shortly after her delivery flight from Ohio.

a false reading, exaggerating the ship's altitude by several hundred feet. And, with the ship falling at a sharp angle of incline, the tail would have been several hundred feet lower than the control car where the altimeter was located. (For example, at an angle of thirty degrees the trailing edge of the tail fin would have been almost 300 feet below the control car.) So, when Lieutenant Calnan called out "eight hundred feet", the lowest part of the ship was actually just above the waves. Seconds later the tail fin hit the water and the *Akron* was finished.

THE ORIGINS OF THE *AKRON* AND HER LATER SISTER THE *MACON*, THE two greatest airships ever built in the United States, can be traced back to 1924, the year Hugo Eckener piloted the soon-to-be-christened *Los Angeles* from Friedrichshafen to Lakehurst. The building of the *Los Angeles* had temporarily staved off extinction for the Zeppelin Company, but prospects remained uncertain. So Eckener was already moving on another front. Just in case the Allies would not permit Germany to build zeppelins, he would find someone else who could. The obvious candidates were the Americans, given their navy's strong interest in lighter-than-air craft. And the logical partner was the Goodyear Tire and Rubber Company of Akron, Ohio, which had been

building blimps for years and whose president, Paul Litchfield, was an enthusiastic believer in the potential of the rigid airship.

A few weeks after the *Los Angeles* flew to Lakehurst, her chief designer, Dr. Karl Arnstein, arrived in the United States with twelve engineers from Friedrichshafen. The short, soft-spoken Arnstein had joined the Zeppelin Company in 1915. He and his "twelve apostles" became the core of the design team for the newly formed German-American partnership, the Goodyear-Zeppelin Company, which held the North American rights to the Zeppelin Company patents. They had to wait another four years for their big chance, but they were ready when it came.

Despite the *Shenandoah* crash, Admiral Moffett and Lieutenant Commander Rosendahl had kept rigid airships on the naval agenda. As chief of the Bureau of Aeronautics, Moffett had a powerful voice. And he believed that the huge rigid airships, with their extraordinary range and endurance, would play a vital role in seagoing reconnaissance, especially in patrolling the vast reaches of America's Pacific sphere of influence.

In 1926 Congress finally allocated the funds and in 1928 Goodyear-Zeppelin won the contract to build two rigid airships of 6.5-million-cubic-foot capacity for the United States Navy for a total of nearly $8 million. While Dr. Arnstein refined his designs for the two 785-foot-long helium-

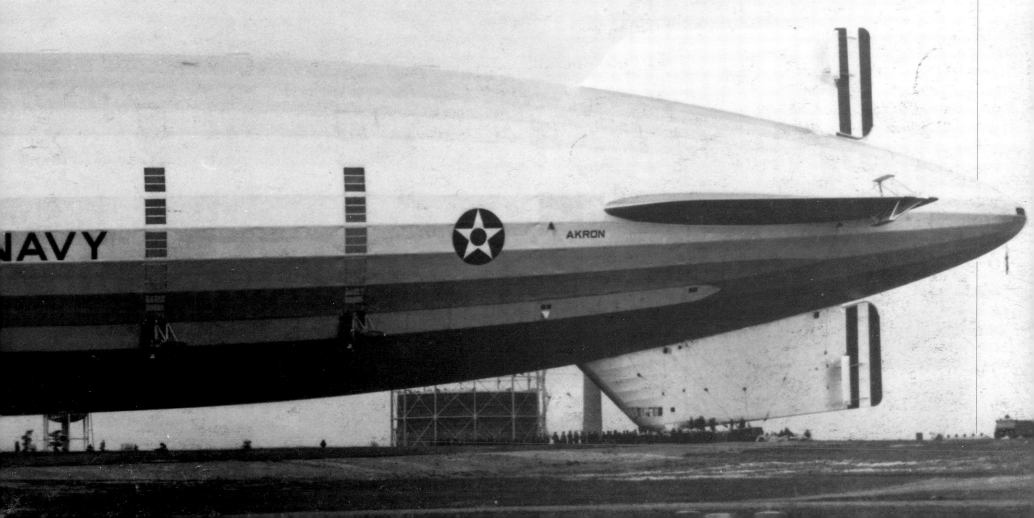

filled ships, Goodyear went to work on a hangar to house them, the huge air dock at Akron. This enormous airship shed with its streamlined shape and "orange-peel" doors was a great improvement over old Hangar No. 1 at Lakehurst. Unlike that earlier structure, at Akron the air dock's axis corresponded to the direction of the prevailing winds, making docking and undocking these unwieldy aircraft far easier. The hemispherical doors, which folded snugly back along the sides of the shed, eliminated much of the local turbulence encountered at a hangar entrance with conventional door arrangements.

Dr. Karl Arnstein (left), chief designer of the *Akron* and the *Macon*, poses with Goodyear president Paul Litchfield.

If the hangar was innovative, however, the massive streamlined shape that grew within it between November 1929 and August 1931 was the most forward-looking rigid airship yet built. And, to the eyes of many, the most beautiful. Liberated from the constraints of zeppelin orthodoxy, but with the full weight of zeppelin experience behind him, Arnstein designed a ship that was superbly suited for the extremes of the American climate. With three keels (one along the top and one along each side of the lower hull), ten tough unbraced main rings of triangular cross-section (similar to the big rings in the *R 101*) and thirty-six longitudinal girders, the *Akron* was immensely strong. No storm over Ohio would break this mammoth baby in pieces, as it had the ill-fated *Shenandoah*. The three keels, as well as adding to structural strength, provided unprecedented access to all parts of the ship's interior. It would no longer be necessary, for example, to clamber along the top of the hull to inspect the gas valves. This could now be done by strolling along the catwalk built into the upper keel.

For the first time an airship was designed from the start with only helium in mind. The engines were housed inside the hull—there was no danger of a spark igniting the inert lifting gas—and fixed to the two lateral keels, eliminating a serious source of drag. Condensers to recover water from the engine exhaust, and so compensate for the loss of weight through fuel consumption, were built

(Left) At a ceremony marking the official start of the *Akron*'s construction on November 7, 1929, thirty thousand people gathered in the still-incomplete Goodyear air dock to watch Admiral Moffett drive a golden rivet into the first main ring. (Top and bottom right) The new air dock with its "orange-peel" doors made docking and undocking a giant airship much easier.

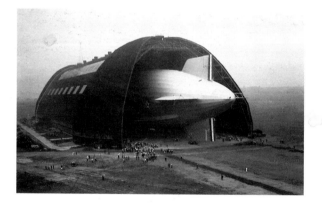

into the sides of the hull. They resembled long rectangular windows ascending vertically above each propeller. And the crew quarters included a smoking area.

Most important of the *Akron*'s many novel features would be her ability to launch and recover airplanes. Up to three Curtiss F9C-2 Sparrowhawk biplanes could be carried in the ship's belly. The plan was for the planes to fly from, and hook on to, a movable trapeze extended below the ship. It remained to be seen how reliable this technique would be and whether the planes could be safely moved into and out of the ship's hull during flight. If these problems could be solved, the Americans would possess the world's first flying aircraft carrier.

But Rosendahl and other American airship commanders strenuously objected to one aspect of the original design, the configuration of the tail fins. Arnstein had made them long and sleek. But this meant that the bottom of the lower fin couldn't be seen from the control car. The future operators of the big airship wanted to be able to see that lower fin with its auxiliary control room when it touched the ground. So Arnstein reluctantly redesigned the fins to be shorter and deeper. This change placed an extra strain on the main frame rings, since the fins now had only two instead of the previous three attachment points. As Arnstein would

comment many years later, "compromise cannot produce excellence." And in this one aspect at least, the *Akron*, as well as her successor the *Macon*, was the product of an unfortunate compromise.

But no one was thinking of compromise when the *Akron* made her debut on September 23, 1931, with Lieutenant Commander Rosendahl in charge. For Rosendahl, this had to be even better than the round-the-world flight in the *Graf*. Now he was in command of the greatest airship the world had ever seen. And on this occasion she didn't let him down. At his command of "Up Ship!" the ground crew let go of the handling lines and pushed up on the hull, sending the *Akron* gracefully into the air before an enthusiastic crowd of 200,000. A few days later, he piloted her to Lakehurst.

Unfortunately, Rosendahl's enthusiasm for airships was not matched by a clear notion of how the navy was going to use them. As yet, no one had developed a definitive strategic operational doctrine for this enormous new naval vessel. And in the early days of the *Akron*'s service, Rosendahl and his boss, Admiral Moffett, both seemed more interested in showing her off to the American public than in getting her down to the more serious business of exercising with the fleet.

At the time of the *Akron*'s launch, neither her trapeze nor her airplanes

Because of objections from American airship commanders, the fins on the *Akron* and the *Macon* were shortened and deepened, reducing from three to two the number of points of attachment to the main rings. Despite criticisms from some, this design was more than adequate to handle predicted aerodynamic loads. (Right) In the *Akron*'s control car, Charles Rosendahl keeps his eye on the nose telegraph for word that the ship has been released from the mast. Meanwhile, the ground crew prepares to push the ship up using long poles in the only known photo of this unusual launching technique.

were ready for use. Yet Rosendahl, a man contemporaries remember as intense, aggressive, even ruthless in pursuit of his objectives, seems to have been unworried by the delay. It wasn't until May 1932, seven months after the *Akron*'s commissioning, that the first plane hooked on to the dirigible in flight. And it wasn't until the fall of 1932, a year after the *Akron* went into service, that a full complement of Sparrowhawks and the crew to fly them were in place.

Without her planes, the *Akron*'s initial tryout with the fleet was disappointing, to say the least. Failing to locate an "enemy" scouting force off North Carolina in January 1932, she was herself spotted by two destroyers. In Pacific fleet exercises in June she managed to sight the enemy, but was swiftly attacked by carrier-launched airplanes. Had his planes been aboard, Rosendahl lamely maintained, it was "perfectly apparent" they would have fended off the thirteen attackers. But others believed that despite her planes and modest armament, the airship presented a huge, slow-moving target for carrier-launched dive-bombers.

Rosendahl and many of the other old hands of the airship service did not want to admit that their vast new ship was ill suited for a center-stage role in naval warfare. But with aircraft carriers now an integral part of the surface fleet, airships would never be able to act alone as front-line scouts using their tiny complement of airplanes to fend off counterattack.

Airships were chiefly suited to act as long-range strategic scouts, using their airplanes to extend their range. In such a role, airships would never intentionally make direct contact with enemy surface units—they were far too vulnerable. But their planes, flying advance scouting formations, would be able to appear out of nowhere in these days before radar. Unfortunately, during the *Akron*'s all-too-brief career, this sensible doctrine was never put into practice, although reliable techniques for hooking on and launching during flight were soon perfected. At least some of the blame for this neglect must be laid at Rosendahl's door.

The *Akron* did exhibit impressive endurance, including accomplishing the difficult round trip across the continental United States. In her seventy-three flights she logged nearly 1,700 hours of flying time. And apart from the teething problems inevitable with any new aircraft, those who flew on her remembered her as a comfortable and reliable ship that sailed through just about everything Mother Nature could throw at her.

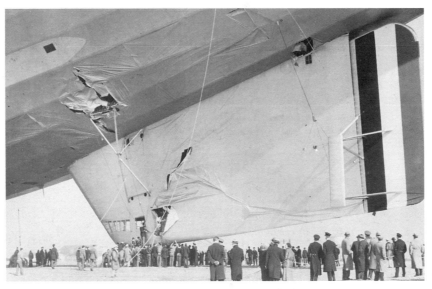

ADVENTURES OF THE *AKRON*

(Above) On February 22, 1932, while being undocked at Lakehurst, the *Akron*'s tail broke free from its stern mooring and bounced repeatedly on the ground as the ship swung into the wind while four visiting congressmen watched in horror. The fin had to be substantially rebuilt. Only a few months later, three members of the ground crew at Camp Kearny, California, were carried aloft when the ship accidentally released ballast during landing. Only one of the three, Apprentice Seaman Bud Cowart (left and above left), managed to hang on for the hour it took the *Akron*'s crew to haul him on board. The other two fell to their deaths. (Opposite) With three Sparrowhawks in attendance, the *Macon* flies over her home base of Moffett Field, California.

ON APRIL 21, 1933, BARELY TWO WEEKS after the *Akron* crash, the *Macon* emerged for the first time. The ship was in most ways identical to her departed sister, but some improvements had been made. She was eight thousand pounds lighter and about eight miles per hour faster (the water recovery panels and radiators had been set into the hull to reduce air resistance) with a top speed of eighty-seven miles per hour. The hangar in her belly could carry up to two more planes—she could carry five planes instead of the *Akron*'s three—and the modified trapeze worked even better. And her crew, all of them trained on the *Akron*, knew what their new vessel could do. By all accounts, the *Macon* was a happy ship right up until her most unhappy end.

Just what was it like to fly aboard the last big American rigid? The routine was very much that on a navy surface vessel. The men stood regular watches. During each watch one of the senior officers would invariably be on duty on "the bridge," the forward part of the control car. Off

duty the men relaxed in their cramped bunk rooms spread out along the two lower keels or played cards and chewed the fat in the mess. The food was plentiful and appetizing.

Unlike the *Akron*, the *Macon* was ready to work with the fleet as soon as she had been broken in. In the fall of 1933 she left Lakehurst for the newly completed airship base at Sunnyvale, California, just south of San Francisco Bay. Named Moffett Field after the *Akron*'s most famous fatality, the new base would have made its namesake proud. With its giant air dock and the latest in ground-handling technology, Moffett Field was "probably the finest lighter than air base in the world," according to William Althoff, author of *Sky Ships*. With the exception of one trip east to take part in Atlantic fleet exercises in the spring of 1934, the *Macon* would be based in California for the rest of her brief life.

O N JULY 11, 1934, LIEUTENANT COMMANDER HERBERT V. WILEY got the job he'd wanted for so long—command of the *Macon*. After the *Akron* crash, Wiley had served a stint with the surface fleet and he knew firsthand just how deep the distrust of the big rigid airships had become. It was thanks only to the fact that Rosendahl had found another good friend in high places that the future of rigid airships in the U.S. Navy remained an open question. This friend was Rear Admiral Ernest J. King, the new head of the Bureau of Aeronautics. Like his predecessor, King was determined to give the big rigids a chance to prove their military potential. But the *Macon* still had to prove herself. In her most recent exercises with the fleet she had been "shot down" nine times. It would take a signal success to turn the tide of negative opinion.

Herbert Wiley took quickly to his new job. The perennial second-in-command suddenly

Lieutenant Commander Herbert V. Wiley

seemed born to be the boss. Not only did he look the part—solidly built and over six feet tall, his thick gray hair brushed brusquely to one side—he played the role, as well. Too well, in the opinion of some. Richard Smith, author of *The Airships Akron & Macon*, describes him as

"an austere personality, especially with his juniors" and says he had a reputation of being something of a martinet. Certainly, as one of his officers later commented, "he ran a damn taut ship." But those who feared he would be too conservative were in for a surprise. Only one week after taking over as captain, he took the *Macon* on a daring unauthorized mission.

Wiley knew that the vacationing President Franklin Roosevelt was sailing from Panama to Hawaii aboard the heavy cruiser *Houston*, escorted by a second heavy cruiser, the *New Orleans*. With nothing more than newspaper reports to go on, the *Macon*'s captain calculated the president's probable route and speed, then plotted an intersect course. He would prove in dramatic fashion the value of the big airship as a long-distance scout.

On the morning of July 18, 1934, the *Macon* departed from Moffett Field and headed southwest. Soon she was far out over the Pacific, navigating by dead reckoning and sun sightings. Just after 10:00 A.M. the next day, Wiley ordered two Sparrowhawks lowered and launched, one after the other. If he'd calculated correctly, the president's small flotilla should now be in range. Sure enough, not long before noon, the two fighters found the two heavy cruisers.

The last thing anyone on board expected was to see airplanes in the middle of the Pacific Ocean, especially given the fact that all of the navy's aircraft carriers were known to be in the Atlantic. On the *Houston*'s bridge, where the two aircraft were spotted just as the watch was about to change, astonishment turned briefly to consternation: the planes appeared to be carrying fat bombs beneath their fuselages. But more knowledgeable eyes quickly pointed out the telltale skyhooks jutting above the upper wings. The "bombs" were actually auxiliary fuel tanks installed in place of unneeded landing gear, a method of increasing the planes' range.

The triumphant pilots radioed their success to Wiley who arrived on the scene, recovered his two planes, then relaunched them with a load of gifts. For the president were the latest San Francisco papers and a selection of national newsmagazines, as well as some souvenir envelopes from the *Macon* crew stamped with a special *Macon* cachet. Wiley knew the president was an avid stamp collector and would be thrilled to own examples of the first mail delivery by an airplane launched from an airship. It was a good thing, however, that the packages were wrapped in waterproof material, since they all landed in the water.

The mail drop was a lovely touch, worthy of Hugo Eckener, who had made a detour in order to drop a wreath over Alberto Santos-Dumont's Brazilian birthplace during the *Graf Zeppelin*'s first flight to South America. Roosevelt was delighted. "The president compliments you and your planes on your fine performance and excellent navigation," the *Houston* radioed.

By the end of her career, the U.S.S. *Macon* (above) had become an efficient aerial aircraft carrier. The most difficult maneuver was actually recovering the F9C-2 Sparrowhawks while in flight. A green flag (bottom left) told the pilot he was cleared to hook on to the trapeze. Note that the Sparrowhawk in this picture still has its undercarriage, whereas the plane hooking on below right has had its landing wheels removed to enable it to carry an auxiliary fuel tank, greatly increasing its range. (Below middle) Once a plane hooked on, the *Macon*'s trapeze became a crane that brought the fighter biplane into the airship's belly.

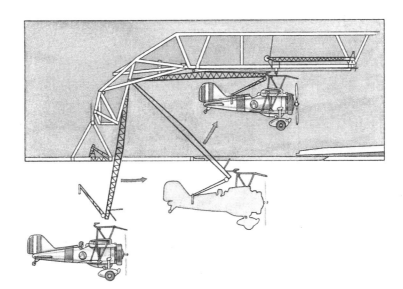

Wiley's superiors weren't nearly so pleased with this display of individual initiative. The *Macon*'s captain had not revealed the airship's true plans and for many hours she had been out of communication. The new commander in chief of the U.S. fleet, Admiral Joseph Reeves, snorted that the flight was "ill-timed and ill-advised" and called it a case of "misapplied initiative." There was talk of disciplinary action. But King and apparently even Roosevelt came to Wiley's defense. Years later the *Macon*'s former captain commented, "They told me to show them that the *Macon* could scout. When I did, they wanted to court-martial me!" When the tempest died down, Wiley was still captain of the *Macon* and more determined than ever to show what his ship could do.

During the summer and fall of 1934, with the American fleet exercising in the far-off Atlantic, the *Macon*'s crew underwent a period of intensive training unlike anything any airship crew had experienced before. Between the end of July and her return to fleet operations in November, she spent 404 hours in the air. Above all she trained with her airplanes. After the success in finding President Roosevelt, Wiley was completely convinced that his Sparrowhawks should be used as scouts, not to defend the airship. And he now had technology that made those planes even more effective: a simple radio-homing device.

Previously the airship-launched scouting planes had been forced to fly a set flight pattern while the airship held a steady course so that the pilots could be confident of returning safely to their moving hangar. Otherwise they could easily become lost over the ocean and run out of fuel. The radio-homing capability made the *Macon* the first—and last—fully effective airborne aircraft carrier. Now her planes could roam more freely, while she could safely change course to avoid enemy attack or dodge an ugly storm. All that remained was for Wiley to demonstrate what he and his crew had learned. Their big opportunity would come during Fleet Problem XVI,

the major exercises scheduled for the spring of 1935. Then the *Macon* would be operating in the wide Pacific west of Hawaii, ideal conditions for long-range scouting.

In Wiley's eagerness to prove himself and his ship, however, he had perhaps unduly discounted one nagging item: some structural problems near the *Macon*'s tail fins. Back in April 1934, the airship had encountered terrible turbulence over Texas while flying to Florida to participate in Caribbean fleet exercises. During the wild ride over the continental divide, one of the main-frame rings became severely compromised when

The U.S.S. *Macon* glides over the Pacific Ocean during one of her intensive series of training flights in the summer and fall of 1934.

two girders broke and a third buckled on its port side. The frame in question, Ring 17.5, happened to be one of the two crucial attachment points for the *Macon*'s huge fins. If this ring had failed, one or more of these fins would have been carried away. Fortunately for the ship and her crew, emergency repairs staved off a more catastrophic structural failure and the ship made it safely to Florida, where a team from Goodyear-Zeppelin made the necessary temporary repairs.

Subsequent analysis determined that the frame at this point was too weak to handle the maximum fin loads the ship might encounter in severe turbulence. Clearly the structure needed reinforcing. But the *Macon* was allowed to continue on active duty. The justification seems to have been that in operations over water, her primary purpose, the airship was unlikely to encounter anything like the air turbulence over west Texas. The recommended structural reinforcements were to be "accomplished from time to time, as opportunity offers, at the discretion of the Commanding Officer." Wiley simply never found the "opportunity" to complete these repairs, and the upper part of the faulty main frame was never strengthened. However, he and his officers never doubted their ship's airworthiness.

Charles Rosendahl, in a subsequent assessment, described the failure to finish the work as "a collective error in judgment." There was no "Admiral" Eckener to order the airship grounded until any doubts about its structure had been laid to rest. The ship's chief designer, Karl Arnstein, vainly sounded the alarm, urging that the ship not fly until the changes were made. But the decision was the navy's, not his.

A crewman stands at the main rudder control, or helm, in the control car.

T OWARD MIDAFTERNOON ON February 12, 1935, Lieutenant Commander Wiley turned the *Macon* homeward with a sense of deep satisfaction. Finally he'd been able to show off his ship's scouting capabilities in front of the surface fleet—and in less than ideal conditions. The previous day his Sparrowhawk fighters had located surface units and reported their positions while remaining unseen. Now he looked forward with even greater confidence to Fleet Problem XVI, during which he planned to supplement aerial scouting with a bit of surprise offense. Unlike carrier-bound aircraft, his planes could operate at night. His idea was to locate and track an "enemy" carrier, then stage a nocturnal dive-bomb attack. That would show the doubting admirals just what the *Macon* was worth.

Finally the tide of opinion seemed to be turning in the airship's favor. In January the Federal Aviation Commission had actually recommended expanded airship operations for the navy, including the building of a new training ship to replace the *Los Angeles*. What's more, the commission had called for a $17-million program of commercial airship building.

As the *Macon* droned steadily northward along the California coast that overcast afternoon, there was a collective feeling on board of accomplishment at a job well done. Within a few hours the ship would be back at Moffett Field. Wiley watched the cloud ceiling grow lower without alarm. As he expected, the ship passed easily through a series of rain squalls. Just before 5:00 P.M. Point Sur lighthouse appeared just off the starboard bow. A few minutes later Wiley ordered, "Left rudder." He had observed a nasty cloud formation to starboard.

The helmsman put the rudder over. Then, suddenly, the ship lurched sharply to starboard, apparently struck by a hammer-like gust. The weather was clearly deteriorating, but Wiley still saw no reason for concern. He had forged the eighty-three men on board into a tight and competent team. And the *Macon* had logged many hundreds of hours since the incident over Texas.

During the moments when the gust took hold, the rudder man and elevator man both briefly lost hold of their wheels, which spun wildly, then reported that they seemed to have regained control. But about a minute after the gust hit, the nose began to tilt upward. The bridge telephone jangled. The coxswain reported ill-defined damage to Ring 17.5, the forward attachment point of the four big fins.

At this moment the fate of the ship hung in the balance. Wiley knew only that there was some structural damage in the aftermost section of the ship; how serious wasn't clear. But the sudden drop in the stern suggested a loss of gas from at least one of the rear gas cells. And the upper rudder controls were gone, implying damage to the upper fin. However, the *Macon* possessed no formal damage-control routine, and Wiley didn't think to send anyone aft to check out the situation further—there didn't seem to be time. He simply reacted instinctively, ordering the release of all the water ballast aft of midships. The telephone jangled again. Cells 0, I and II were all losing helium. Release the aft slip tanks, Wiley ordered. Idle the engines. And dispatch an SOS.

The ship fell, perhaps 100 feet, paused and then shot skyward, remaining at a sharp angle throughout her hair-raising ascent. Either Wiley had dropped too much ballast, or the order to slow the engines was delayed in reaching the men tending the eight powerful 560-horsepower Maybachs. (The subsequent naval inquiry attributed the *Macon*'s rapid rise to dynamic lift from her engines.) Up and up the ship flew, past her pressure height of 2,800 feet. As she rose, helium automatically bled out of the still-intact cells through the emergency valves. Helplessly the captain watched the altimeter needle move: 3,000 feet, 3,500 feet, 4,000 feet, 4,500 feet. Manual valving of helium failed to stop the rise. Finally at almost 5,000 feet the ship slowed and stopped.

Interminable minutes passed as more helium leaked into the surrounding air. Wiley now knew his ship was doomed by the excessive loss of lifting gas. During the wild ascent he'd ordered all hands into the bow in the vain hope that their weight would correct the ship's trim. Now he ordered them to prepare to abandon ship. Thanks to the lesson of the *Akron* disaster, the ship carried a full complement of life jackets and life rafts. He would break the fall as best he could by pitching the propellers downward and by dropping all remaining ballast. But the best he could hope for was a reasonably soft landing in the ocean.

Finally, inevitably, after a full sixteen minutes above pressure height, the plunge began and Wiley felt the floor fall away from under his feet like a skyscraper elevator plummeting out of control.

Meanwhile, the keeper of the Point Sur lighthouse had seen what Commander Wiley could not. When the giant airship first came into view he had trained his field glasses on her

(Above) An Italian magazine illustrator created this dramatic depiction of the *Macon*'s final moments. As the airship sinks into the Pacific the crew escapes in inflatable life rafts.
(Below) As he had following the *Akron* disaster, Herbert Wiley once again found himself explaining an airship crash to members of the press after the loss of the *Macon*. By this time, the American public had lost its faith in the rigid airship.
(Opposite) A lone blimp waits in vain in Hangar No. 1 at Moffett Field for the return of the *Macon* on February 12, 1935.

and followed as she came abeam. Suddenly her stern dropped. A moment later the leading edge of the upper fin appeared to pull away from the hull surface, then the whole fin simply disintegrated. He watched in horror as the crippled airship sailed in a helpless circle while a stream of fuel and water ballast poured from her tail area like blood spurting from a wounded animal. A few moments later she disappeared into the gray overcast on her fatal rise above pressure height.

No one witnessed the *Macon*'s final descent into the sea. The tail hit first, then the rest of the giant aircraft, longer than two football fields, settled into the water. Soon the ocean was dotted with rubber rafts and bobbing heads held up by life jackets. The *Macon*'s crew had ringside seats as their great ship gradually disappeared beneath the waves.

Rescue was swift and merciful. Nearby navy ships involved in the fleet exercises had rushed to the scene as soon as the *Macon* sent her SOS. All but two of the eighty-three men on board went home alive. Among the survivors was the now twice-spared Herbert Wiley.

THE COMMANDANT OF THE LAKEHURST Naval Air Station paced endlessly up and down his office. As he paced, he repeatedly uttered the worst expletive in his arsenal: "Goddammit! Goddammit! Goddammit!" He was not one to raise his voice, but the sharp syllables shot from his mouth like bullets. Everything he had worked for lay in ruins. His dream had crashed with the last great American navy airship.

Yet even in his darkest hour, Charles E. Rosendahl would not give up the fight for the rigid airship. This time, however, not even friends in high places could save his crusade. With previous crashes there had always been another ship to take the lost one's place. Now there was none.

The crash of the *Macon* brought to a close

the American chapter in the saga of the giant airships. New schemes would be floated over the next few years, even a plan for a gigantic ship with a gas volume of 10 million cubic feet that could carry a whole squadron of planes, but all were doomed by the *Macon* disaster and the subsequent arrival on the aviation scene of amphibious airplanes that could take on the role of long-range strategic scouting.

Still, a tantalizing possibility floats unresolved. Had Wiley managed to pilot the *Macon* safely to ground—by no means an impossible task—the rigid airship might well have gone on to play an important role in World War II. With her proven endurance and with even better planes for scouting, it is tempting to imagine a small fleet of these aerial aircraft carriers patrolling the waters west of Hawaii on a certain day in December 1941, when wave after wave of Japanese planes sped toward Pearl Harbor on their mission of destruction. Airship-launched scout planes might have spotted the attacking enemy, saving the United States from the devastating loss of the core of its Pacific fleet.

In February 1935, when the *Macon* met her end, there was still one flyable rigid in the U.S. Navy. In the big shed at Lakehurst sat the venerable *Los Angeles*, idle since her official decommissioning in June 1932. Her helium cells had recently been reinflated and both Admiral King and Commander Rosendahl were agitating for her use on experimental flights. But it was not to be.

His promising career on hold, Rosendahl found himself the manager of America's only international airport for airships, which was otherwise a navy backwater. He would be there to shake Hugo Eckener's hand at the end of the first transatlantic voyage of the *Hindenburg* in the spring of 1936, but neither he nor any other American would ever command one of the great rigid airships again.

Many considered it an ill omen that when the *LZ 129* emerged from her building shed in March 1936 she bore no name, having not yet been christened.

CHAPTER SEVEN

SHIP OF DREAMS

"Due to its light construction and the vulnerability inherent in its large size, it can thrive and exist only in an atmosphere of unclouded peace.... It is like one of those opalescent butterflies, which fascinate as they flutter in the summer sunshine, but seek a sheltered corner whenever a storm blows up. Often, when people greet it so enthusiastically as it appears in the heavens, I have felt as if they believed they were seeing in it a sign and symbol of lasting peace, or at least a symbol of the universal dream of lasting peace among peoples."
—Hugo Eckener

"The Hindenburg *represented Eckener's dream of the ideal transatlantic airship."*
—Douglas H. Robinson

ERNST LEHMANN CURSED SOFTLY TO HIMSELF. IT WAS NOT YET dawn on March 26, 1936, but a gusty east wind had sprung up, making an airship undocking extremely risky. Ordinarily he would not have even considered attempting to bring the *Hindenburg* out of its new operating hangar at Löwenthal (a suburb of Friedrichshafen) in such conditions. The new ship, named after the late German president, Paul von Hindenburg, was even bigger than the *Graf Zeppelin* and had been flying for less than a month.

On the other hand, this was no ordinary test mission, but a flight for the fatherland. None other than Dr. Joseph Goebbels, Hitler's propaganda minister, had decreed that the *Hindenburg* and the *Graf* would together make an aerial tour of Germany to campaign for a "yes" vote in the March 29, 1936, referendum. Patriotic music would blare from specially mounted loudspeakers and thousands of leaflets in support of the Third Reich's recent occupation of the Rhineland would be dropped over every important population center.

Lehmann had not joined the Nazi party, but like many patriotic Germans—especially those who had fought in World War I and lived through the humiliating peace that followed—he was forced to admit that the new regime had not only brought order and restored the German economy, but had given his countrymen a new sense of pride and self-confidence. What's more, it was the Nazis who had finally provided the Zeppelin Company with enough money to complete the first commercially viable transcontinental airship.

Lehmann and Hugo Eckener may have had their differences, but they were united in their devotion to the zeppelin cause. Still, Dr. Eckener had been horrified at the prospect of his zeppelins being subverted into vehicles for propaganda. "If the airships are to be used for political purposes, it will be the end of the airship," he had announced angrily. But the old man's pronouncements no longer carried the weight they once had. The Nazis had made Ernst Lehmann director of the recently formed Deutsche Zeppelin-Reederei, which now owned both the *Graf Zeppelin* and the *Hindenburg* and ran the transatlantic service. Hugo Eckener, less acceptable than Lehmann to the government in power, had been handed the honorary position of chairman of the board of the new airline, effectively ending his control over passenger operations. Nonetheless, the great aviation pioneer was still head of the Zeppelin Company, remained immensely popular within the ranks of airshipmen—not to mention ordinary Germans—and continued to enjoy international acclaim, especially in the United States.

Around 6:00 A.M., Lehmann felt he could wait no longer. If anything, the wind would likely grow stronger once the sun came up. He ordered the ground crew to walk the great ship from its shed while he watched from his command position in the control gondola. This was a smaller, more streamlined affair than the gondola on the *Graf Zeppelin*, which had also housed the passenger dining lounge and sleeping quarters. On the *Hindenburg* the far more spacious passenger decks had been built inside the bottom of the hull.

Everything went well until the ship was safely out of the shed and preparing for takeoff. Since the mouth of the hangar opened to the west and the wind that day blew from the east, this would be a somewhat difficult downwind maneuver, but Lehmann wasn't unduly worried. He'd directed such takeoffs many times before. Then a gust caught the stern, a restraining line broke, and the tail of the huge ship soared upward, out of control. The bow, struggling to follow, slipped from the grasp of its handlers. The forward half of the huge craft—one-sixth of a mile long—seesawed up, the stern half came down, and the bottom of the lower stabilizing fin and lower rudder smashed heavily into the ground, accompanied by the crunch of girders and the ripping of canvas. The whole ship

shot upward and suddenly Lehmann found himself in command of the biggest free balloon that had ever flown. He hastily ordered the engines started and brought the *Hindenburg* under control, but it was almost three hours before he could bring her back down to earth and see to the damage.

Waiting for him was a furious Dr. Eckener. For a moment they became teacher and pupil once more. The big older man with his shock of close-cropped white hair and goatee towered over the delinquent student.

"How could you, Herr Lehmann, order the ship to be brought out in such wind conditions?" he thundered. "You had the best excuse in the world for postponing this idiotic flight; instead, you risk the ship merely to avoid annoying Herr Goebbels. Do you call this showing a sense of responsibility towards our enterprise?"

Lehmann's exact response to this tongue-lashing has not come down to us. In his memoirs he dismisses the whole incident in a few sentences. He coolly told Eckener that the damage was not too serious and that he would have it repaired quickly.

"So is that your only concern," Eckener answered bitterly, "to take off quickly on this mad flight and drop election pamphlets for Herr Goebbels? The fact that we have to take off for Rio in four days and have made no flights to test the engines apparently means nothing to you!" (The final full-power trials had been canceled to make way for the propaganda tour.)

Eckener stormed off, leaving Lehmann to direct temporary repairs. These were, as he had predicted, effected in short order. The *Hindenburg* took off a few hours later, and the propaganda flight went ahead as

The *Graf Zeppelin* and the *Hindenburg* soar over Berlin's Brandenburg Gate during their controversial propaganda tour in late March 1936.
(Left) From the *Hindenburg*'s control car Ernst Lehmann directs the ground crew prior to takeoff.

planned. On referendum day, in a special polling station established on board the new zeppelin, all 104 passengers and crew cast ballots in favor of the Rhineland annexation, which passed by a 99 percent vote throughout Germany. Eckener, with typical acerbity, wondered aloud why the on-board vote hadn't been even higher.

Precious few had the courage or clout to stand against the Nazis. Until now, Hugo Eckener had been one of them. But this time, perhaps, he had gone too far.

SOON AFTER THE *GRAF ZEPPELIN* WAS LAUNCHED IN 1928, PLANNING had begun for the next great airship in the zeppelin line, the *LZ 128*. At 761 feet and slightly over 5 million cubic feet in gas capacity, this was to have been a fattened version of the *Graf*, a ship resembling the two big British dirigibles. But then came the disastrous crash of the hydrogen-filled *R 101* in October 1930. Had the *R 101* held inflammable helium, few, if any, lives would have been lost. Plans for the hydrogen-filled *LZ 128* were shelved in favor of the *LZ 129*, whose larger and longer design compensated for the fact that helium possessed less lifting capacity than hydrogen.

In the end, however, the giant that emerged from the new building shed at the Zeppelin Company works at Friedrichshafen on March 4, 1936, had only hydrogen inflating its sixteen gas cells. The Americans, fearing others might use helium for military purposes, refused to rescind the Helium Control Act of 1927, which prohibited the export of the lifting gas over which the United States still exercised a monopoly. And in fact the Germans never formally requested helium for use in the *Hindenburg*.

The safety-conscious Eckener was fully aware of the risk of operating with hydrogen. But by 1936 the unbroken passenger safety record of the German zeppelins made its danger seem exaggerated. Eckener himself regarded gasoline as a greater threat to airship safety. In fatal airship accidents, it was usually the fuel that ignited first, setting the hydrogen on fire. Of the handful of hydrogen-filled airships that had accidentally burned in the air, two were known to have been struck by lightning in a thunderstorm while

valving gas. And a third, the French *Dixmude*, was thought to have suffered the same fate. From this experience had come the firm operational dictum: "Never blow off gas in a thunderstorm." Since World War I, German zeppelins had survived every imaginable type of bad weather and had been struck by lightning more than once. All had survived.

Nonetheless Eckener knew perfectly well that no piece of technology was perfect and that human beings made human errors. He would have preferred helium, but in his view hydrogen was safe—as long as experienced crews handled their ships with care.

At 803.8 feet in length and 135.1 feet in diameter at its fattest point—with a gas capacity of 7,062,100 cubic feet—the *Hindenburg* was indeed the largest aircraft that had ever flown. But, as Harold Dick points out in his book *Graf Zeppelin & Hindenburg*, "the basic design and structure were thoroughly conventional." Ludwig Dürr and the other *Hindenburg* engineers pooh-poohed the innovations their former colleague Karl Arnstein had worked into the *Akron* and the *Macon*. Instead they built conservatively on the foundation of the long tradition of German zeppelin design.

Because of the initial plans for using helium, Dürr and his colleagues had experimented with various water-recovery techniques in order to minimize the necessity for valving gas, but in the end used gutters like those recently installed on the *Graf Zeppelin* to collect rainwater for ballast. One innovation did imitate an American advance. Instead of being lined with impermeable goldbeater's skin, the gasbags were coated with a gelatin solution similar to the inner lining used for the gas cells on the *Akron* and the *Macon*. In the main, however, the *Hindenburg* was an airship Count Zeppelin would have clearly recognized as one of his own grandchildren.

Where the *Hindenburg* surpassed all previous dirigibles was in her passenger accommodations, which have never been equaled in a commercial aircraft. On two decks inside the hull just aft of the control gondola, fifty people could live in the style and comfort of a grand hotel. The twenty-five two-berth passenger cabins that occupied the center of the upper deck (A deck) were in themselves nothing special—a first-class railway sleeping car easily matched these. In fact, veterans of the *Graf* complained about the lack of

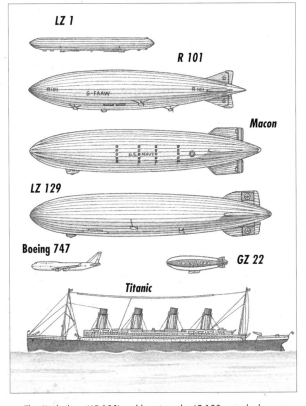

The *Hindenburg* (*LZ 129*) and her sister the *LZ 130* were the largest aircraft that ever flew, dwarfing both modern jumbo jets and Goodyear's most modern blimp, the *Spirit of Akron* (*GZ 22*). In fact, the *Hindenburg* was only 78 feet shorter than the 882-foot-long *Titanic*.

A LEVIATHAN IS BORN

Construction of the *LZ 129* began in the autumn of 1931, soon after completion of a huge new building shed in Friedrichshafen, and was finished by early 1936. (Above left) The axial walkway is clearly visible in the completed nose framework, to which the first piece of outer cover has been affixed. (Above right) Just aft of the bow, workmen lace cover sections together. The bow itself has already been laced and given its final coat of aluminum dope. (Below left) Once the frame was completely covered, several coats of clear dope were applied to the fabric. (Below middle) A gas cell is hung for fitting. (Below right) Final work on the tail and fins.

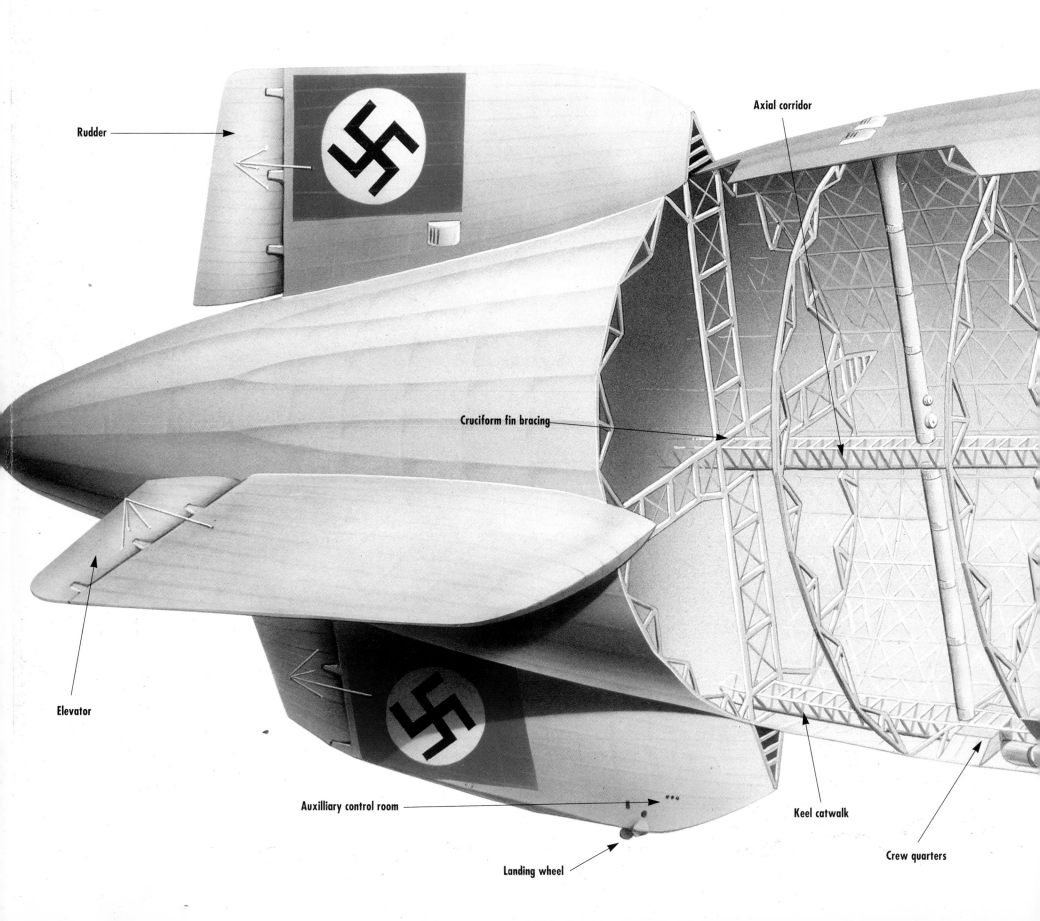

Rudder

Axial corridor

Cruciform fin bracing

Elevator

Keel catwalk

Auxilliary control room

Crew quarters

Landing wheel

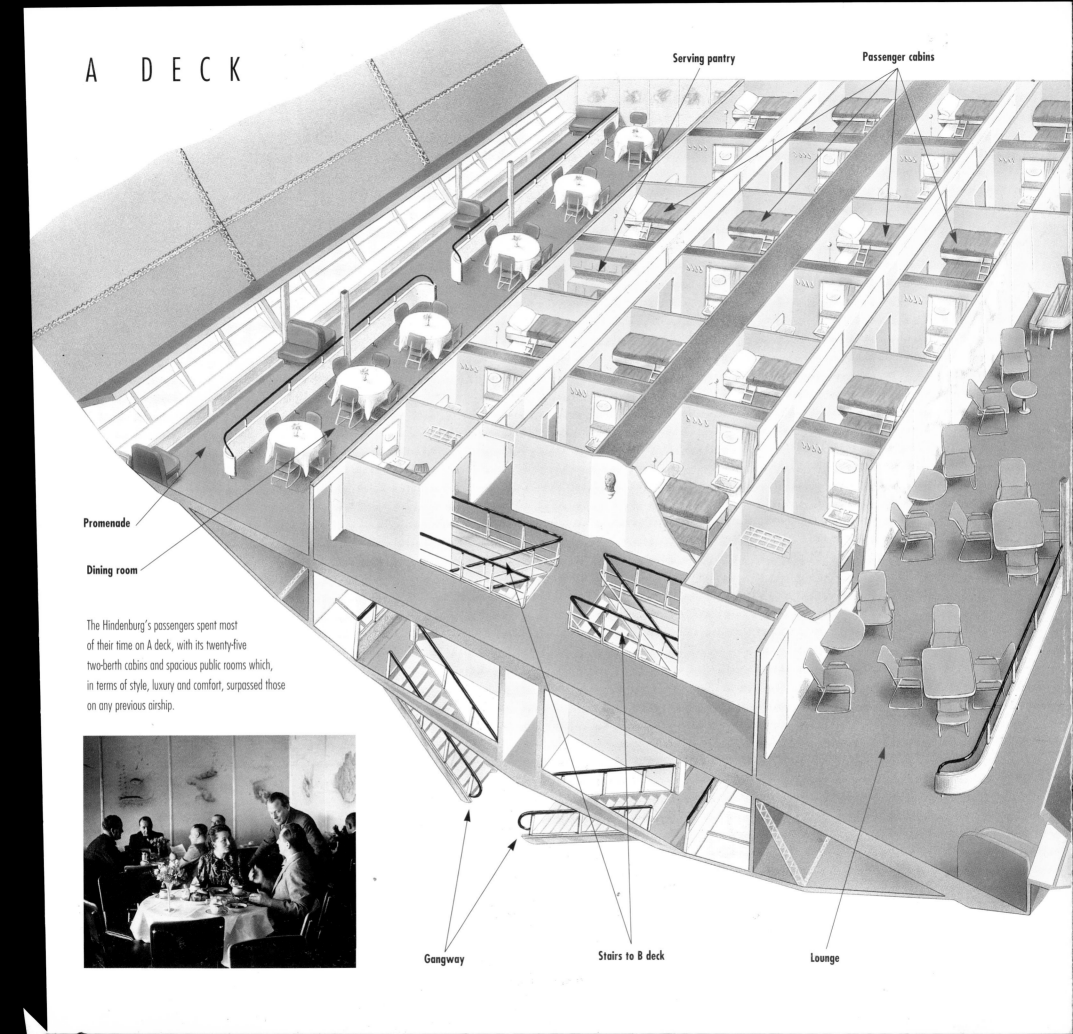

A DECK

Serving pantry

Passenger cabins

Promenade

Dining room

The Hindenburg's passengers spent most of their time on A deck, with its twenty-five two-berth cabins and spacious public rooms which, in terms of style, luxury and comfort, surpassed those on any previous airship.

Gangway

Stairs to B deck

Lounge

U R G

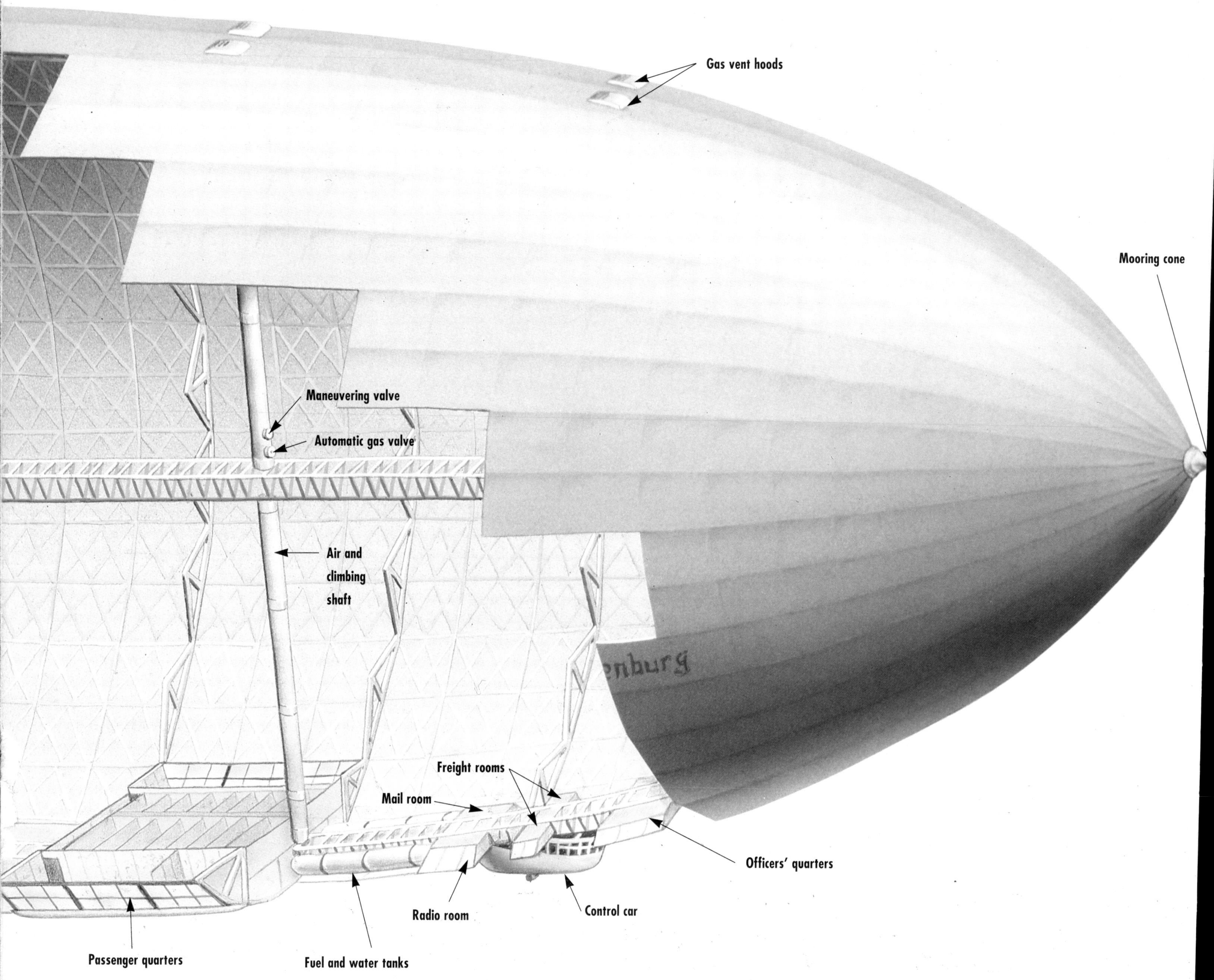
Gas vent hoods
Mooring cone
Maneuvering valve
Automatic gas valve
Air and climbing shaft
enburg
Freight rooms
Mail room
Officers' quarters
Control car
Radio room
Passenger quarters
Fuel and water tanks

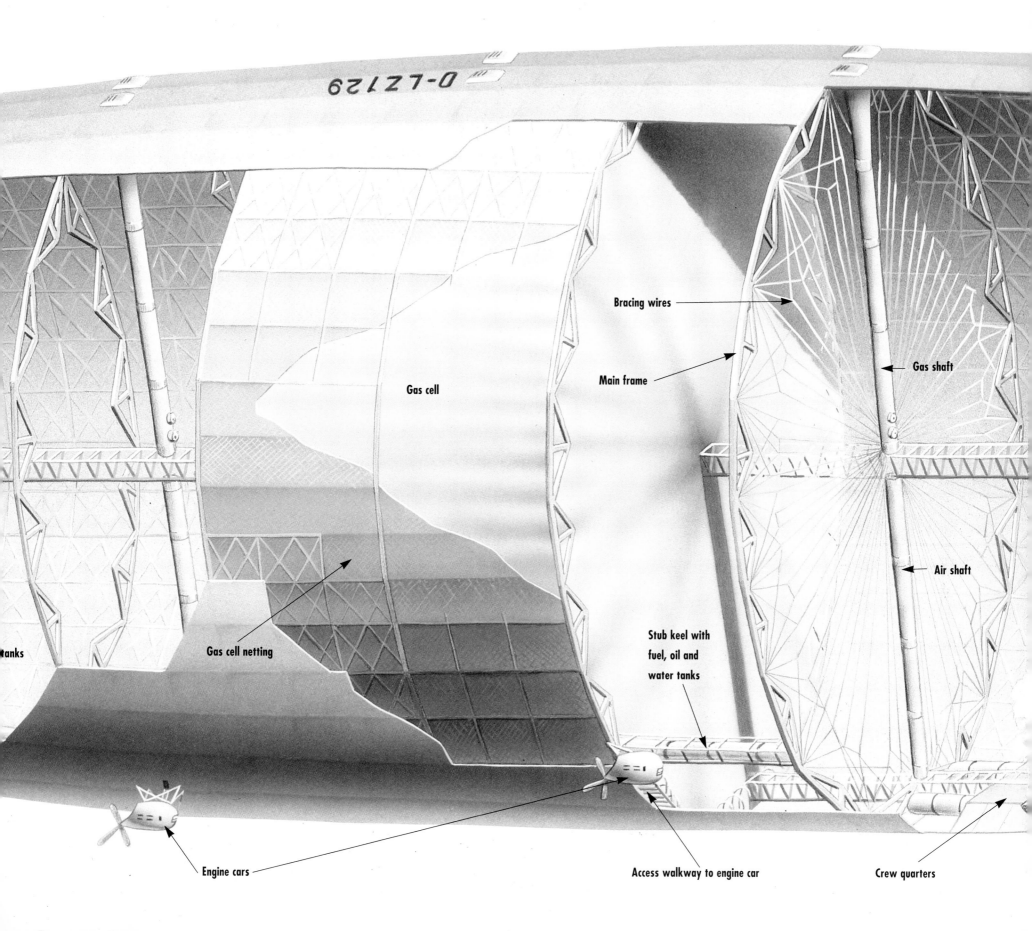

D-LZ129

Gas cell

Bracing wires

Main frame

Gas shaft

Air shaft

Gas cell netting

Stub keel with
fuel, oil and
water tanks

tanks

Engine cars

Access walkway to engine car

Crew quarters

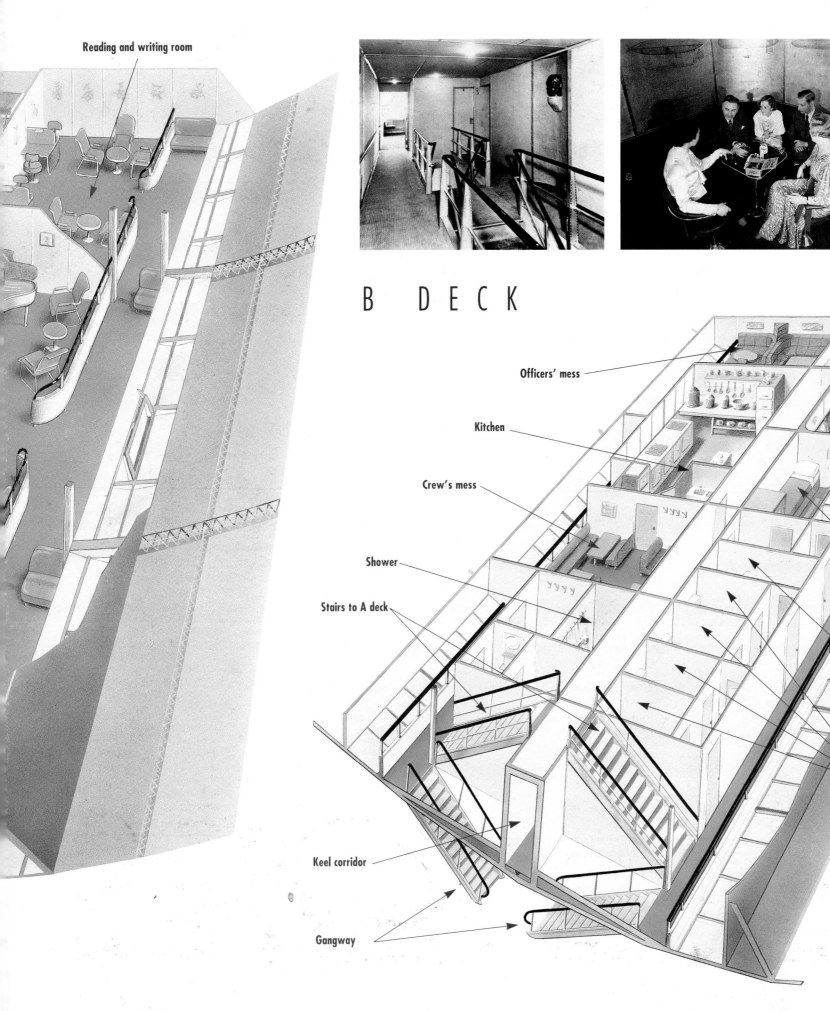

Reading and writing room

Passengers boarded the ship by way of retractable stairs that brought them onto B deck. Then they proceeded up one of the two staircases to A deck (far left). B deck's main attractions were the smoking room (left) and the first-ever shower on board an airship.

B DECK

Smoking room

Officers' mess

Kitchen

Crew's mess

Bar

Air lock door

Shower

Chief Steward's cabin

Stairs to A deck

Urinals

Toilets

Keel corridor

Gangway

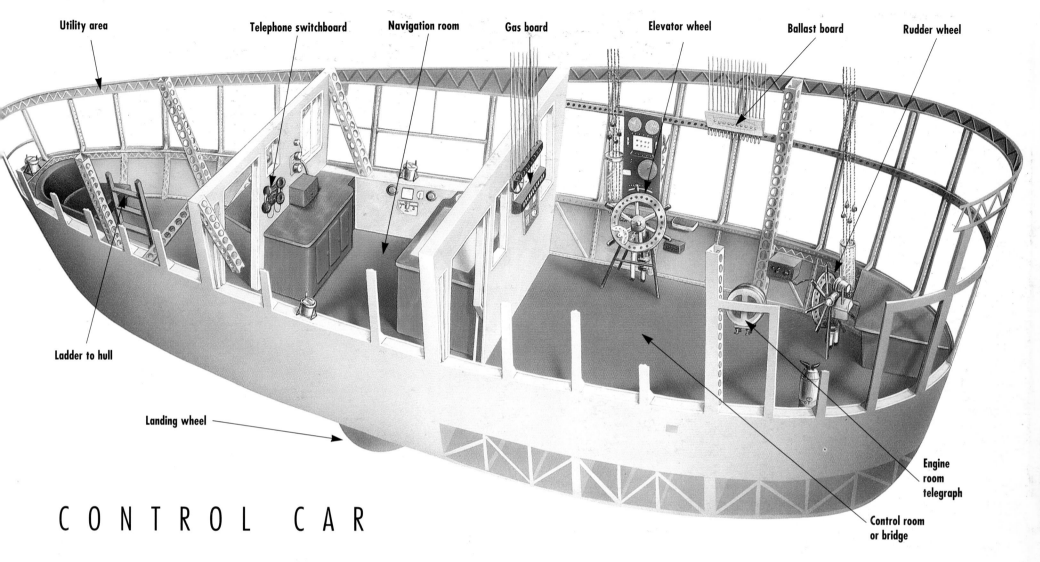

Utility area   Telephone switchboard   Navigation room   Gas board   Elevator wheel   Ballast board   Rudder wheel

Ladder to hull

Landing wheel

Engine room telegraph

Control room or bridge

C O N T R O L   C A R

The nerve center of the vast airship was the small control car where the duty officers and crew kept the *Hindenburg* on course and out of trouble. Unlike the *Graf Zeppelin,* the *Hindenburg*'s rudder could operate on automatic pilot, but did so only during calm conditions. (Below left) At all times both the rudder man, at right, and elevator man, at left, were at their posts. The elevator man, standing parallel to the centerline of the ship so that he could immediately sense any change in its angle, kept a constant eye on the panel in front of him, which included the inclinometer, a gas-cell-pressure monitor and the altimeter. A ladder led from the utility room up into the radio room (below right), where a radio operator was on duty twenty-four hours a day.

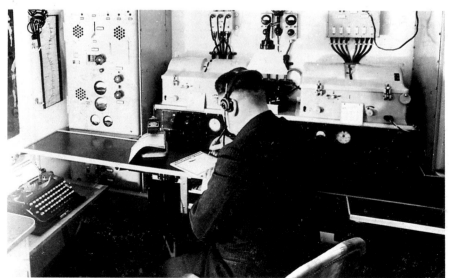

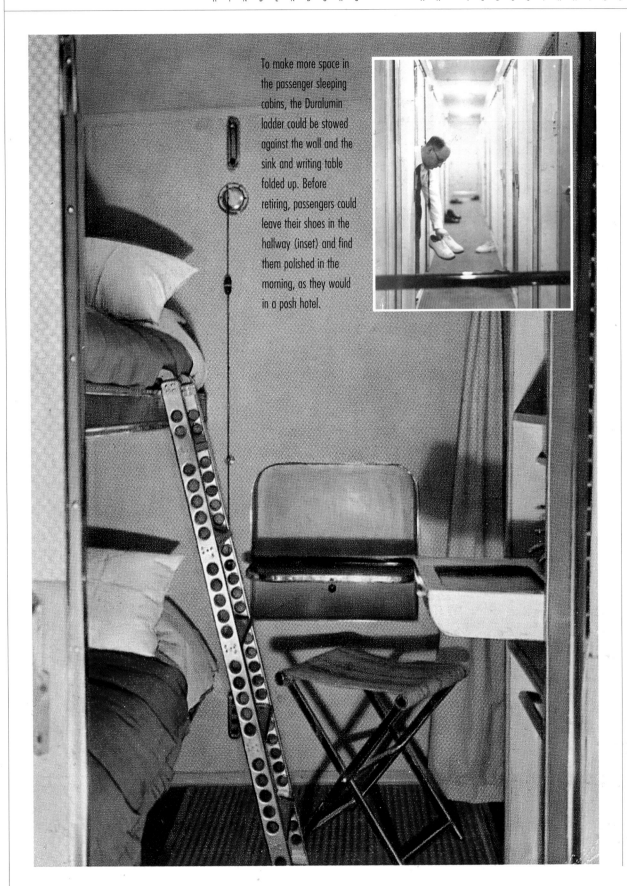

To make more space in the passenger sleeping cabins, the Duralumin ladder could be stowed against the wall and the sink and writing table folded up. Before retiring, passengers could leave their shoes in the hallway (inset) and find them polished in the morning, as they would in a posh hotel.

windows, but at least these berths were heated. No, it was the spacious public rooms, where the passengers spent most of their time, that gave the *Hindenburg* such elegance and élan.

Along both sides of A deck ran the splendid promenade with its comfortable seating and big slanted windows that gave a panoramic view of the scene passing below. These windows could be opened and, even at cruising speed, ordinarily created no draft inside the zeppelin, no hint that the airship was racing along at nearly eighty miles per hour. Just inboard of the port-side promenade was the long, attractive dining room, its walls adorned with paintings by Professor Otto Arpke, showing picturesque scenes from a flight of the *Graf Zeppelin* between Friedrichshafen and Rio. Here the passengers could sit at tables draped in white napery, adorned with tasteful Deutsche Zeppelin-Reederei silver and china created especially for the *Hindenburg*, and decorated with freshly cut flowers. If one's table seat faced outboard, it was possible to view the passing skyscape while dining on such delicacies as "Fattened Duckling, Bavarian Style, with Champagne Cabbage" or "Venison Cutlets Beauval with Berny Potatoes," accompanied by a good French Burgundy or a fine German Mosel. It was discovered that at an inclination of ten degrees a wine bottle tipped over, so the elevator men were under strict instructions to limit the aerial ups and downs to no more than five degrees off a perfect level.

In the spacious starboard-side lounge, passengers could relax with a drink while listening to Ernst Lehmann or another of the musically gifted on board play the Blüthner baby grand piano (travelers on the *Graf* had complained that a piano was the only embellishment their after-supper parties lacked). Made mostly of aluminum and covered in yellow pigskin, it weighed a mere 397 pounds. And on the impressive wall mural—a huge map of the world—they could trace the routes of famous explorers, from the first voyage

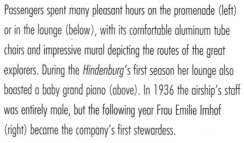

Passengers spent many pleasant hours on the promenade (left) or in the lounge (below), with its comfortable aluminum tube chairs and impressive mural depicting the routes of the great explorers. During the *Hindenburg*'s first season her lounge also boasted a baby grand piano (above). In 1936 the airship's staff was entirely male, but the following year Frau Emilie Imhof (right) became the company's first stewardess.

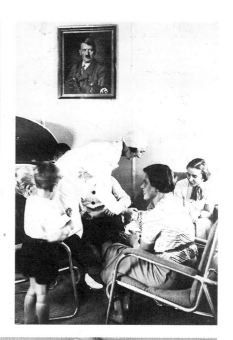

DINING
ABOVE THE CLOUDS

A meal aboard the *Hindenburg* surely represented the acme of airship elegance. The food was excellent and the wine list (above) included both French and German vintages. The captain and his senior officers generally joined the passengers, as did Hugo Eckener whenever he was on board (top right). Dishes traveled via dumbwaiter from the spacious kitchen on the deck below (middle and bottom right), furnished with an electric stove, baking and roasting ovens, a refrigerator and an ice machine. On a typical Atlantic crossing the chef went through 440 pounds of fresh meat and poultry, 800 eggs and 220 pounds of butter.

The reading and writing room (above) provided peace and quiet for those, such as Lady Grace Drummond Hay (top right), who sought it.
(Right) One of many special *Hindenburg* covers prized by stamp collectors. (Opposite) A corner of the smoking room on B Deck.

of Columbus to the round-the-world flight of the *Graf Zeppelin*.

Those in search of greater peace or intimacy could repair to the reading and writing room next door, with its soothing gray walls and paintings depicting the development of the world postal service. When a letter was written on *Hindenburg* stationery and sealed in a *Hindenburg* envelope, one needed only to drop it in the mailbox, whose contents were emptied twice a day and carried to the nearby mail room.

B deck, in the narrower space below A deck, held a cozy preserve known as the smoking room. To enter, one had to pass through a cramped antechamber that doubled as the room's bar. There a steward stood watch until 3:00 A.M., granting admission through the air lock door—the room was pressurized to prevent any hydrogen from entering—and dispensing libations. The specialties of the house included the *LZ 129* Frosted Cocktail—gin with just a dash of orange juice—and the Maybach 12—recipe unknown, but undoubtedly of considerable horsepower.

The rest of B deck housed more functional facilities: lavatories for the passengers, the kitchen, messes for both the officers and crew and a first

on any aircraft, the shower. To conserve water this was timed to stop after a very brief interval, and its pallid, prickly spray left much to be desired. But it was a shower, nonetheless.

All in all, the *Hindenburg* put the cramped passenger quarters of the *Graf Zeppelin* to shame and far excelled the relatively lavish appointments of the ill-fated *R 101*. Here, at last, was the ship of Hugo Eckener's dreams.

ON MARCH 31, 1936, ONLY TWO DAYS AFTER COMPLETING ITS controversial propaganda flight, the *Hindenburg* set off for Rio de Janeiro. For the first time since the death of Count Zeppelin, Hugo Eckener was not in command of a passenger zeppelin on its maiden voyage. This honor fell to Ernst Lehmann, his star now rising fast. It was not Eckener's advancing age—he would celebrate his sixty-eighth birthday in August—but his waning influence that explained the break with tradition.

So Eckener flew to Rio as a passenger with no operational authority.

HEISSLUFT-BALLON MONTGOLFIER
1783

WASSERSTOFF-BALLON
VON PROF CHARLES
1783

But he remained the media star. When reporters asked him why he wasn't in command, he gave politely evasive answers. This pose became more difficult when, midway over the southern Atlantic, a reporter from an important English newspaper came up to him: "I have just received a radio message from my paper asking me to inquire the reason for the 'declaration of banishment' which Dr. Goebbels has imposed on you. I would like to send five hundred words about this." Eckener was astonished— this was the first he had heard of it— but halfway between two continents he was unable to find out exactly what had happened.

In fact, word of Eckener's intemperate remarks to Captain Lehmann after he'd damaged the *Hindenburg*'s lower fin had reached Joseph Goebbels himself. Hitler's powerful propaganda minister was not pleased. At his next press conference, he pronounced Hugo Eckener an unperson: "Dr. Eckener has alienated himself from the nation. In the future, his name may no longer be mentioned in the newspapers, nor may his picture be further used." Papers outside Germany soon picked up the story. By the time the *Hindenburg* arrived in Rio, foreign press reports had created something of a stir in the sizable German community there.

At the welcoming banquet of the German Club of Rio, Eckener listened with considerable amusement as the local Nazi leader delivered a diatribe against the "vileness of the foreign Press" which was defaming his good name by suggesting that he had "fallen into disgrace with the Nazi Government!" Eckener rose to set the record straight: "I had to explain to the nonplussed and very embarrassed gentleman that 'for once' the foreign Press was accurate . . . I could not restrain myself from adding that I was in no sense a National Socialist and that I greatly regretted the tensions and divisions which the local organization had caused in the German

A poster publicizing the addition of the *Hindenburg* to the South American service. She made seven round trips to Brazil during the 1936 season.

colony in Rio." These words, which would inevitably reach the authorities in Germany, were hardly calculated to make his homecoming any easier. But by this point Eckener seems not to have cared.

On the return flight to Friedrichshafen, Eckener's concern that the propaganda flight had prevented crucial full-power tests proved well founded. On the trip out, one of the *Hindenburg*'s four big diesel engines had broken down. It was repaired as well as possible at Recife, but could not be run at full speed on the trip home. As the ship approached the Cape Verde Islands off the coast of Africa, another engine failed from exactly the same type of wrist-pin breakage. Clearly there was a design flaw in these new engines, the first diesels to be used in a German zeppelin. While the mechanics took the broken engine apart, yet another engine failed.

The *Hindenburg* was now flying on two motors, one of them incapable of full power, just as the ship ran into the northeast trade winds blowing at more than thirty miles per hour. Should another engine fail, the ship would no longer be able to make any forward progress. This was a serious situation. To the east lay the Sahara Desert, hardly an ideal spot for an emergency landing. To the west lay the broad expanse of the Atlantic. The only option was to attempt to climb above the head winds in search of the so-called counter-trades. These winds usually blew only above 5,000 feet, well beyond pressure height for the heavily loaded *Hindenburg*. But on this occasion luck was with her. At a mere 3,600 feet she found the following breeze and began to pick up speed toward home.

It took sixteen hours for the mechanics to restore partial power to the first of the two broken engines, thirty to patch up the second well enough so that it could be used in an emergency. Fortunately none occurred and the *Hindenburg* limped safely home to Friedrichshafen. Before the early

THE PRIDE OF THE REICH

It was the Nazis who came up with the money to complete the construction of the *Hindenburg* and, despite Hugo Eckener's opposition, she and the *Graf Zeppelin* inevitably became identified as symbols of the new regime. The flag of the Deutsche Zeppelin-Reederei (left), the airline that owned and operated the two ships, bore the Nazi swastika, as did the two ships' giant tail fins. The first use of the *Hindenburg* for propaganda purposes came in March 1936, shortly after her launch, when she and the *Graf* appeared over every German city with a population of more than 100,000 (top left), dropping campaign leaflets and broadcasting from loudspeakers in support of the referendum on Hitler's recent occupation of the Rhineland. At the beginning of August, the *Hindenburg* made a triumphal appearance at the opening ceremonies of the Berlin Olympics. And in mid-September she added her powerful aura to the annual Nazi Party congress in Nuremberg (top far left and bottom left), where Hitler (right foreground) received the adoration of the faithful.

May trip to Lakehurst that was to inaugurate regular passenger service to America, all four diesels were overhauled by the Daimler-Benz company. They never again gave any problems.

As for the news of Dr. Eckener's "banishment," it proved to be somewhat exaggerated. At Air Minister Goering's suggestion, Eckener wrote a letter to Goebbels explaining his "technical" reasons for objecting to the propaganda flight, reasons now fully borne out by the incident off Africa. Nonetheless, he remained in official disfavor for some time. Still, his ideal airship was up and flying. And as far as the world was concerned, zeppelins and Dr. Eckener were inseparable.

ALL DAY PASSENGERS HAD BEEN ARRIVING in Friedrichshafen by train and airplane for the *Hindenburg*'s first flight to America. They gathered at the elegant Kurgarten Hotel, where Count Zeppelin had lived for much of the last part of his life. On the Kurgarten's lovely terrace, looking out over Lake Constance toward the snow-capped Swiss Alps, a distinguished international assembly soaked up the warm spring sun. Some, like the journalists Lady Grace Drummond Hay and Karl von Wiegand, and Sir Hubert and Lady Wilkins, were old zeppelin hands. Others, like Louis P. Lochner, Berlin bureau chief for the Associated Press, were voyaging on an airship for the first time. Regardless of their past experience, however, all shared in the sense that they were making history. For this was May 6, 1936, and they were about to inaugurate the first scheduled passenger air service between Europe and North America.

After an early dinner at the hotel, the passengers arrived by bus at Löwenthal. The huge hangar loomed grandly in the gathering dusk. Its great doors had already slid open, like curtains on a proscenium arch, to reveal the vast, silvery nose of the airship and beneath it, like Lilliputians,

Each item of baggage taken aboard the *Hindenburg* was identified with a luggage tag (below) and a sticker (above) bearing the first letter of the owner's surname, allowing the crew to sort the bags alphabetically on landing. (Opposite) The *Hindenburg* releases water ballast to slow her descent in front of the new Frankfurt hangar and (bottom right) the ground crew grasps spider lines as the ship comes in for a landing. (Right) Friends and relatives crowd forward to greet the arriving airship.

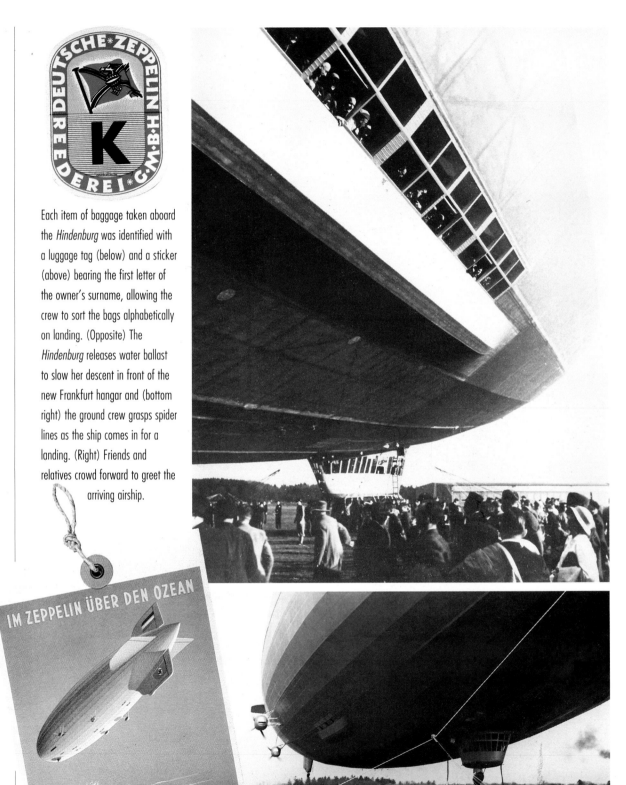

the tiny figures of the ground crew, the invited guests, the press, the photographers, and the uniformed customs officials. Even those who had flown on the reliable old *Graf* were impressed. So were the thousands of sightseers already on hand, bursting with pride at what their countrymen had created. Before boarding, matches, lighters—anything combustible— were confiscated, as were cameras (the German authorities wanted no one snapping pictures of secret military installations).

To the embarking passengers the two small aluminum stairways must have seemed extraordinarily puny as they followed them up into the vast belly of this enormous silver whale. Louis Lochner later noted in his diary that it was "almost like getting on a small ocean steamer." The passengers quickly climbed up the interior stairs from B to A deck, nodded toward the bust of the late German president Paul von Hindenburg, then made a brief stop in their cabins to drop off hand luggage before proceeding to the promenades, where they leaned out the open windows. Those who had traveled on the *Graf* marveled at the spaciousness of the attractive public rooms.

With everything in readiness, the Friedrichshafen town band struck up a sentimental farewell tune, "Muss ich denn zum Städele hinaus" ("Must I leave my beloved home town") followed by "Deutschland über Alles," the stirring German national anthem, and finally the "Stars and Stripes Forever." Then, at Captain Lehmann's shouted command, "Zeppelin marsch!" the ship began to move slowly out of the shed into the falling darkness. Soon onlookers could see the airship's name, emblazoned just aft of the bow in scarlet Gothic script and, a few moments later, the interlocking multicolored rings symbolizing the 1936 Berlin Summer Olympics. Then the giant tail fins finally emerged, their jet black swastikas set off against a circle of white inside a scarlet rectangle. For a moment, even those who had seen the *Hindenburg* fly before doubted that this unbelievable craft, as long as an ocean liner, and as high from fin tip to fin tip as a thirteen-story building, would ever get off the ground.

"Schiff hoch!" called Lehmann, leaning from the control-car window. "Up ship!" At this order the web of handling lines was thrown off, and the ground crew lining the gondola handrails gave the ship an upward push. A few tons of ballast water splashed groundward, dousing—to the amusement of the onlooking passengers—several hundred spectators who had ventured too close. Then, accompanied by a jubilant chorus of shouts and cheers, the *Hindenburg* rose slowly above the throng. To United Press correspondent Webb Miller, she ascended "as gently as thistledown." There was no sensation like it, this feeling of effortless power, of great weight rendered weightless.

The four big diesel engines sputtered to life and then settled into a powerful, pulsing thrum; the ship began to move forward, slowly at first, and to rise ever more quickly into the night sky. Some passengers felt slightly dizzy as the ground receded rapidly and the figures below grew tinier. But the sense of disorientation was fleeting. The *Hindenburg* felt solid, immensely reassuring. Most still lingered by the windows, watching the darkened fields and forests of southern Germany, lights glimmering here and there from a farmhouse or perhaps an ancestral castle. A full moon had already risen, bathing the landscape in silver mystery for their nocturnal ride to the sea.

Those new to airship travel couldn't get over the smoothness and quietness of what one American newspaper would soon refer to as this "galleon of the air." Journalist Lochner, an old friend of both Lehmann and Eckener, waxed poetic when he was conducted to the "seaman's rest," an aerie perched snugly in the point of the bow that was free of the slightest trace of engine vibration: "You feel as though you were carried in the arms of angels," he later confided to his diary.

Even on the passenger decks the faint drone of the engines far astern was barely audible. Later, when the *Hindenburg*'s transatlantic crossings had become routine, some travelers would miss the takeoff entirely, deceived into thinking their great ship was still on the ground, so imperceptible was its motion. The Zeppelin Company's American representative, Willy von Meister, particularly enjoyed recounting one such incident that took place at the beginning of a flight from Lakehurst later in 1936.

On this occasion the airship had arrived late in the United States and its evening departure was therefore delayed from 8:00 P.M. until 10:00. Two ladies, who had traveled that day from the American midwest, were so worn out that once they were finally allowed on board they retired directly to bed. After midnight, von Meister was passing by their cabin, perhaps on his way to the smoking room for a nightcap and one last cigarette, when he noted that the signal light beside the door was lighted. Just then a steward came running down the corridor. One of the two ladies opened the door. She was dressed in a lovely silk nightgown and wore a sleeping cap on her head.

"Steward," the lady asked. "When are we leaving? It's half past twelve."

"Why madam," the steward replied, "we left over two hours ago. We're over Cape Cod."

"I don't believe you!" the lady snapped. Then, oblivious to her rather

informal attire, she ran down the corridor and across the lounge to the promenade windows to see for herself that the ship truly was in flight and about to leave the New England coast.

So stable was the *Hindenburg* in flight that it became something of a game to see how long a pen or pencil could be stood on end without falling over. Eventually, most tired of waiting. Even when passing through rough weather, no one ever got airsick on the *Hindenburg*. Compared to the noisy, often bumpy ride on a modern jumbo jet it was indeed feather soft, feather quiet.

By midnight, after passing the ornate silhouette of the Cologne cathedral, most of the passengers had retired for the night. Sleep came easily unless a snorer inhabited the adjoining cabin, for the walls were merely a single thickness of foam covered by fabric. But some passengers stayed on in the smoking room, sharing the single electric lighter and tapping their ashes into the automatically self-sealing ashtrays. There they lingered until the wee hours, occasionally catching sight of lights far below through the Plexiglas panels set in the peachwood floor—wood burned less easily than carpet—drinking toast after toast to those master mariners of the air, Ernst Lehmann and Hugo Eckener.

Eckener's official status was mysterious. The doctor's name appeared at the head of the officer-and-passenger list, distributed shortly after embarkation, unaccompanied by any title, whereas the name just beneath, that of Captain Lehmann, was designated "commander." But Eckener spent long hours in the control gondola, especially when his son, Knut, was standing watch, and he never seemed to sleep. Those who retired late were as apt to encounter him prowling the corridors as those who rose early. He may not have been in command, but this ship belonged to him.

By breakfast the next morning the easy conviviality of an ocean voyage prevailed on board. The passengers were all people of means. At $400 for a one-way fare—the cost of an automobile—and $720 to travel both ways, this mode of travel remained far beyond the ordinary pocketbook, but less than a first-class ticket on the *Queen Mary*, the fastest and most luxurious liner on the transatlantic run. No one seemed bored. When passengers were not writing the hundreds of postcards promised to friends and relatives, they were gazing out the promenade windows at the sky and seascape. "To voyage in an airship high over the ocean is never monotonous, and is always delightful," Eckener later wrote, "because the picturesque scene of sea and cloud is always rapidly changing." For a time that

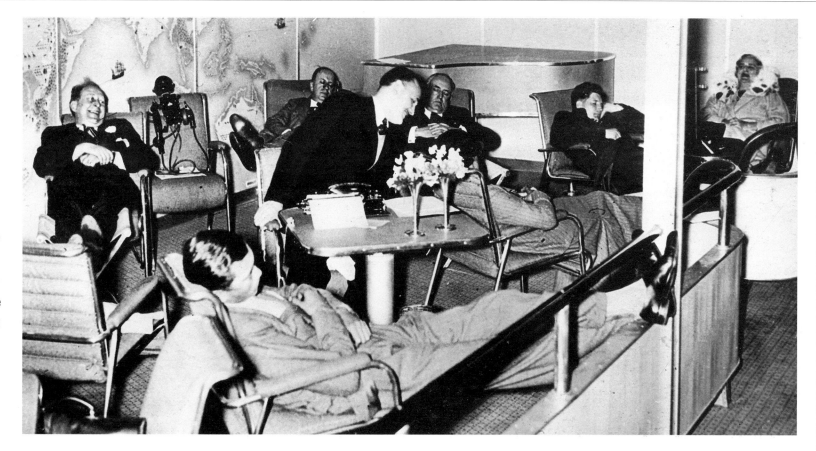

(Opposite left) The white plastic passenger cabin sink provided hot and cold running water. (Opposite right) Hugo Eckener (in background) joins other passengers gazing out the promenade windows. (Right) Passengers relax in the lounge during the first voyage to Lakehurst. One of the few not actually dozing is Associated Press journalist Louis P. Lochner (at extreme left), who kept a fascinating diary of the flight.

morning they sailed in sunshine over an endless field of fleecy clouds. Occasionally the black shadow of the ship passing below was aureoled by a 360-degree rainbow, a phenomenon that had long delighted passengers on the *Graf*. Except when weather dictated otherwise, the *Hindenburg* maintained an altitude of around 650 feet, giving the passengers incredible views of passing steamers, breaching whales and, occasionally, an iceberg. This low cruising height minimized the need for valving gas and made conditions more comfortable for the crew who lived and worked in unheated parts of the ship.

Every passenger who so wished received a guided tour of the ship from control gondola to giant fins. One commented that the inside of the ship resembled a "titanic Meccano set." Webb Miller's guide was Captain Lehmann himself, who turned puckish as they ambled down the walkway along the keel. To demonstrate the strength of the outer cover, the veteran of a thousand zeppelin flights jumped off the catwalk and onto the fabric skin, bouncing as happily as a schoolboy. Later, climbing down the flimsy-looking ladder into one of the engine gondolas in the full rush of the eighty-mile-per-hour slipstream, Miller learned to crook his elbow around the ladder's windward edge so as to keep from being blown right off. He wore a padded helmet, just like the mechanic on duty, but the engine noise still deafened, and it felt "as if we [were] being shot through the air inside a huge artillery shell with open windows."

That evening of the first full day, an impromptu musical group formed around the Blüthner baby grand and promptly named themselves the *Hindenburg* Quartet. Providing the vocals were Lady Wilkins, the popular English novelist, Leslie Charteris—creator of that most debonair of detectives, the Saint—and Charteris's "witty and oh! so attractive, wife," Pauline, to quote passenger Hans Hinrichs. Their showstopper was Irving Berlin's "Cheek to Cheek" with its immortal chorus, "Heaven, I'm in heaven."

Even a bit of rough weather couldn't dampen the good spirits on this landmark Atlantic crossing. During Thursday lunch, with Captain Lehmann sitting at the head of one table and Hugo Eckener at the other, rain and hail began to lash the ship. The vases holding the fresh flowers shook slightly and the ship rolled gently, a little like a huge fish swimming slowly in deep water. Many were disappointed that the storm didn't last for more than a few minutes. Early the next morning, off the North American coast, another wilder storm rocked the *Hindenburg* for roughly half an hour, but in Webb Miller's cabin not a drop spilled from the full glass of water on his night table. Later a number of passengers confessed to having slept through the whole thing.

When the *Hindenburg* approached Manhattan on the morning of

A MECHANIC'S LIFE IS NOT A QUIET ONE

The noisiest job on the *Hindenburg* belonged to the mechanics who stood rotating watches inside the four engine cars, two hours during the day and three hours at night. (When off watch, the mechanics were often assigned other duties.) Each engine had three men assigned to it—one of whom was always on duty in this age before automatic monitoring systems—to keep an eye on engine revolutions, water and oil temperature, and oil pressure. Apart from the noise, the heat could also become intense, especially on the flights to South America, when temperatures in the car could reach 113 degrees Fahrenheit. Communications from the bridge appeared on the engine telegraph dial (lower left) and the mechanic adjusted engine speed or reversed engines accordingly. Between shifts the mechanics ate one of four hearty daily meals or snoozed in their bunks near the stern, where the noise of the engines remained their constant companion. In fact, the monotonous drone became so predictable that the men woke up whenever one of the Daimler-Benz diesels was temporarily shut down, for example, for midair repairs.

The *Hindenburg* arrives over New York during one of her ten flights to the United States during the 1936 season.

the third day, the city that never sleeps must have seemed a sorcerer's conjuring, its forest of impossibly tall spires looming magically in the predawn half-light. Despite the early hour, and the fact it was Saturday, the great ship was greeted by "a deafening roar of vessel and factory whistles," wrote Lochner. In a typically rakish gesture, Lehmann passed only a few hundred feet above the pinnacle of the Empire State Building, then headed south to his final destination. By this time, the ship's supply of gin having run out, Pauline Charteris came up with the brilliant idea of making dry martinis with Kirschwasser—cherry-flavored schnapps. The result met with general approval.

The *Hindenburg* touched the ground at Lakehurst at 6:10 A.M. local time, caught indelibly in the memories of every onlooker by the first rays of the rising sun. Her transatlantic passage had lasted 61 1/2 hours, far better than the *Graf* had ever managed. Not surprisingly it was the famous unperson on board whom the reporters most wanted to question. Eckener fended them off with smiles and platitudes until they came to the subject of his impending visit to President Roosevelt. He would be taking the president a specially stamped envelope commemorating this inaugural trip to North America. Eckener never seems to have missed a public-relations trick. It was, after all, FDR who had made possible the use of Lakehurst

at a nominal fee. Otherwise the series of "test" flights scheduled for 1936 would never have been feasible. If all went well, construction could soon begin on an American commercial airship port to match the new facility at Frankfurt where the *Hindenburg* would be based following her return flight from Lakehurst. And the men who now ran the Zeppelin Company were already talking about an ambitious ten-year plan that would see a fleet of thirty-six to forty giant airships operating a global passenger service by 1945. In America and around the world the *Hindenburg* and her builder, Hugo Eckener, seemed the unchallenged masters of the skies.

DURING THE 1936 SEASON THE *HINDENBURG* MADE ALL TEN OF HER scheduled round-trip flights between Germany and the United States, as well as seven nonstop flights to Rio de Janeiro. Meanwhile, the *Graf* still regularly plied the southern route, establishing a sturdy record for punctuality and reliability. In her first year of operation the *Hindenburg* carried more than 1,600 transatlantic passengers and, including test flights, traveled nearly 200,000 miles without serious incident before holing up for the winter in the new hangar at Frankfurt. More important, her passenger accommodations had been virtually sold out, and the ship had come remarkably close to breaking even, proving that the transatlantic operation could be commercially viable.

In the flight record for 1936 only two real brushes with danger are recorded. The first came during the second trip to Lakehurst, when watch officer Heinrich Bauer took the ship through an Atlantic storm front with an inexperienced man at the elevator. Mechanics in the after engine gondolas later estimated that at one point the lower fin skimmed barely fifty feet above the water.

Later, on the third flight to North America, the *Hindenburg* crossed the southwestern part of Newfoundland near Cape Race in a thick fog. On this occasion the ship's new sonic altimeter proved its worth. The time lapse between the altimeter's two beeps suddenly began to get shorter and shorter, indicating that the ground below was rising fast. The officers in the control car ordered the elevator man to bring the ship up as quickly as possible, but the beeps soon merged into one unbroken tone that meant the ground was too close for the instrument to measure. The ship kept climbing—and no crash came.

But the *Graf*, too, had had her near misses. As far as the general public was concerned, not a single blot marred the impressive performance of the two big passenger zeppelins.

Just to be sure, however, that none of his American friends had missed the point, Dr. Eckener devised one final public-relations coup to close out the 1936 season. The Millionaires' Flight took place on October 9 during the *Hindenburg*'s Lakehurst layover on her last round trip of the year. On board as Eckener's guests were seventy-two of the richest and most powerful men in the United States, brought to Lakehurst from Pennsylvania Station in specially chartered Pullman cars, then chauffeured by limousine to the airship itself. The prominent names included Nelson Rockefeller, powerful public utility executive Thomas McCarter and

(Above) Zeppelin Company posters promised a speedy and comfortable voyage to America. (Overleaf) In April 1936 the *Hindenburg* joined the regular passenger service between Germany and Brazil, where a new airship hangar had recently been completed just south of Rio.

Winthrop Aldrich, chairman of the board of the Chase Manhattan Bank. According to John Toland, in his book *The Great Dirigibles*, "more than a billion dollars were riding in the *Hindenburg*" that day. NBC radio announcer John B. Kennedy, broadcasting from the airship as it headed north for New England and the splendid fall colors, told his listeners, "We've got enough notables on board to make the *Who's Who* say what's what."

The *Hindenburg* was already renowned for the quality of her cuisine. The highlight of the maiden flight to America had been the final supper of fresh Black Forest brook trout washed down with a selection of excellent wines from the ship's "cellar." But the luncheon served on the Millionaires' Flight put all previous airborne repasts to shame. It began with Indian swallow nest soup, then a cold course of Rhine salmon with spice sauce and potato salad, accompanied by a lovely 1934 Piesporter Goldtröpfchen. This was followed by the hot course: tenderloin steak with goose liver sauce, chateau potatoes and green beans à la princesse served with a lovely sparkling 1928 Feist Brut. Next came a Carmen salad, iced California melon and Turkish coffee, cakes and liqueurs.

The food, the gorgeous scenery, the stately progress of the massive airship and its aura of invincibility duly impressed the wealthy guests. When they disembarked at Lakehurst after ten hours in the air, one can imagine Hugo Eckener and Paul Litchfield, Goodyear's president, exchanging smiles of great satisfaction. Prospects looked ever more promising for the rapid expansion of the North American service to include four passenger zeppelins.

IN OCTOBER 1936 TWENTY-NINE-YEAR-OLD Harold Dick arrived in Frankfurt on the *Hindenburg*'s last flight of the season, then traveled down to Friedrichshafen. He found a marked change in the atmosphere at Zeppelin headquarters in the several months he had been away. As Goodyear-Zeppelin's liaison to the Zeppelin Company since 1934, Dick had spent most of the

(Above) A brochure promoting the North American service and (below) a 1936 passenger ticket from Lakehurst to Frankfurt.

previous two years haunting the company works in Friedrichshafen or flying on the *Graf* and the *Hindenburg*. In all he had made twenty-two transatlantic crossings. He spent much of his free time mountain-climbing with Dr. Eckener's son, Knut, who had become a close friend. Although an American, Dick had by now been accepted as a member of the Friedrichshafen family and so was uniquely placed to observe what was happening there.

"One obvious and understandable alteration," he later wrote, "was the confident, even arrogant, attitude of everyone connected with both the Reederei and the Luftschiffbau Zeppelin following the dazzling success of the *Hindenburg*'s first season." And Dick particularly noted this arrogance in the prevailing attitude toward Goodyear-Zeppelin, which was slated to build the two American-owned ships for the transatlantic service. This had more to do, in Dick's opinion, with the rising tide of Nazi chauvinism than with justifiable professional pride. It was certainly completely alien to Eckener's longtime attitude toward his American friends. As far back as 1924 and the delivery of the *Los Angeles*, he'd been criticized in some nationalistic circles for sharing Zeppelin Company "secrets" with foreigners, but he had gone ahead and done so. Now, however, Dick found that information he might previously have had simply by asking was no longer available to him.

But he was privy to the accelerated airship building schedule now underway. The new *LZ 130*, sister ship to the *Hindenburg*, was already under construction at Friedrichshafen and looked to be complete by September 1937. Immediately thereafter, construction would begin on the *LZ 131*, lengthened to accommodate nearly a million more cubic feet of lifting capacity, enabling her to comfortably carry eighty passengers. At 863 feet, the *LZ 131* would be too long for the Friedrichshafen shed, which would be extended at one end while construction on the airship began at the other. And with the opening of a second shed at the Frankfurt airship base, which was eventually to include three huge hangars linked by a revolving docking shed that could deliver a ship into any one, the Löwenthal hangar near Friedrichshafen would become a construction site for the *LZ 132*, sister to the *LZ 131*.

As for the *Hindenburg*, she gained ten passenger cabins over the winter of 1936–37. Since the ship had originally been designed for helium and so had lift to spare, the added weight posed no problem. Located in space previously occupied by crew quarters just aft of the existing B deck, and all with windows, these would add twenty-two berths, including one four-berth cabin designed for a family with children. The Zeppelin Company works had not been this busy since the glory days of World War I.

By May 3, 1937, the *Hindenburg* was ready to begin an ambitious new season of North American passenger service—eighteen flights to Lakehurst were scheduled. Earlier that spring she had already made a successful round trip to Rio under her new captain, Max Pruss. Lehmann had withdrawn from hands-on airship command to become the full-time director of the Reederei, responsible for overseeing all passenger operations and the recruiting and training of airship crews. The age of safe, efficient and comfortable airship travel had arrived. And there seemed no reason not to think that it would be years before heavier-than-air craft could truly compete with these giant rulers of the skies. No airplane would carry paying passengers across the Atlantic until 1939, and then in nothing like zeppelin luxury. Soon distant corners of the globe would be linked by regular, reliable airship service. It was obvious, inevitable. And long overdue.

On May 14, 1936, upon the *Hindenburg*'s return from her first flight to North America, she landed at the new airship station at Frankfurt, where the first of several planned sheds had been completed. As the main German passenger terminal for the growing zeppelin airline, Frankfurt had the advantage of its more central location, with excellent road and rail connections and an altitude about a thousand feet lower than Friedrichshafen. The greater air density at this lower altitude meant the *Hindenburg*'s hydrogen could lift nearly seven additional tons of payload.

"OH, THE HUMANITY..."

"Please inform the Zeppelin company in Frankfurt-am-Main that they should open and search all mail before it is put on board prior to every flight of the Zeppelin Hindenburg. The Zeppelin is going to be destroyed by a time bomb during its flight to another country."
    —Letter from Kathie Rauch of
    Milwaukee to the German embassy in
    Washington, D.C., April 8, 1937

"Tomorrow's arrival will be the first of eighteen this summer. Slight interest in the Hindenburg is being shown by persons other than naval officers. Arrival and departure of the world's largest lighter-than-air craft on schedule is now taken here as a matter of course."
    —Newspaper report
    of May 5, 1937

HUGO ECKENER WAS NOT ON BOARD THE *Hindenburg* on the evening of May 3 when she left Frankfurt to begin her first 1937 voyage to the United States. At the end of April he had begun a motor trip in Austria that would include delivering a couple of lectures, one in Vienna, the other in Graz, the country's second-largest city—harmless enough activity that kept him out of the limelight and where he couldn't cause trouble. Eckener still retained his job as head of the Zeppelin Company, and would do so as long as the Nazis allowed him. He had briefly flirted with the notion of emigrating to the United States

rather than living in a Germany run by Hitler, but had ultimately decided to stay in his homeland and do what he could to save Count Zeppelin's company and his cause. To this end he had nearly completed a biography of the rigid airship's inventor, which would be published the following year, the centenary of the count's birth.

The lecture in Vienna had been well received, but Eckener had been perturbed by increasing signs that the Austrians favored military occupation by Germany. The next morning, May 6, he was unpleasantly surprised to discover that someone had attached a swastika flag to the car that waited in front of his hotel. As soon as the car was safely out of town, he removed it. When would people learn that politics and zeppelins were not to be mixed?

After lunch in Graz, Eckener paid a call on a well-known sculptor whom he greatly admired, Gyslings Ambrosi. Not ordinarily a superstitious man, Eckener was deeply affected by the visit. First the sculptor himself, who turned out to be deaf, had a remarkably expressive face from which "there shone a pair of overpoweringly illuminated eyes in which there burned an almost mystical fire," like some Old Testament prophet's, Eckener later wrote. But even more compelling was the sculpture the old artist was so anxious to show him.

It was an image of a prostrate young man reaching desperately skyward with arms that wore disintegrating wings. The young man was Icarus, the mythological Greek figure who flew too close to the sun and plunged to his death in the Aegean Sea. "Was this intended as a warning, a premonition?" Eckener wondered. He attempted to shrug off the incident.

ON THE NORTH AMERICAN SIDE OF THE ATLANTIC THE MORNING of May 6, 1936, broke as gloomily as had the two previous dawns. "Our trip on the *Hindenburg* in May was the most uneventful journey I ever undertook in an airship," wrote fifty-six-year-old Leonhard Adelt. Adelt, a German journalist traveling as a guest of the Deutsche Zeppelin-Reederei, had just collaborated with Ernst Lehmann on his memoir, *Zeppelin*, already published in Germany and soon to be available in the United States. As he stared out the promenade windows before breakfast, he could see nothing. The great airship floated as if suspended in time, "a gray object in a gray mist, over the invisible sea."

Leonhard Adelt and his wife, Gertrud, also a journalist, were not the only nonpaying guests on board. Unlike the 1936 flights, which had turned away passengers on both sides of the Atlantic, there were quite a few empty berths on this first crossing of 1937—only thirty-six passengers out of a possible seventy-two. Presumably this was at least partly the fault of an increasingly unsettled political situation at home. The return flight, however, was fully booked, largely by people planning to attend the May 12 coronation of King George VI.

The fact that the ship wasn't full and the passenger list less than glittering undoubtedly contributed to the somewhat subdued atmosphere on board during the first two days of the trip. There was little of the elegant jollity that had characterized the maiden voyage of 1936. Ernst Lehmann, in particular, was not his usual self. The jaunty energy and self-confidence that sometimes bordered on arrogance had been replaced by a sad sobriety. Behind the habitual politeness, he seemed withdrawn. And for good reason. Only a few weeks earlier, his only son, Luv, had died of pneumonia.

Lehmann was on board only as an observer—Max Pruss was in command—but it was a relief to be flying on the *Hindenburg* and to have his mind occupied with professional matters. There had been another bomb threat before the flight, but he didn't take it seriously. Since the Nazis had come to power, the swastika-emblazoned zeppelins seemed to have attracted the notice of the lunatic fringe.

Lehmann spent many hours quietly observing in the control car as Pruss battled the persistent head winds that had pushed the *Hindenburg* almost half a day behind schedule. Instead of the advertised 6:00 A.M. arrival, Pruss had radioed Lakehurst to expect him around 6:00 P.M. Assisting Pruss were Captain Albert Sammt, the first officer, and Captain Heinrich Bauer, the second officer. Along with Lehmann and Anton Wittemann, another on-board observer, that made five captains in all. Between them they had accumulated many thousands of hours of experience flying airships in every kind of weather.

Like the Adelts, the passengers who gathered for their final breakfast—some casually dressed in pajamas and bathrobes—were disappointed to find that the weather still hadn't broken. But as the *Hindenburg* skated down the fog-enshrouded coast of Maine, the mood on board became more buoyant. The excitement that comes inevitably with the approaching end of a

A gallery of zeppelin officers from the final flight: Ernst Lehmann (opposite), Max Pruss (left), Anton Wittemann (right), Albert Sammt (middle right) and Heinrich Bauer (far right). (Above) The ship's navigator sits at his chart table, his logbook at his left elbow, various radio direction-finding instruments on the panel in front him. The control car's bridge area is visible through the open door and windows.

long voyage—even longer than expected—began to take hold.

Fifty-nine-year-old Margaret Mather had "slept like a child." She "awoke in the morning with a feeling of well being and happiness such as one rarely experiences after youth has passed." The feeling had been a long time coming. A great fan of air travel, Mather had experienced "a strange reluctance" to board the *Hindenburg*, although she had previously longed to make an airship crossing of the Atlantic because she suffered terribly from seasickness. Then the baggage search at the Frankfurt hangar had been unusually thorough, and she became quite irritated by the charge levied for fifteen kilos of overweight luggage even though, as she pointed out to the officials, at barely five feet tall and ninety-eight pounds, she weighed twenty kilos less than the average male passenger.

Miss Mather made a few acquaintances during the trip (she particularly enjoyed the company of some of the young single men on board) but had spent much of the time reading or writing letters and watching the Doehner boys—eight-year-old Walter and six-year-old Werner—playing with their toys on the floor of the lounge. The boys were so well behaved. They didn't even make much of a fuss when the steward confiscated their metal toy truck because its clockwork motor made sparks.

Mather, who lived in an apartment near the Spanish Steps in Rome, would have been quite at home inside a novel by Edith Wharton. She was a well-born, properly educated New Yorker who had spent her childhood summers at the family country house on Cape Cod. Now that her father was dead—she had cared for him during his retirement in Italy—she traveled widely and dabbled in poetry. She tried to get home at least once a year and was particularly looking forward to seeing her favorite brother, who taught art and architecture at Princeton University.

The first concrete visual evidence that the *Hindenburg* was indeed nearing its final destination came near noon, when the city of Boston emerged briefly out of the mist. By this time Margaret Mather had finished packing and sat writing a few last postcards. "A great

(Above) Provisioning the *Hindenburg* during a Lakehurst stopover in 1936. (Right) Each member of Lakehurst's civilian ground crew wore an identification button like this one.

U.S. NAVAL AIR STATION
LAKEHURST, N. J.
1937
GROUND CREW
PASS NO. 97
TRANSATLANTIC AIRSHIP SERVICE
C.R. Rosendahl
COMMANDER, U. S. N.
COMMANDING

elation seized me," she later wrote, "joy that I had flown—that I had crossed the sea with none of the usual weariness and distress. 'It is ridiculous to feel so happy,' I said to an American, who replied that her delight was as great as mine."

COMMANDER CHARLES ROSENDAHL, STILL THE COMMANDING officer of the Lakehurst Naval Air Station, had been popping in and out of the aerological building all morning. Since the building housed both the meteorological and communications centers, this was the quickest way to get updates on the *Hindenburg*'s position and keep on top of the changing weather. It was up to him to make sure conditions on the ground were right for a safe landing. The latest word from Captain Pruss was that he hoped to be over the field by 4:00 P.M. But Rosendahl could see from the weather map that this would almost certainly coincide with a spring storm front moving through from the west.

Age had only added distinction to the commander's patrician good looks, and it had not lessened his zeal for lighter-than-air flight. The *Shenandoah*, *Akron* and *Macon* had all met catastrophic ends. Although the *Los Angeles* still emerged periodically from her hangar to spend a few days floating at the mooring mast for tests, she would not fly again. Nonetheless, Rosendahl still believed that the navy brass would once again relent, that Congress would come up with more funds, that somehow another great rigid airship would fly under the navy ensign. In the meantime he was a man with too little to do.

At 2:57 P.M., Lieutenant George Watson, the base communications officer, walked out of the radio room and handed Rosendahl the *Hindenburg*'s latest missive: RETURN OF LAUNDRY NOT NECESSARY STOP WILL SAIL AS SOON AS POSSIBLE. Watson informed his commanding officer that the airship, which had been flying down Long Island Sound in good visibility and moderate winds, was about to reach Manhattan.

Rosendahl immediately understood the subtext of the *Hindenburg*'s mundane message: Captain Pruss intended to make the fastest possible turnaround. With luck he could begin the trip back to Europe only a few hours late. Rosendahl had enormous admiration for the German airshipman, but he doubted very much whether Pruss would manage to get away before midnight. That worrisome line of thunderstorms was rapidly moving in on Lakehurst.

"NEW YORK SWAM INTO VIEW. THE rain had stopped, but there were black clouds behind the tall buildings. We flew over the Bronx and Harlem, then along Fifth Avenue," recalled Margaret Mather. The sun briefly caught the *Hindenburg* as she sailed over the Empire State Building, low enough that the passengers could wave to the tourists on the observation deck and see photographers taking pictures. After such a long, dull crossing, Captain Pruss wanted his charges to get their money's worth. He took the ship right down to the foot of Manhattan, where they could glimpse the Statue of Liberty, looking as "small as a porcelain figure," according to Leonhard Adelt, then looped back up the East River. Half an hour later, just past 4:00 P.M., the ship was over Lakehurst.

Rising dramatically above the flat scrub oak and pine woods that grow in the sandy soil of south-central New Jersey, the vast, arched shape of Hangar No. 1 presented a startling silhouette against the dark overcast. It dwarfed the figures of the spectators, photographers and reporters. Some of them had been waiting all day for the arrival; now the ship had been delayed once again. Leaning out a promenade window, Margaret Mather noted that the ground crew had not yet assembled and that the weather seemed to be getting worse.

In the control gondola Pruss had just received the latest weather report from Lakehurst: GUSTS NOW 25 KNOTS. Like Mather, he could see for himself the glowering, wind-whipped sky. Clearly these were

(Top) The *Hindenburg* over Manhattan at about 3:00 P.M. on May 6, 1937. (Above) While waiting for the weather over Lakehurst to clear, Captain Pruss steered the ship along the beaches of the New Jersey shore.

not the conditions for a safe landing. He would ride out the storm and wait for calmer weather. He signaled his intentions to Rosendahl, and the *Hindenburg* continued southeastward, passing over Toms River to reach the coast at Seaside Heights. There Pruss turned northward, sailing along the almost-deserted New Jersey beaches as far as Asbury Park. At that point he turned inland, then south again, waiting for word from Lakehurst.

Most of the passengers seem to have been unperturbed by the further delay. Joseph Späh took advantage of the postponement to pay one last visit to his dog, Ulla, a prize Alsatian bitch he was bringing home as a surprise for his three children whom he hadn't seen for three months. Späh, who described himself as an "acrobatic vaudeville actor," performed under the stage name Ben Dova. His specialty was impersonating a rubber-kneed drunk, an act that culminated in a hilarious attempt to light a cigarette from a street lamp, from which he dangled at various impossible-seeming angles.

Ordinarily passengers weren't allowed unescorted into the body of the ship, but the stewards had given up worrying about Späh. He was a charming little man and he obviously cared about his dog very much. Ulla and the other dog on board lived in wicker cages in the rear of the ship, where the noise from the engines made sleep difficult for man or beast. But she had survived the trip fine, as had the many pets that had previously made a zeppelin crossing. Späh could hardly wait to see the expressions on his kids' faces. Undoubtedly they were waiting for him impatiently on the field at Lakehurst.

GIVEN THE UNSETTLED WEATHER, COMMANDER ROSENDAHL WAS anxious to see the big airship safely moored to the mast and her passengers disembarked. Restlessly he paced his spartan office, stopping frequently to peer out the window at the late afternoon sky. At 5:00 P.M. he'd given the order for Zero Hour to be sounded. A series of loud, deep blasts on the station siren, which could be heard in the nearby town of Lakehurst, summoned the 92 navy and 139 civilian personnel who comprised the landing crew. The civilians earned a dollar an hour for their services—not to be sneezed at during these late depression days. But if they sat around for a few hours, the cost to the Reederei could get quite steep. Rosendahl hoped he'd guessed correctly.

Just before 6:00 P.M. a heavy rain fell on the station, soaking the ground crew as they ran for cover. Then the skies began to clear. At 6:12 Rosendahl radioed Pruss: CONDITIONS NOW CONSIDERED SUITABLE FOR LANDING. With any luck the *Hindenburg* hadn't strayed too far. The barometer began to rise and the winds lulled. Clearly the main storm front had passed through. Two more messages went out to the airship. Finally the *Hindenburg* replied: POSITION FORKED RIVER, only fourteen miles to the south. At 7:10, a little like a school teacher urging on a tardy student, Rosendahl radioed: CONDITIONS DEFINITELY IMPROVED RECOMMEND EARLIEST POSSIBLE LANDING.

The Lakehurst commander ordered the ground crew back out onto the field and left his office to drive to the edge of the landing circle. As he reached the small crowd of officials already on the scene, he nodded a greeting to Willy von Meister as he came up to stand beside him. As always, the Zeppelin Company's American representative was on hand to meet the ship and see that the arriving and departing passengers were properly looked after. In a few minutes Rosendahl would be congratulating his old friend Lehmann on the successful start of another passenger season. Voices shouted, "There she is!" Almost dead ahead of him, coming in from the south, he saw the great gray shape of the *Hindenburg*.

THE CONTROL GONDOLA WAS CROWDED AS THE *HINDENBURG* made a preliminary pass over the field in a lightly falling rain. Besides the helmsman, the elevator man, the watch officer (monitoring gas pressure) and the man operating the engine telegraphs, all five captains were present in the cramped bridge area: Lehmann, Wittemann, Pruss, Sammt and Bauer. Since this was First Officer Sammt's watch, he was in nominal charge of the landing operation, but Pruss had final say. Second Officer Heinrich Bauer stood at his usual place to the rear of the elevator man, were he could keep an eye on both the elevators and the boards that monitored hydrogen and ballast. Ernst Lehmann and Anton Wittemann kept out of the way, sticking to their roles as observers. Everyone in the cramped bridge area had been through this operation hundreds of times before.

The same could not be said for twenty-four-year-old Richard Kollmer, who stood with three others in the bottom of the tail fin as part of the crew responsible for releasing the stern mooring lines and lowering the rear landing wheel. In command of the party was Chief Engineer Rudolf Sauter, who was on the telephone to the bridge and would relay orders as they came in. Kollmer, who had only joined the Zeppelin Company in 1935 to work on the *Hindenburg*'s construction, was extraordinarily proud to have been invited to join the crew—the airship elite.

While the men in the tail fin waited for their commands, the *Hindenburg* described a swift circle north and then west of the landing area, repeatedly valving gas to lower altitude and "weigh off" so the landing would be on a perfectly even keel. Captain Pruss, apparently in a hurry to take advantage of the temporarily favorable weather conditions, made a sharp left turn at full speed before slowing down as he came back in over the field. Reversed engines rapidly braked the ship's forward progress as she moved in from the west and dropped lower. Then she made a final sweeping right turn into the wind for the last approach to the mooring mast.

As she did so, instruments on the bridge indicated the ship was roughly one thousand kilograms stern heavy. For some reason the *Hindenburg* was slightly down by the tail. To correct this Albert Sammt immediately ordered ballast released from the stern. Heinrich Bauer pulled one toggle, waited a few moments, then pulled another: the water from two 300-kilogram ballast bags splashed groundward. But the ship

Navy and civilian ground crew take up their positions as the *Hindenburg* draws near.

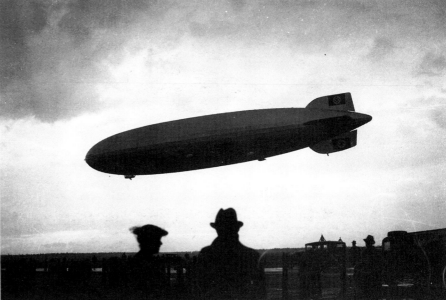

As the *Hindenburg* makes her final approach from the north she slows to a crawl and gradually loses altitude.

remained tail-heavy. Bauer released another 500 kilos, this time drenching some surprised spectators. When this action still failed to fully correct the trim, Sammt ordered six crewmen forward into the bow, hoping their weight would solve the problem.

Unheard and unseen by the spectators, a young announcer with radio station WLS in Chicago was describing the scene for a later broadcast to the folks back home. His sound engineer, Charlie Nehlson, recorded every word he spoke onto big metal disks. The two had set up shop in a small airplane hangar next to Hangar No. 1; its large windows gave Herbert Morrison a good view of the *Hindenburg*'s final approach.

"Here it comes, ladies and gentlemen," he had begun, "and what a sight it is, a thrilling one, just a marvelous sight. It is coming down out of the sky pointed toward us, and towards the mooring mast. The mighty diesel motors roar, the propellers biting into the air and

Herbert Morrison

throwing it back into gale-like whirlpools . . . No one wonders that this great floating palace can travel through the air at such a speed with these powerful motors behind it. The sun is striking the windows of the observation deck on the eastward side and sparkling like glittering jewels against a background of black velvet."

The *Hindenburg* was now less than a thousand feet from the mast, moving slowly forward about three hundred feet above the ground. At 7:21 P.M. the starboard handling line dropped from her bow hatch and hit the ground, sending wet sand flying. Then the port line splatted down. The second rope became temporarily tangled as the ground crew rushed to grab both lines. Finally the port line was hooked onto a larger ground line attached to a capstan. The Germans ordinarily preferred to bring their ships gently to earth and then walk them to the mooring mast. But this required even more men than the 231 ground crewmen assembled for this occasion. As a cost-saving measure, Pruss had agreed to try a "high landing" or "flying moor" during this first Lakehurst arrival of 1937.

From the windows of both promenade decks people leaned and waved happily, like passengers arriving on a luxury ocean liner. Joseph Späh trained his movie camera on the spectators, searching through the viewfinder for the faces of his wife and children. The young man standing beside Margaret Mather snapped away madly on his camera, confiding to her that he had taken an astonishing eighty photographs during the trip. Captains Pruss and Lehmann leaned out of the port windows of the control gondola and shouted a cheerful greeting to Rosendahl as the

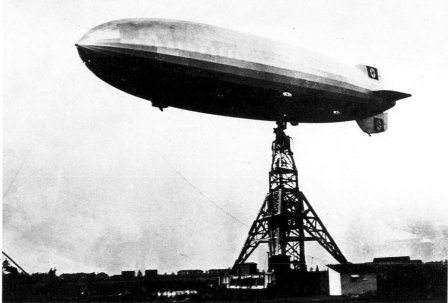

At the edge of the mooring circle, about 800 feet from the mast, the *Hindenburg* comes to a stop and the two heavy hemp handling lines drop from the bow to the ground.

ship came to a hovering halt above the waiting crowd. A light drizzle was still falling and a faint breeze pushed the *Hindenburg* gently to starboard. Off to the west, the sky was beginning clear.

Charles Rosendahl waved back to Pruss and Lehmann, marveling once again at the power of a great airship to impress and humble the onlooker. "There, in imposing, majestic silence, the vast silvery hulk of the *Hindenburg* hung motionless like a framed, populated cloud," he later wrote.

Leonhard Adelt, standing at a promenade window on the opposite side of the ship from Rosendahl, remembered this moment, too: "Suddenly there occurred a remarkable stillness. The motors were silent and it seemed as if the whole world was holding its breath. One heard no command, no call, no cry."

N THE BOTTOM OF THE *HINDENBURG*'S LOWER fin, Richard Kollmer had finished lowering the landing wheel. There was nothing left for him to do except wait for the ground crew to draw the ship gently to earth. About forty feet above him, Hans Freund stood over the open fin on the keel walkway, at a point just aft of Cell No. 4. He was paying out a steel mooring cable, which had become briefly tangled. Helmut Lau, who had been helping

One of the last photographs taken from the *Hindenburg* shows the ground crew just before the first mooring lines are dropped.

unsnag the line, was about thirty feet below Freund on a catwalk running along the lower port side of the fin. Near Lau, Rudolf Sauter watched this operation from his position at the auxiliary steering station. Both Sauter and Lau could see up beyond Freund to the aft panel of Cell No. 4. Four minutes had passed since the first bow rope had dropped to the field.

Lau was still keeping an eye on the mooring cable when he heard a muffled detonation—it reminded him of someone turning on the burner of a gas stove. Instantly, he turned and looked upward. Cell No. 4 was lit up from inside somewhere above and beyond his line of sight—he could only see a bright reflection against the lower starboard part of the cell's forward panel. Sauter, who looked up at almost the same moment, thought the combustion seemed to originate near the center of the cell, where the axial walkway tunneled through, but everything happened so fast there was no way he could be sure. Freund, who was closest to the faint explosion, had his back turned, so he had no clue where the fire actually started. The next thing he knew he was surrounded by flames.

In instants the hydrogen-fed fire grew from a flicker into a huge blaze that engulfed Cell No. 4, which simply disintegrated before their eyes as the fire spread to the adjacent gasbags. The ship shook.

181

Only a few seconds after the first flame appeared near the tail, almost half the ship is ablaze.

Freund scrambled down from his perilous perch and, with his comrades, dove for any available cover in the bottom of the fin. All four wanted to get as far away from the flames as they could. They shielded their heads with their hands as pieces of molten aluminum and burning fabric rained down on them and the tail of the ship began to fall rapidly toward the ground.

Nearly six hundred feet forward in the control car, Heinrich Bauer saw

that something was wrong just before he felt it. From his position on the port side, monitoring both water ballast and hydrogen, he noticed Hangar No. 1 suddenly light up brightly.

When Anton Wittemann felt the shock, his first thought was that one of the anchor lines had failed.

"Is a rope broken?" he asked the captain.

"No," replied Pruss. In this brief moment none of the officers yet understood what was happening. They looked at each other, these five zeppelin veterans, as if hoping that from somewhere in their collective experience they could summon forth a solution to this puzzle. Then Captain Sammt, who was leaning out the port window beside Bauer, cried out: "The ship's on fire!"

The *Hindenburg* began to tilt sharply toward the stern, then it began to fall. Next to Bauer, the man at the rudder wheel started to make a horrible moaning noise. It was a sound the second officer would never forget.

"Should I release water?" shouted Bauer. Without waiting for the answer he desperately tore away the ballast control toggles—anything to soften the crash landing they all now knew was only seconds away. Captain Lehmann called out, "Everyone look to a window." There was nothing else that any of them could do except wait for the right moment to jump. As Heinrich Bauer later recalled, "In the gondola there was an oppressive calm; some crewmen were groaning, others fell to the floor and everyone attempted to hold onto something as the pitch became steeper."

T O MOST OF THE ONLOOKERS, the first sign that there was anything amiss came when a burst of flame appeared just forward of the upper fin. To Rosendahl it looked like "a mushroom shaped flower bursting speedily into bloom." In seconds the flames engulfed the tail and began moving forward like a huge "fluorescent tube lighting up," in the words of Willy von Meister. The ground crew shrank back as the fire roared toward the bow and the tail began to fall. Through the flames figures could be seen dropping to the ground. The tail hit first, then the rest of the ship came crashing down. Men and women, some with their clothes on fire, emerged from the inferno. Some crawled. Some ran. Some stumbled and fell. Between the first flash of fire and the crash, only thirty-four seconds had elapsed.

In that unbelievable half minute, broadcaster Herb Morrison suddenly found himself reporting the biggest story of his life—and it was almost too much for him. His smooth delivery became a jumble of impressions as the emotion of the unfolding disaster took hold: "It's burst into flames . . . get this, Charlie, get this, Charlie. . . . Get out of the way, please, oh, my, this is terrible, oh, my, get out of the way, please! It is burning, bursting into flames and is falling on the mooring mast and all the folks we . . . this is one of the worst catastrophes in the world! . . . Oh, it's four or five hundred feet into the sky, it's a terrific crash, ladies and gentlemen. . . . Oh, the humanity and all the passengers!"

The moment Rosendahl saw the first mushroom-burst of flame, he

A group of spectators, who had come to witness a routine landing, watch in horror as the disaster unfolds.

knew the *Hindenburg* was doomed. Instinctively, he, Lieutenant Watson and Willy von Meister moved backward. The slight wind blowing at their backs kept the flames away, but they felt the intense heat as the great airship was consumed. Rosendahl's mesmerized gaze followed the front edge of the fire moving forward along the hull until the flames erased the name *Hindenburg*, letter by scarlet letter. As the ship fell, the forward section telescoped slightly toward the tail, then crashed to the field.

In barely half a minute it was all over. (Left) As the now-blazing stern falls groundward, a huge fountain of flame erupts from the doomed ship, silhouetting the mooring mast and the ground crew below it. (Right) With the stern half of the ship grounded and completely consumed by fire, the forward section still points skyward, with flames shooting out of the bow, which had become like the chimney outlet of a hydrogen furnace. Only three of the men clinging to girders in the bow section managed to keep their grip and survive.

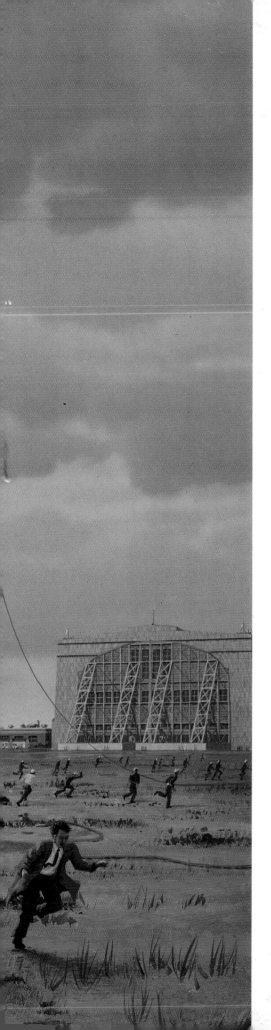

SOME OF THE PASSENGERS LINING THE windows noticed the ground crew below them stiffen, then begin to retreat. Others heard a distant, muffled explosion just before a violent lurch threw most of them off their feet. It sent Margaret Mather sliding down the length of the port-side promenade toward the wall, where she found herself pinned against a bench and suffocating beneath a pile of passengers. The jumble of bodies struggled to its feet and the individuals fought to climb away from the stern. But Mather was transfixed by the macabre poetry of the scene: "The flames blew in, long tongues of flame, bright red and very beautiful." As the fire licked in through the rear bulkheads and the ceiling, she watched the other passengers leaping against the bucking ship, blood streaming from cuts and burns, some jumping from the windows. One man let out a terrible cry in German: "It is the end!"

"But I sat just where I had fallen," she later wrote, "holding the lapels of my coat over my face, feeling the flames light on my back, my hat, my hair, trying to beat them out, watching the horrified faces of my companions as they leaped up and down." It seemed to her "like a scene from a medieval picture of hell."

Meanwhile Joseph Späh had used his movie camera to smash out a window. Now he dangled by one hand outside the promenade in a grisly parody of his vaudeville act. With the ship still a hundred feet up in the air, a man hanging on beside him lost his grip. He grabbed at Späh's jacket and tore off a lapel as he fell, but the acrobat held on. He waited until the ground was about forty feet away, then let go. Späh tried to roll like a gymnast to cushion his fall, but he landed hard on his left leg. Then he limped away as quickly as he could, feeling the heat of the flames on his back.

On the starboard side, Leonhard and Gertrud Adelt clung desperately to a promenade window as they waited for the airship to hit the ground. "Its impact threw us from the window to the stair corridor. The tables and chairs of the reading room crashed about and jammed us like a barricade," Leonhard later wrote.

(Left) The last passengers escape from the *Hindenburg*'s promenade as officers jump free of her control gondola and flames envelop the bow.
(Above) Spectators and ground crew turn to avoid the heat of the burning airship.

"Through the windows!" he shouted to the other passengers, then pulled his wife over to the nearest opening. Afterward neither of them remembered jumping, only the feeling of their feet touching "soft sand and grass. We collapsed to our knees, and the impenetrable darkness of black oil clouds shot through with flames enveloped us."

When the midsection of the flaming *Hindenburg* hit the ground, Margaret Mather was still sitting against the bulkhead shielding her eyes

from the flaming debris with her upturned coat collar. Then someone called, "Come out, lady!" and she looked up to see several men standing outside the promenade windows, beckoning her. As she stood up, she instinctively used her foot to search for her handbag. "Aren't you coming?" a man called. This snapped her back into focus and she ran out of the burning wreck to safety, leaving her bag behind.

RICHARD KOLLMER WAS THE FIRST TO ESCAPE FROM THE TAIL section, which had crashed violently to earth amid collapsing girders and tearing canvas. He tried the hatch door in the side of the lower fin, but it wouldn't open, so he simply ripped his way through a tear in the outer cover and ran. "I could have won an Olympic gold medal," he joked fifty-six years later. The other three men followed on his heels. Rudolf Sauter, who came last, had blood streaming down his face from a bad cut on his forehead; Freund was badly burned on one cheek and on the back of his head. But none of the four was seriously hurt. As Kollmer ran, he glanced back at the ship. The flames had almost reached the tip of the bow, which still pointed into the air. He thought of the crewmen trapped there. Surely none of them could survive.

In fact, nine of the twelve men caught in the bow met horrible deaths. Everyone held on desperately as the flames roared closer and the metal girders grew hotter. The heat was unbearable: the interior of the ship had become a vast chimney for a hydrogen-fed blast furnace. One by one the men fell into the well of fire until only electrician Josef Leibrecht, cook Alfred Grözinger and navigator Kurt Bauer (no relation to Heinrich) remained. But they did not give in to the blaze, even when they felt its tentacles reach out to grasp them. Then, as the bow hit the landing field, they finally let go and ran out through the sea of flames.

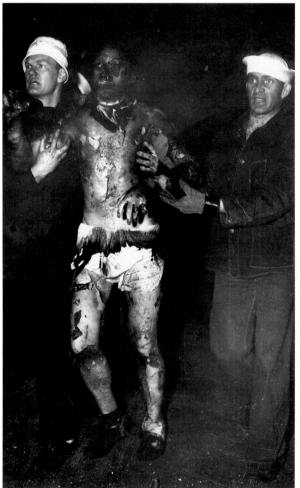

(Far left) Among the witnesses to the *Hindenburg*'s spectacular destruction was Commander Rosendahl's wife, Jean (with two unidentified onlookers). (Above) First Officer Albert Sammt (second from right) links arms with two rescuers, who help him and another survivor stagger toward safety. (Left) Two sailors help a desperately burned man.

(Above) A bloodied passenger, his face stiff with shock, is given first aid before being taken to a hospital. (Opposite) A photographer with a Lieca loaded with recently introduced Kodachrome slide film arrived in time to take this rare color shot of the burning wreck on the ground.

ANATOMY OF A CATASTROPHE

1) At 7:25 P.M., with the ship stationary approximately 260 feet above the ground, a tiny mushroom-burst of flame appears on the top of the outer cover, just forward of the vertical fin.

2) For the first few seconds, while the flames spread rapidly forward and the ship begins to fall, she remains almost level.

3) Then, as the stern accelerates downward, the bow shoots up and a huge flaming geyser erupts from amidships.

4) Thirty-four seconds after the first sign of fire, the entire ship lies on the ground, a blazing inferno from bow to stern.

ALL CATASTROPHES SEEM TO BE DEFINED BY MOMENTS OF SPECIAL courage or self-sacrifice, and the burning of the *Hindenburg* was no exception. One such moment belongs to Frederick J. Tobin, one of the petty officers in charge of the ground crew. Like Rosendahl, Tobin had survived the breakup of the *Shenandoah*. He was a classic navy chief whose foghorn voice and bearlike build had earned him the nickname Bull. Now, as he saw his crew retreat like a line of infantry breaking before an enemy attack, his voice roared out, "Navy men, stand fast!" The retreating ground handlers, both enlisted men and dollar-an-hour civilians, stopped dead. "We've got to get those people out of there," the human bullhorn bellowed. The men turned and followed Bull Tobin back to the burning ship.

The first figures George Watson observed emerging from the wall of flames were a woman and two children. At first Watson thought they were spectators who had somehow broken through to the ship. Then he saw that they

Ground crewmen stoop to lift a body recovered from the wreck.

were badly burned. The woman was Matilde Doehner, the children her two boys, Walter and Werner, whom she had thrown out the promenade windows into the arms of waiting ground crew before the ship hit. (Her husband, Hermann, died inside the ship. Her sixteen-year-old daughter, Irene, was rescued, but later died of her burns.) The three were quickly rushed to the base hospital, which would soon be overflowing with casualties.

Both Watson and Rosendahl moved toward the control car to lend what assistance they could to their fellow officers. The flames still burned fiercely and black billowing smoke filled the air. A man staggered forward, his clothes burned off, his skin burned black. Before they could reach him, he fell and died. Then Ernst Lehmann emerged from the wall of fire, his white captain's cap singed, but seeming otherwise not seriously harmed. Reflexively, Watson saluted, but Lehmann looked right through him. "I don't understand, I don't understand," he muttered as he walked by. Watson turned and saw Lehmann's naked back was a black

By the time fire trucks reached the scene (above) there was no one left to save, but the fire, mostly fueled by diesel oil, would continue to burn for several hours.

mass of horrible burns. Rosendahl rushed to his friend's side and led him away.

It seems a miracle, but all but one of those in the control car managed to escape the burning wreck. Heinrich Bauer pushed two crewmen out a window, then jumped after them. As he leapt away, the skeleton of the ship crashed behind him and the heat of the flames burned the hair off the nape of his neck. After pausing for a few moments to catch his breath, he turned back toward the passenger area to look for survivors. Anton Wittemann at first found himself blocked by the flames but eventually located an opening on the port side of the ship. He was not seriously hurt.

Pruss and Sammt jumped together from the navigation room window, but soon became separated. Sammt closed his eyes and ran the red-hot gauntlet of falling wires and crashing girders. By the time he was clear of the ship, his uniform was afire. Frantically he rolled in the damp grass and sand to douse the flames. Only when the fire was out and he stood up did he dare to open first one eye, then the other. He could see! Then he pulled on each ear. They were still there! And his cap still sat on his head, although the badge had been ripped off.

When Sammt looked back toward the wreck he saw a man wearing a long coat coming toward him. The man had lost his hat and his hair was completely burned away.

"Pruss, is that you?" Sammt called to him.

"Ja," he replied. "My God, what a sight you are!"

"But you do not look much better," Sammt shot back.

Of the two, Sammt had been the more fortunate. His burns were slight. The badly scorched commander of the *Hindenburg* was in serious danger, and he would linger near death for days.

The few minutes between the first spark and the last escape from the burning wreck would

A Lakehurst officer briefs reporters the night of the crash. The blackboard lists passengers and crew known to have been saved.

later seem like hours in the memories of survivors and witnesses, so much life and death were telescoped into such a short space of time. George Grant of London, England, a passenger agent for the Hamburg-America line traveling as a guest of the Zeppelin Company, leapt out of a window and landed unscathed. But as he was struggling to his feet, another passenger jumped on top of him, injuring Grant's back and sending him to the hospital for several months. Rosendahl observed one "elderly woman passenger" who "as though walking in her sleep" stepped down one of the gangway stairs, which had dropped on their own, and walked through the flames and falling metal virtually unharmed. Eighty-year-old Otto Ernst and his wife, Elsa, descended the same steps arm in arm. (Otto later died in a nearby hospital.) The ship's fourteen-year-old mess boy, Werner Franz, jumped to the ground through a hatch in the ship's bottom, but found himself trapped and choking in smoke and flame. Then a water tank broke open above him, doused the fire and

enabled him to escape, soaking wet but without a scratch.

None of the ground crew would ever forget the day their routine task turned into a dangerous and horrifying rescue mission. Terrible images, as searing as the heat from the blazing ship, burned permanently into their brain cells: a man walking away from the wreck, his flesh hanging in tatters, wearing nothing but his shoes; a severed hand, described by John Toland in *The Great Dirigibles*, "stuck to a white-hot girder like an empty glove." Herbert Rowe, a survivor of the *Macon* crash, bent down to pick up a badly burned body, then dragged it away from the wreck. After Rowe set the figure gently down in the sand, he noticed chunks of burned flesh clinging to the front of his rain slicker. Only then did he realize the person he'd just rescued was dead.

Alongside the scenes of horror were graphic scenes of comic relief: a seventy-year-old spectator not only outran everyone else in his zeal to aid those stumbling from the wreck, he managed to hold his umbrella firmly first female crew member to work on a zeppelin, perished on only her second flight.

As darkness fell, flames still flickered and smoke rose skyward from the blackened skeleton of the *Hindenburg*. Soon the last ambulances had departed and the landing field of Lakehurst Naval Air Station lay deserted, except for the cordon of guards who stood watch throughout the night.

The injured crowded every cranny of the small naval station infirmary. "Its rooms swarmed with excited people like a disturbed ant heap," observed Leonhard Adelt. "In the corridors on tables, stretchers and chairs lay the seriously wounded. An ambulance orderly with a morphine syringe the size of a bicycle pump ran about and wanted to give everyone an injection." Gertrud Adelt refused the morphine. Her burns didn't seem that bad and she didn't want to lose track of her husband.

In one room Margaret Mather found herself near a man with terrible burns who sat stoically swabbing himself with picric acid. If someone hadn't told her who it was, she would never have recognized Captain Lehmann. Occasionally, when the pain in her burned hands became more intense, she reached for the bottle and he handed it to her politely. When she returned it, he would murmur, "Danke schön." Otherwise no words passed between them. "It was a strange, quiet interlude," she remembered, "almost as if we were having tea together."

According to Heinrich Bauer, an "unnatural calm" pervaded the room where many of the least injured survivors were gathered. Despite the pains in his chest and the burn blisters on his hands, which grew more painful with each passing hour, he occupied himself compiling lists of the survivors and the missing. Then he sketched a plan of the final approach, noting from memory the radio signals received and sent. A doctor wrapped his chest to ease the pressure on his cracked breastbone, then dressed and wrapped his hands so he could keep on working. As he later wrote, "There would be no sleep for me in 'this night of misfortune.'"

The next morning Americans awoke to screaming newspaper headlines and riveting pictures of the *Hindenburg*'s fiery fall. Never before had photographers and newsreel cameramen been present to record every second of a disaster. Soon theaters around the world were showing the amazing thirty-four-second sequence as the famous airship burst into flames and plunged to earth. As much as the images, however, Herbert Morrison's emotion-choked reportage brought home the horror. Many thousands of people who heard its first broadcast the following afternoon on NBC would later swear they'd been listening in during the actual moments when Hugo Eckener's dream ship met her terrible, untimely end.

Commander Rosendahl answers questions from the press gathered outside Paul Kimball Hospital in nearby Lakewood, where many of the injured were treated.

over his head to keep off the light rain that continued to fall. And there were heart-rending twists of fate. Burtis Dolan, a perfume importer from Chicago, in Europe on a four-month buying trip, hadn't told his wife he would be returning on the *Hindenburg*—she'd made him promise that he would never fly. But the German airship seemed so safe, and the trip would allow him to be home in time for Mother's Day. Instead his wife spent the day in mourning.

Given the horrific speed with which the *Hindenburg* burned and the intensity of the hydrogen-fed conflagration, an amazing number of people lived to tell the story—sixty-two out of a total complement of ninety-seven. The thirty-six dead would include thirteen passengers, twenty-two crew members and one member of the ground crew who hadn't moved fast enough to escape the falling ship. Stewardess Emilie Imhof, the

CHAPTER NINE

AFTER THE FALL

"Though sabotage could have produced the phenomena observed in the fire that destroyed the Hindenburg, there is still in my opinion no convincing evidence of a plot, either Communist- or Nazi-inspired. The one indisputable fact in the disaster is that the Hindenburg burned because she was inflated with hydrogen."
—Douglas H. Robinson

"Thus of all the chemical or mechanical agents which conceivably might be employed to start hydrogen aflame, an ordinary photo flash bulb would be the most ideal. In addition to the great heat developed, it also carries its own oxygen supply, without which hydrogen simply cannot be kindled."
—A.A. Hoehling

THE SOUND CAME FROM SOMEWHERE VERY far away. Slowly it moved closer, a harsh ringing that was impossible to ignore. Finally the noise dragged Hugo Eckener out of his deep sleep. Where was he? Oh, yes, a hotel in Graz, Austria. He groped for the telephone.

The voice on the line belonged to the Berlin correspondent for the *New York Times*, a man Eckener knew.

"Herr Eckener," the voice began, "I felt it necessary to inform you at once that I have just received a message from my office in New York, according to which the airship *Hindenburg* exploded yesterday evening at 7:00 P.M. above the airfield at Lakehurst."

"That can't be!"

"I'm afraid it is, Doctor. We've got a confirmation on it."

Wide awake now, Hugo Eckener sat up in bed, turned on the light and looked at his watch. Two-thirty in the morning. How had that reporter been able to find him so fast? At Lakehurst it was now just past 8:30 P.M., an hour and a half after the alleged time of the accident. Maybe the phone call was a nasty joke. It wouldn't be the first time someone had made a false report about a zeppelin disaster. But he knew the man and he knew the *New York Times*—not an organization that spread spurious rumors.

How could this have happened? The *Graf Zeppelin* and the *Hindenburg* had made between them more than six hundred flights without serious mishap. They'd been struck by lightning, survived terrible squalls and landed safely after storms. Reluctant as Eckener was to consider the possibility, he wondered whether the cause could be sabotage. There were many, within Germany and without, who might take joy in the destruction of what had unfortunately come to be viewed as an emblem of Nazi power.

Reporters had already gathered outside the hotel when Eckener emerged for the drive back to Vienna. Perhaps, he told them, sabotage was to blame for the catastrophe, but he would need more information before passing any kind of judgment. In Vienna a special airplane provided by the air ministry took him directly to Berlin and a meeting with Hermann

Many of the first news reports of the disaster raised the specter of sabotage (above), but the ship's blackened skeleton (opposite) revealed no clues. Two diesel fuel tanks (right foreground) appear to have survived the fire intact.

Goering. Among the reporters who met him at Tempelhof Airport was Louis Lochner, who had been on board for the *Hindenburg*'s maiden flight to Lakehurst the year before. "I shall never forget the pathetic figure of Dr. Eckener," he wrote to his son and daughter. "A life's work ruined! And yet, do you know that my faith in the dirigible is such that I'd fly again if I had the chance?"

At the air ministry, Goering told Eckener there was to be no further talk of sabotage and ordered him to recant his ill-advised comment in a national radio broadcast. The Nazis had no interest in suggestions that their regime faced any internal opposition. An American commission of inquiry was in the process of being formed; the Germans would co-operate fully. Eckener would lead their delegation, which would include Ludwig Dürr, the *Hindenburg*'s chief designer, and professor Max Dieckmann, an expert on electrostatic electricity.

The next morning Eckener flew to Cherbourg, where he met the other members of his team and boarded the passenger liner *Europa*. He carried with him only the clothes he wore, not having found time to pack even a toothbrush. Before sailing he ordered the *Graf Zeppelin* grounded until further notice—over Captain Hans von Schiller's strenuous objections. The *Graf* had been returning from Rio when she received word of the *Hindenburg* accident; von Schiller had wisely withheld the information from both passengers and crew until just before landing in Germany. But Eckener would take no chances. Until the calamity at Lakehurst had been thoroughly investigated, no zeppelin would again climb the skies.

ON THE MORNING OF MAY 7, 1937, THE DAY FOLLOWING THE crash, Lakehurst Naval Air Station had a desolate air. The crowds were gone. The bodies of the dead were stored in the press room, now converted into a makeshift morgue. The towering facade of Hangar No. 1, its huge doors shut tight, looked broodingly down on the black and twisted framework of the *Hindenburg*. Heinrich Bauer, his bandaged hands still throbbing painfully, walked slowly across the flat sandy field to where the remains of his ship now lay. As the highest ranking officer without serious injuries, it fell to him to

So near and yet so far: the *Hindenburg* wreck lies roughly 700 feet from the Lakehurst mooring mast.

investigate the wreck site. He walked up and down the ship's length, staring in melancholy wonder at the utter destruction. The fire seemed to have consumed everything except the twisted maze of Duralumin rings and girders. Then something caught his eye. He stooped down, brushed the ashes aside and picked up a flat oval object. For a moment his mind could not relate the piece of warped and blackened metal in his hand to the luxurious ship on which he'd served so proudly. Then he realized he was looking at a silver-plated serving platter. On its underside he could make out the insignia of the Deutsche Zeppelin-Reederei. This would be his remembrance of the *Hindenburg*.

Many souvenirs had been plundered from the *Hindenburg* wreck by spectators before the guards cordoned it off the night before. Postal inspectors had worked late into the night salvaging mail, most of which had been destroyed. But some of it, badly charred though still readable, was posted to the addressees. Now customs inspectors picked through the wreckage for personal effects, and investigators searched for evidence of foul play.

Beyond a few scorched wallets, purses and briefcases, personal effects were few. Six-year-old Werner Doehner's toy truck, confiscated during the voyage, had lost its shape from the heat but was still recognizable. A Luger pistol, from which one shell had been fired, caused the more sensational newspapers to speculate that an officer or crewman had committed suicide. Joseph Späh's movie camera survived with the celluloid inside intact.

The day after the *Hindenburg* crash, Ernst Lehmann lay poised between life and death, his scorched body swaddled in bandages. His burns, though horrible, did not seem as severe as those suffered by Max Pruss, but he appeared to have lost the will to live.

That morning Charles Rosendahl sat by Lehmann's bedside. They talked for a while of their families and adventures they had shared. According to Rosendahl, Lehmann did not seem to be suffering much and his mind remained "crystal-clear." Inevitably, their conversation turned back to the devastating events of the previous day, and together they searched for an explanation. Finally, "as if to summarize his judgment of the case, not with rancor but as if sick at heart that humanity could be so cruel," Rosendahl wrote, "he said to me soberly, 'It must have been an infernal machine.'" In his final hours Lehmann had concluded that only an act of sabotage could have destroyed the *Hindenburg*.

"But of course, regardless of the cause, the next ship must use helium," Lehmann whispered. In his mind there was no doubt that there would be a next ship, that this setback, too, would be overcome.

Lehmann's death later that day affected Rosendahl deeply. Here was a man whose life, like Rosendahl's, had been dedicated to the advancement of airships. To Rosendahl fell the honor of writing a description of the

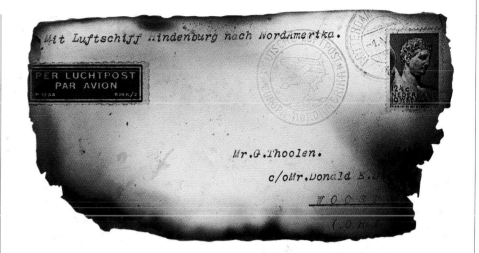

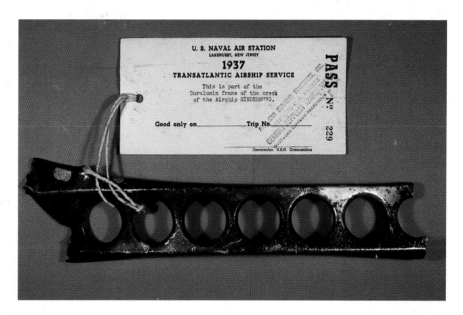

A few of the objects salvaged from the wreck. (Top) A letter postmarked in Holland and bearing a special zeppelin cachet. (Middle) A girder fragment attached to a visitor pass permitting entry to the Lakehurst base on May 6, 1937. (Above) A blackened fish knife. (Left) A teacup and saucer.

Hindenburg disaster for the final chapter of the English edition of Lehmann's book. In the book's foreword he penned a glowing tribute to his friend of fourteen years: "Dapper, polished, suave, conversant with world affairs, a talented linguist" and an authoritative captain who "never had to raise his voice above a conversational tone." But above all, a champion of lighter-than-air flight: "His whole existence was bound up in a great ideal—the perfection of the Zeppelin principle of airships for the commercial transportation of the peoples of the world."

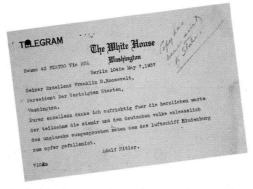

The day after the catastrophe, President Roosevelt received this telegram from Adolf Hitler, thanking him for his expression of sympathy to the German people.

Others who had survived the fire succumbed to their injuries in the days that followed but, astonishingly, Max Pruss was not among them. The *Hindenburg*'s captain pulled through, thanks in part to the services of a Jewish-German doctor who had fled Hitler's Germany and moved his practice to New York. When Willy von Meister asked the doctor for his bill, he replied, "In an emergency of the German people there is no charge for my services." Hermann Goering subsequently wrote the doctor a thank-you note.

Albert Sammt's burns did not prevent him from testifying at the inquiry, which opened on the Monday after the fire. Anton Wittemann, who escaped with minor injuries, was well enough to return home with the bulk of the crew on a passenger steamer ten days later. Richard Kollmer's first act on escaping the burning ship was to send a telegram to his parents. They received it even before they heard of the crash. Joseph Leibrecht, one of the three who survived from the burning bow, carried permanent scars, but lived out a long life in his home town of Lindau on Lake Constance.

Margaret Mather's coat was full of burn holes, but only her hands had suffered from the flames. Both Leonhard and Gertrud Adelt also recovered from their relatively minor injuries. And acrobatic actor Joseph Späh hobbled from the flaming airship straight into the arms of his waiting family. (His dog, Ulla, died in the fire.)

Four days after leaving Cherbourg, the liner *Europa* arrived in New York carrying Hugo Eckener, Ludwig Dürr, Max Dieckmann and the other members of the German investigating team. As Eckener once again entered the gates of Lakehurst Naval Air Station his mind reeled with the memories of past triumphs: the arrival of the *Los Angeles* in 1924, the *Graf*'s 1929 world flight, the first landing of the *Hindenburg* the year before.

"Now Lakehurst was dead. The ground crew had been transferred, the few remaining stood by the barracks, idle and dejected . . . ."

The investigators who sifted through the ship's remains found no evidence to suggest sabotage. The FBI was called in to follow up on any passenger who had exhibited suspicious behavior. An obvious target was Späh. His profession as a touring performer made him an ideal candidate for espionage; as well, he had made several unaccompanied trips to the stern of the ship to visit his dog. Although he now made his home on Long Island, Späh remained a German national. But after a preliminary investigation, which included interviewing his neighbors, the bureau was unable to turn up any evidence that he was involved in the ship's destruction.

Joseph Späh with his wife and children after his escape from the airship. The FBI found no evidence he had anything to do with the crash.

Crank theories, however, abounded. Someone had shot a ray gun or incendiary bullets from the pine woods as the ship made her final approach. A rare kind of bacteria had somehow both eaten away a gas cell and ignited the hydrogen. Best of all was the New England inventor who claimed he had shot off a rocket from his village in the Berkshires only twenty-five minutes before the *Hindenburg* burst into flames—just the

amount of time it would take his creation, which was traveling in "a southerly direction," to reach the scene.

But there were precious few clues to the real cause of the crash. One moment the *Hindenburg* had been coming in for a perfectly normal landing; the next there was a muffled explosion, the ship lurched, flames roared forward from the tail, and the ship fell to the ground. Apart from the four crewmen in the lower tail fin, no survivors had been close to the origin of the blaze. But some spectators had observed the first flash of flame on the top of the ship just forward of the tail. A few witnessed a fluttering in the outer cover near the same spot but before the fire appeared. Others, among them Willy von Meister, noted that the ship had dropped water ballast three times as it approached the mast and that she looked heavy at the tail. This fact was confirmed by survivors from the control car, including Heinrich Bauer.

In his testimony before the commission, Eckener concluded that the disaster was due to an unusual combination of accidental causes. He argued that the evidence suggested one of the rear gas cells had begun to

(Opposite left) Investigators pore over the wreck in search of clues to the cause of the fire. (Opposite right) Colonel South Trimble, Jr., chair of the American inquiry, makes a point to Hugo Eckener and Ludwig Dürr (at right).

(Right) On May 10, the U.S. Department of Commerce opened a public inquiry into the cause of the *Hindenburg* disaster with testimony from Charles Rosendahl (in center of picture). The hearing room was a section of the Lakehurst hangar that had been set aside as a waiting area for *Hindenburg* passengers but had most recently served as a temporary morgue.

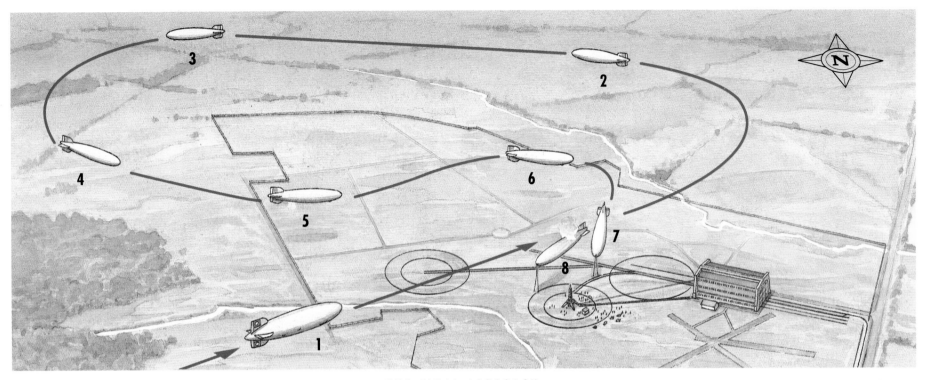

THE FINAL APPROACH

1) About 7:00 P.M., altitude 650 feet. The ship approaches from the southwest for an inspection pass over the landing area.

2) 7:08 P.M. The ship has just made a full-speed left turn to circle the landing field to the west.

3) 7:11 P.M., altitude 590 feet. Still moving at full speed, the ship turns back toward the landing area and valves gas for 15 seconds, the first of several releases of hydrogen to gradually reduce altitude.

4) 7:12 P.M. All engines idle ahead and the ship begins to slow.

5) 7:14 P.M., altitude 394 feet. Aft engines full astern, the first of several reverse engines to brake the ship as it approaches the mast.

6) 7:18 – 7:19 P.M. In quick succession, 300 kg, 300 kg and 500 kg of water ballast are released aft to correct a slight stern heaviness.

7) 7:21 P.M., altitude 295 feet. The first mooring line drops from the bow.

8) 7:25 P.M. The first flame appears.

leak just prior to the landing. This was indicated both by the flutter in the cover and the marked tail heaviness. He noted that Pruss had made a sharp left turn at full speed to begin his final approach. Perhaps the strain had caused a bracing wire to snap, slicing an opening in one of the rear cells. All that was then needed was a spark. Max Dieckmann, the scientific expert on the German team, argued convincingly that the conditions were right for a discharge of static electricity into the atmosphere.

Dieckmann pointed out that because of the recent thunderstorm, there would have been a significant difference in electrical charge between the clouds above the airship and the ground. As soon as the first mooring line hit the field it became an electrical conductor that began to ground the ship. As the hemp ropes grew wet

An American expert attempts to demonstrate how static electricity could have caused the *Hindenburg* fire.

with rain they became better electrical conductors, but it took several minutes before the ship acquired the same electrical charge as the ground. (In fact, four minutes elapsed between the first line being dropped and the first flash of flame.) There then existed a marked difference in electrical potential between the ship and the clouds above, exactly the conditions for a so-called brush discharge, also known as St. Elmo's fire. Then, as electricity discharged into the atmosphere, it ignited the leaking hydrogen. Disaster followed. According to this theory, had the ship come in for the traditional low landing the difference in electrical potential would not have been sufficient to generate such a spark.

In the end the American commission found no evidence of sabotage and agreed with Eckener and Dieckmann that a hydrogen leak ignited by a spark of static electricity was the "most probable" cause of the accident, even though no witness had seen any evidence of a brush discharge. Years later, however, Douglas Robinson met a Princeton professor who had been standing just outside the main gate when the *Hindenburg* approached the mast. The man told Robinson he distinctly remembered seeing the dim blue flame of St. Elmo's fire "flickering along the airship's back a full minute before the fire broke out." To this day, this remains the only eyewitness evidence for the brush discharge theory.

The ensuing German inquiry, even more eager to dismiss any hint of foul play, took essentially the same position, although by this time Dieckmann had changed his story slightly. The fatal spark had come, he now argued, when electricity leapt from the fabric cover, a poor electrical conductor, to a nearby piece of the metal framework. In his German laboratory Dieckmann had run some tests comparing the cover of the old *Graf Zeppelin* with that of the *Hindenburg*, which had been treated with a new doping solution. Each time he used a piece of the new cover, he was able to produce a hydrogen explosion. With the *Graf*-type cover, nothing happened. Key details of Dieckmann's findings were suppressed at the time, but the Zeppelin Company was paying attention. The lacings for the cover on the new *LZ 130*, the *Hindenburg's* sister, were treated with graphite to make them good electrical conductors that would quickly equalize the charge between the cover and the nearest girders, eliminating the chance of sparking. And when the *LZ 130* began flying, it became standard procedure to monitor the electrical gradient between the ship and the ground before landing. Whatever the men at Zeppelin headquarters ultimately believed had caused the fire, they were taking no chances.

But the debate over the true cause of the *Hindenburg* disaster continues to this day. Former officers and crew lined up on both sides of the argument. Max Pruss, who believed sabotage was the only answer, maintained that the stern heaviness was

GOING HOME

(Above) Fourteen-year-old mess boy Werner Franz (center front), the youngest member of the *Hindenburg*'s crew, poses with other surviving airshipmates prior to embarking on the *Europa* to sail back to Germany. (Below right) The flag-draped coffins of the German dead await departure from New York aboard the *Hamburg*. (Bottom right) The *Hamburg*'s captain salutes Ernst Lehmann's coffin. (Below left) A coffin being brought ashore at the German port of Cuxhaven.

nothing out of the ordinary and doubted that the bow lines had become wet enough to conduct electricity fast enough to ground the ship by the time the first flame appeared. As for the sharp left turn, the *Hindenburg* had stood up to far worse structural stress many times before. Eckener, on the other hand, who might have withheld his real opinion at the time to keep from angering the Nazis, kept to the accident story when he published his memoirs after the war.

Two books and the movie based on them have espoused the sabotage theory. After all, it makes for a more dramatic tale than an accidental spark of static electricity. A.A. Hoehling, in his 1962 book *Who Destroyed the Hindenburg?*, fingered a shy young crewman named Erich Spehl as the culprit. The basis of Hoehling's reasoning seems to be the innocent fact that very little was known about Spehl, one of the crewmen who died in the ship's bow. He was new to the *Hindenburg* and kept very much to himself. What's more, as one of the ship's three riggers, Spehl had regular access to the axial walkway and so could easily have planted a tiny time bomb, no more powerful than a flashbulb, on the side of a gasbag. His motive? Hoehling claims Spehl had anti-Nazi friends. He expected, of course, to be off the ship before the blast, but the delayed landing spoiled his plan. Ten years later

Michael Mooney repeated Hoehling's thesis in his book *The Hindenburg*, which formed the basis of the 1975 Robert Wise movie starring George C. Scott and Anne Bancroft.

Many of the men most closely involved with the ship that day remained convinced that sabotage was the only answer. Not only Pruss, but Ludwig Dürr, Charles Rosendahl and the majority of the surviving crew members held that this was the only plausible explanation, given the previous safety record of commercial zeppelins. The crew, however, firmly rejected any suggestion that the saboteur came from within their ranks. The sabotage adherents may be right, but their adamancy hints at an unwillingness to accept the possibility that their beloved airship contained a fatal flaw.

Still, one can't help but wonder. How could it be that for the first and only time in the history of rigid airships a spark of static electricity caused an explosion? How could this have happened to the best zeppelin ever built? There also remains the troubling testimony of the two men in the lower tail fin who saw the first sign of the fire. Both said the fire came from Cell No. 4, and one claimed its point of origin was the cell's center, where a ladder meets the axial gangway that runs through the center of the ship—a perfect spot for a tiny time bomb.

A poster promoting the 1975 movie, *The Hindenburg*.

"I WAS NEVER MUCH FOR AIRSHIPS," HERMANN Goering had remarked to Hugo Eckener during their meeting the day after the *Hindenburg* disaster, "but now we *have* to persist with them." The zeppelin story could not end with a German failure. And the Nazi air minister saw a propaganda opportunity in the bad news from Lakehurst. "Now with renewed vigor we will utilize all our experience to reestablish air service between Germany and the United States with complete safety and forever," he proclaimed to the German people. He would use the new *LZ 130* as a focal point for German patriotism, drawing on the seemingly inexhaustible reservoir of German affection for their zeppelins. In fact, Goering's ploy worked even better than he had anticipated. As they had after the crash of the *LZ 4* at Echterdingen, ordinary people sent in contributions. Some came from as far away as Brazil. But the interior ministry quickly quashed this spontaneous financial outpouring, apparently fearing it might enhance the prestige of the still hugely popular Dr. Eckener. The Nazis would pay for the new zeppelin themselves.

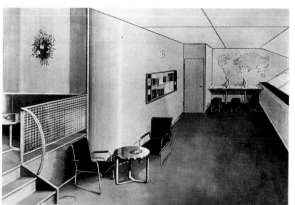

The most noticeable differences between the *LZ 130* and the *Hindenburg* were the larger engine cars (with tractor instead of pusher propellers) and the redesigned passenger spaces.

Eckener's main concern was that the Berlin government foot the bill for nonflammable helium, assuming he could persuade the Americans to release it to him. "No matter what the circumstances," he wrote to his wife, "we must get helium." Before he returned to Germany from the United States, Eckener traveled to Washington to present his case to Congress. In this he was aided by American public opinion which, riveted by the graphic newsreel images of the great zeppelin in flames, had now turned staunchly in favor of exporting helium to Germany. The legislators accepted Eckener's arguments and the Helium Control Act was amended to permit helium export for nonmilitary uses. Eckener returned to Germany believing he had won.

By June 1937 construction on the *LZ 130* was well advanced, but much of what had already been done needed to be undone as part of the helium conversion. Two goals became paramount: weight-saving and water recovery. The new ship needed to be lighter because helium has less lifting capacity than hydrogen. An efficient water-recovery system was required to conserve helium, still extremely costly. The engine gondolas had to be totally rebuilt to accommodate the six tons of water-recovery

equipment which, in a signal advance over the American rigids, recaptured one hundred percent of the weight of the fuel burned. The basic structure of the ship remained virtually identical to that of the *Hindenburg*, but the partly finished passenger accommodations had to be ripped out and rebuilt for only forty passengers instead of the *Hindenburg*'s seventy-two. The result was, in the opinion of the builders, an aesthetic improvement—and thirteen of the twenty double cabins had outside windows—but some luxurious touches were eliminated. Wine would still be carried, but heavy beer bottles were out.

By March 12, 1938, when German troops marched into Austria and annexed it to the Third Reich, the revamped *LZ 130* was virtually complete. But the Austrian Anschluss made the idea of helping the Nazis in any way extremely unpopular in the United States. Secretary of the Interior Harold L. Ickes, who had to sign the contract before the sale of helium could go through, refused to do so. Publicly he worried that the Germans would use helium for military purposes. While a German freighter waited impatiently at the port of Galveston, Texas, to receive its first load of the lifting gas, Eckener traveled once more to Washington. He met first

with Secretary Ickes and then with President Roosevelt, pleading with them to release the helium into German hands, but to no avail. He returned to Friedrichshafen bitterly disappointed. Eckener felt betrayed by FDR, whom he had long admired. "Not once during the meeting did he look me in the eye," he told Harold Dick, "you cannot trust him."

Now the Zeppelin Company faced a difficult decision. Eckener had sworn never to fly passengers again without helium. The *Graf Zeppelin* had already been permanently retired to a Frankfurt shed where she had become a popular local tourist attraction. Once again the Nazis came to the rescue. On the surface it seemed innocent enough. The air ministry agreed that the *LZ 130* could be inflated with hydrogen and used for training and propaganda flights. In time, perhaps the Americans would change their minds. But the Luftwaffe actually had a very different use in mind for the newest rigid airship.

On September 14, 1938, Hugo Eckener christened the *LZ 130* the *Graf Zeppelin*. Although often referred to as the *Graf Zeppelin II*, no numeral appeared after the name that appeared on the ship herself.

Instead of the traditional champagne, he used a bottle of liquid air. The doctor had not lost his public-relations flair. Later the same day the new *Graf* was walked out of the Friedrichshafen shed and, with Eckener in command, took off for her first flight. Captain Heinrich Bauer served as his first officer. On most of her remaining flights, Albert Sammt assumed command, having recovered from the injuries he'd suffered at Lakehurst.

For almost a year, the *LZ 130* flew over Germany and occasionally over the North Sea. Much was made of her local appearances, where she was greeted by brass bands and received the salutes of paramilitary units. Once again Germans flocked to see their zeppelin. Goering's belief in the ship's political value seemed fully vindicated. But frequently, particularly when flying near the German frontier or off the coast of England, the new ship suffered from unexplained engine failures or met contrary winds that pushed her out of German airspace.

During what was officially a demonstration flight to Vienna, on September 22, 1938, the *LZ 130* flew along the Czech frontier, escorted by four Messerschmidt fighters camouflaged as civilian police planes.

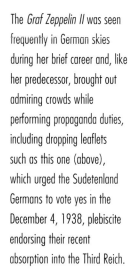

The *Graf Zeppelin II* was seen frequently in German skies during her brief career and, like her predecessor, brought out admiring crowds while performing propaganda duties, including dropping leaflets such as this one (above), which urged the Sudetenland Germans to vote yes in the December 4, 1938, plebiscite endorsing their recent absorption into the Third Reich.

Although this was the last time Hugo Eckener commanded an airship, he does not mention the occasion in his memoirs. Perhaps he was embarrassed to recall it, for the flight represented the final betrayal of his oft stated belief that the zeppelin was a vehicle of peace. Like many of the flights of the second *Graf Zeppelin*, its purpose was electronic espionage.

With war approaching, the German Luftwaffe wanted to know everything it could about the air defenses of its potential antagonists, above all Britain's. What better secret agent than the innocent-seeming zeppelin, whose failures in World War I had disqualified it in most European minds from having any military application? Under the direction of Ernst Breuning, a hotshot young engineer who now ran electronic surveillance for the German air force, a section of the passenger quarters was secretly converted into a radar detection unit. Radar was then in its infancy, and neither side knew the other's detection capabilities, but the Germans did know the British were up to something. Commercial airline pilots had spotted suspicious-looking radio towers along Britain's east coast.

However, the airship-borne spies immediately discovered that the metal framework of the *Graf II* dispersed the incoming signals, making it impossible to pinpoint their source. Someone had the brilliant idea of bringing Ernst Lehmann's World War I invention, the sub-cloud car, now nicknamed the swallow's nest or spy basket, out of retirement. A surviving example was borrowed from a museum and furnished with the necessary direction-finding equipment.

Not until early August 1939 did the British finally catch on. In this instance the *LZ 130* brashly drifted over the coast near Aberdeen, Scotland. Immediately a squadron of Spitfires took off to meet her, catching the *Graf* with her spy basket down. There was brief pandemonium on board as some crewmen frantically reeled in the several hundred yards of cable while others madly snapped pictures of the new British airplanes. The airship rapidly retreated from British airspace.

When the *LZ 130* approached her Frankfurt base the next afternoon, she received a puzzling message from the ground: "Landing before nightfall is not possible." Captain Sammt flew over the airfield; the weather was fine and no trouble was evident. In fact, the British had lodged a diplomatic protest and the Germans had agreed that the ship could be inspected after landing. Under cover of darkness, Sammt brought the *LZ 130* down on an unlighted area of the Frankfurt field. The waiting ground crew quickly spirited away the sub-cloud car and every piece of radio-detection equipment. By the time the British inspectors arrived, they found a local Storm Troop unit on board, talking avidly of the wonderful sightseeing trip they had just been on.

Ironically, all this trouble came to naught. The aerial spies had been listening on the wrong frequencies. Despite repeated entreaties from Breuning, the Luftwaffe had refused to cease experiments that unwittingly jammed the frequency range of the British radar signals. The jamming prevented the zeppelin from listening in.

The outbreak of World War II on September 1, 1939, brought to an end both the spy flights and the brief operational life of the second *Graf Zeppelin*, which would have been easily shot down by the military aircraft of the day. Like her smaller namesake, she was deflated and hung up in the second shed at Frankfurt. Construction of the *LZ 131* got no further than the building of the first rings. Still many airshipmen held out hope that after the war the *Graf II* would fly again and that the other great airships on the drawing boards would join her.

Hermann Goering had other plans. As long as the "gasbags" served his purposes, he had tolerated them. Now his underlying contempt surfaced. In March 1940 he ordered that both the *Graf Zeppelin II* and her namesake be demolished. The pretext? Their metal frames could be melted down and used in airplanes. The loyal zeppelin crews refused to perform this task, so a Luftwaffe construction battalion did the deed. Then, on May 6, three years to the day after the *Hindenburg* burned at Lakehurst, both new airship hangars at Frankfurt were dynamited, supposedly because they interfered with bomber takeoffs. The highly trained zeppelin crews dispersed, and the Zeppelin Company turned its expertise to building aircraft components. It later produced

In the spring of 1940, the demolition of the *Graf Zeppelin II* (above) was soon followed by the destruction of the two new Frankfurt airship sheds (right).

part of the assemblies for the V-2 rocket. Allied bombing in the spring and summer of 1944 destroyed the Friedrichshafen sheds.

DIRIGIBLES DID, HOWEVER, PLAY A SMALL BUT IMPORTANT ROLE IN World War II—on the Allied side. Although the American navy had given up on rigid airships—the *Los Angeles* was finally scrapped in late 1939—it had not completely abandoned nonrigid pressure ships, which it had been flying since World War I. These smaller airships had the advantages of being much cheaper to build and requiring smaller crews in the air and on the ground. With war looming, the blimp program was geared up again; a total of 168 were built during the war. The U.S. Navy blimps more than proved their worth as antisubmarine escorts for merchant ships. Over the course of World War II, no convoy they escorted lost a single ship to enemy torpedoes, and only one blimp was shot down.

The revival of the military airship gave Charles Rosendahl his last hurrah. He spent the months following the Japanese attack on Pearl Harbor helping to select airship bases and setting up a training program for the airship crews that would fly the new generation of blimps rapidly coming into service. He was then transferred to sea duty long enough to command the U.S.S. *Minneapolis* at the Battle of Tassafaronga off Guadalcanal in November 1942. (The ship's bow was blown off by a Japanese torpedo, but Rosendahl piloted her to safety, for which action he received the Navy Cross.) In the spring of 1943, when he returned to Lakehurst to take over naval airship training and experimentation, he'd earned his promotion to rear admiral. At war's end, with roughly a hundred blimps still in the air, he could with some justice believe that a new era had opened for airships, for which he would continue to lobby in civilian life. One of his last acts before retiring from the navy in 1946 was to send an envoy in search of Dr. Hugo Eckener.

"MAY I SUGGEST, LIEUTENANT, THAT WE TALK IN English. It will be easier for you. I am naturally out of practice but I can still get along." The speaker's voice was heavily accented, guttural, his figure stooped with age. But even at seventy-eight, Hugo Eckener made an indelible impression.

"We sat down, he near the window. His powerful dynamic profile, silhouetted against the pane, made me think at once of the strength of character and determination for which he was so well known and admired among American airship people. From where I was sitting, I could see a magnificent oil painting hanging on the wall. It showed him as captain of the *Graf Zeppelin*, binoculars and all. The artist had captured to an unbelievable extent the magnetism, confidence, and presence which made up the man."

The young lieutenant sitting in the living room of a house near the shore of Lake Constance that hot summer day in 1946 was Gordon Vaeth. He handed the old man a box of Havana cigars, a gift from his boss, Admiral Rosendahl. Eckener lit one with evident pleasure, his first cigar in a long time. Then Vaeth got down to business. What remained of the last zeppelins and their innovations? And who among the surviving airship personnel might be willing to come to America and work on new airships? Eckener answered freely. And he indicated that he still hoped to play a role. Like Rosendahl, he had not quite given up on the zeppelin.

Later that year, at the invitation of Goodyear, Hugo Eckener arrived in America for one last time. During his seven months in the country, he contributed his expertise to Karl Arnstein's ambitious plan for a huge new helium ship, 950 feet long, with 10 million cubic feet of gas capacity, that would become the prototype for a fleet of postwar zeppelins. Able to voyage 7,000 miles without refueling and achieve an unprecedented ninety miles per hour, it would have enough lift to carry 232 passengers in Pullman-type quarters (similar to the berths on the *Hindenburg)* or 112 passengers in the height of luxury.

The new airship plans never got beyond the drawing board. Neither government nor private buyers could be found. Eckener returned to Germany for good and finished his memoirs, which he had begun working on at Willy von Meister's urging. He watched the heavier-than-air craft catch up with and ultimately surpass the rigid airship as a vehicle for long-distance passenger transportation. Before his death at the age of eighty-six in 1954, even he had to admit, "The Zeppelin has given way to the airplane; a good thing has been replaced by a better."

The nonrigid airship played an important naval role in World War II. (Above) A K-type blimp flies along the Hudson River in October 1945 and (right) a formation of L-type blimps over Moffett Field in February 1944.

CHAPTER TEN

BUOYANT FUTURES

"If the airship is not revived in our lifetime, future generations will have to reinvent it." —J. Gordon Vaeth in 1963

"The large rigid is too fragile, too ponderous, too slow and too unproductive to exist in the competitive world of today alongside the modern aeroplane, the heavy-lift helicopter and the container ship."
—Sir Peter G. Masefield in 1982

THE NOISE OF IDLING ENGINES FILLS THE SMALL CONTROL CAR as the eight-man ground crew backs the blimp away from the mooring mast. At a hand motion from the crew chief, the three crewmen gripping the car rails lift the ship in the air, then let go—the traditional "weigh off" that precedes every airship flight. The double-tired landing wheel beneath the car immediately sinks back to the ground, indicating that the ship is already heavy enough to compensate for the lost weight of the fuel that will be burned during the flight. Satisfied, the pilot radios the airport control tower for permission to take off.

Another signal from the crew chief sends the three men at the control car scrambling clear. The pilot revs the engines, and the blimp begins to move slowly forward, helped by four crew members still handling the two nose lines. As the airship starts to gather speed, they, too, let go and run sideways. The blimp is on her own now, bouncing faster and faster along the grassy landing strip just like a small plane taxiing for take off. A few final jolts and the airship is airborne, swooping and swaying upward into the autumn sunshine. She easily clears a stand of trees at the end of the runway then rises exhilaratingly and turns northward. Destination: Berlin.

So begins a routine advertising flight of a Lightship A-60 Plus, built by the American Blimp Corporation but owned and operated by Virgin Lightships. It is Saturday, September 18, 1993. For the next several hours she will sail over the German capital displaying the name of a local newspaper, *Der Tagesspiegel*, to shoppers on the fashionable Kurfürstendamm, to the crowds gathered to watch a football match at the Olympic Stadium, to families strolling in the famous Tiergarten. The pilot, Alan Burrows, a former RAF navigator and a relatively recent convert to the pleasures—and pitfalls—of lighter-than-air travel, is fascinated to learn just how much airship history he will be flying over on today's trip. In homage to his little blimp's illustrious forebears he does a slow circle around the Brandenburg Gate, just as the *LZ 6* did on August 29, 1909. On that occasion two million people poured into the streets and onto the rooftops to cheer Count Zeppelin's amazing invention on its first visit to the capital. Now Berliners glance up curiously, but without awe or surprise, as the 132-foot-long blimp passes overhead.

One-half the volume of the smallest airship operated by the U.S. Navy in World War II, the Lightship can only hint at the sensation of flying in one of the giant zeppelins. In fact, the feeling is more like that of sailing a small boat in heavy swells, riding each gust of wind, each up or down draft, very much like a waterborne vessel rides the waves. (Airsickness, unheard of on a passenger zeppelin, is very much a possibility in a small blimp on a windy day.) The pilot rides these aerial swells by playing almost constantly with the rudder pedals (something like the pedals on a paddleboat) and the elevator wheels (mounted on both sides of his seat in roughly the position of the wheels on a wheelchair).

Only when the pilot eases back on the throttle in a patch of still air does the airship acquire something of the sense of majestic omnipotence that those standing in the control car of the *Hindenburg* must have felt. All at once the little blimp seems lordly, massive, inexorable as it slowly moves over the Berlin cityscape.

Later, when the clouds move in and the afternoon draws toward dusk, one gains an inkling of how it must have felt to sail high above the

A Lightship A-60 Plus, built by the American Blimp Corporation and operated by Virgin Lightships, rests at its mobile mooring mast prior to taking off from an airfield south of Berlin on September 18, 1993.

Channel in a World War I zeppelin bomber. The unheated cab of the Lightship grows uncomfortably cold. Unprepared, the passengers have worn only sweaters or light jackets. Even worse, there is no toilet on board, and the trip has lasted six hours. How did those men endure the awful conditions during bombing runs to London and back, sometimes airborne for twenty-four hours or more?

The sun is setting as the airship comes in for a landing, descending quickly but gently down to earth. The pilot expertly aims for the throat of the V formed by the waiting ground crew, which is oriented to tell him the precise direction of the wind at field level. He has judged the landing right and is almost able to taxi right up to the portable mooring mast. The crew, cooling its heels since the takeoff, spurts into action with military precision. In a minute or two the bow has been cranked into its socket at the mast, a routine ending to a routine flight in the life of one of the world's growing number of commercial nonrigid airships.

The number is not growing very fast, however. Discounting the tiny one- or two-person hot-air blimps used mostly for aerial photography, there are in 1993 fewer than twenty blimps regularly flying worldwide. They carry passengers only for sight-seeing, functioning mostly as TV camera platforms during news and sporting events or as flying billboards. But things have been far worse for the airship. As recently as the end of 1962 there were only two blimps flying anywhere in the world—one Goodyear blimp in the United States and one German-made WDL blimp in Europe.

(Opposite) The Fuji airship (a Skyship 600) sails over San Diego on an advertising mission.
(Above) The ZPG-3W, the biggest blimp ever built and flown, carried sophisticated radar that formed part of America's Cold War defense system.

I N THE FIVE YEARS FOLLOWING the end of World War II, virtually all of the U.S. Navy's blimps were scrapped or sold. But when the Korean War erupted in 1950 the navy scrambled to buy back a handful for war duty. During the ensuing Cold War, blimps enjoyed a brief military renaissance. In addition to their proven role in anti-submarine warfare, some became flying platforms for early warning radar designed to detect a Soviet nuclear bomber attack. The largest Cold War navy airship, the ZPG-3W, was also the biggest nonrigid airship ever flown. It stretched 403 feet from bow to tail and held 1.5 million cubic feet of helium.

Soon after purchasing four ZPG-3Ws, the last in 1960, the U.S.

Navy again changed its mind about airships. In 1961 it announced that the blimp fleet would be terminated. By that time intercontinental ballistic missiles had replaced over-the-pole Soviet bombers as the likely mode of nuclear attack. These missiles, smaller and more difficult to detect than bombers, required huge ground-based radar arrays.

Since 1962, when the last navy blimp was dismantled, the pressure airship has made a gradual comeback, but not as a military vehicle. The OPEC energy crisis of the 1970s gave rise to an upsurge of interest in lighter-than-air craft because of their obvious energy efficiency. Once again the airship's many virtues were widely touted: it could travel long distances without refueling; it could remain on station for long periods in almost any weather; it could lift heavy loads with minimum fuel expenditure. With the advent of strong but light space-age materials and new propulsion technologies, it seemed that airships once again had a bright future.

When it came to airship schemes, the sky was literally the limit. There were new designs for rigid airships, including one cargo-carrying monster of 40-million-cubic-foot capacity (almost six times as big as the *Hindenburg*). No hangar existed remotely big enough to construct it; one idea was to put a temporary roof over a canyon. NASA, the U.S. Navy and the U.S. Air Force considered developing unmanned remote-controlled solar-powered airships for high-altitude surveillance and communications that would be able to patrol at 70,000 feet for forty-five days. Forestry and oil interests floated various schemes for short-range heavy-lifters that could transport timber or help lay pipelines in remote areas. There were deltoid-shaped ships, disc-shaped ships and ships that were part airplane, part gasbag. Engineering students at Boston University even designed a

(Left) The Cyclo-Crane in the former navy blimp hangar at Tillamook, Oregon, where she was built, and (above) on a brief test flight after her tail was modified to incorporate an outer ring.
(Opposite) A rare photograph of Frank Piasecki's Heli-Stat just before it crashed at Lakehurst in July 1986. The envelope, which had once belonged to a navy ZPG-2 type blimp, bears the name of the U.S. Forest Service, which had agreed to purchase the Heli-Stat. After the crash, Piasecki was willing to try again but, not surprisingly, the Forest Service was no longer interested.

nuclear-powered zeppelin capable of carrying four hundred passengers in the lap of luxury. Some of the many visionary schemes reached the construction stage, then ran out of money. None ever flew—for long.

Two that did get off the ground, however briefly, belonged to a new school of airship design attempting to supplement the buoyancy of helium with heavier-than-air technology to produce a heavy-lifter with much more load capacity than a helicopter, but with all of a helicopter's controllability. The more bizarre-looking of the two, the Cyclo-Crane, gained aerodynamic lift from four airfoils projecting at right angles from the ship's axis. These four small wings, each powered with its own tiny propeller, could rotate as fast as thirteen times a minute, doubling the payload the helium-filled envelope could carry. This awkward contraption looked something like a giant eggbeater turned on its side. The first prototype crashed, was rebuilt, and survived some early tests before a second accident put it permanently into mothballs. It now forms one of the displays at the airship museum in Tillamook, Oregon, where it was built.

At first glance more promising was the Heli-Stat, designed by helicopter pioneer Frank Piasecki. To save money, Piasecki's prototype employed four surplus army helicopters attached by a metal framework to a twenty-five-year-old navy blimp bag. During a test at Lakehurst in July 1986, one of the helicopter pilots mistakenly increased power to full throttle. The change in rotor speed caused a sympathetic vibration in the Heli-Stat's frame, which began to shake apart, the errant helicopter broke free, the whole ship crashed, and the blimp collapsed. Four crewmen suffered injuries and one man died. So did interest in the Heli-Stat.

By the end of the 1980s, when the dust from these and other

In the public mind, airships are still inextricably linked to the Goodyear Tire and Rubber Company. But for how much longer? The *Spirit of Akron* (above), with its distinctive X-configuration tail fins, is one of only three Goodyear blimps still flying and was the last ship to be built by a company bearing the Goodyear name. Just over 60 feet long and with a gas capacity of almost 250,000 cubic feet, it can carry a pilot and as many as nine passengers at speeds up to 65 miles per hour. (Left) In the gondola the pilot checks his instruments before takeoff, and (right) ground crew walk the ship along the landing field.

experiments had settled, the only new airships flying were surprisingly conventional in basic design and familiar in their uses. They were nonrigid pressure ships that looked the way blimps have looked since well before World War II, and they mostly flew either simple surveillance missions or carried commercial advertising and pleasure-seeking passengers.

Perhaps the most surprising thing about the airship scene at this writing is the disappearance of Goodyear as an airship manufacturer. In 1987, as part of an effort to avert a hostile takeover, Goodyear Tire and Rubber Company sold off its airship-building subsidiary, Goodyear Aerospace, to Loral Defense Systems, a contractor interested in Goodyear's expertise in military electronics. Thus came to an end the longest continuous program of airship construction in the world, the enterprise that built the *Akron* and the *Macon* as well as almost every U.S. Navy blimp to have flown since World War I. The last blimp built by Goodyear Aerospace was bought by Goodyear Tire soon after, bringing to three the number of blimps that still ply the skies displaying the company name. This last airship, named *Spirit of Akron*, carried the design designation GZ-22 (Goodyear Zeppelin 22), the twenty-second design in a line that began with Karl Arnstein's plans for the GZ-1, which became the *Akron* and the *Macon*.

A few months after Goodyear Aerospace changed hands, it lost out on a contract to build a new battle-surveillance airship for the United States Navy, which had once again come to the conclusion that the airship had military usefulness. The winner of this competition was a new player on the airship scene, Westinghouse-Airship Industries, an American-British joint venture whose Sentinel 5000 design represented the last word in airship technology. At this point any residual interest that Goodyear Aerospace (now called Loral Defense Systems Inc.) held in blimps faded away.

The Sentinel 5000 was a direct descendant of the Skyship developed by British airship designer Roger Munk, the cofounder of Airship Industries. In the early 1980s Munk built a state-of-the art nonrigid pressure airship constructed with space-age materials and employing sophisticated "vectored-thrust propulsion"—propellers that swivel for greatly increased maneuverability. From the beginning Munk's goal was to sell his ships for military surveillance. Instead, the Skyship 500 (with a

helium volume of 181,000 cubic feet) and the Skyship 600 (with a 235,000-cubic-foot volume) were used mostly as flying billboards. Two now fly as police surveillance vehicles—one in Japan, the other in Korea. Airship Industries was never able to sell enough of them to turn a profit.

Unfortunately for Munk, Reagan-era budget cuts put the navy's airship plans on hold. Meanwhile his own company folded and Westinghouse Airships Inc. has since acquired its technological expertise and the rights to build any future Skyships. But its primary interest remains the Sentinel

This prototype of the 350,000-cubic-foot Sentinel 1000 is the only member of the Sentinel series that Westinghouse has actually built and flown.

series, whose technological innovations include a much more durable envelope impervious to ultraviolet light (long the bane of airship maintenance), which means the Sentinel can be stored outdoors indefinitely. Westinghouse designs now include the Sentinel 1000, a roughly 350,000-cubic-foot ship, and the twenty percent larger Sentinel 1240. Both are intended for military and civil surveillance tasks. As for the Sentinel 5000, it has grown into the 3-million-cubic-foot Sentinel 9000, which Westinghouse hopes the navy will use as a radar platform to warn surface ships of a cruise missile attack.

Despite all this development activity at Westinghouse, there is only one company in the world now actively making airships—American Blimp Corporation of Hillsboro, Oregon. If the Skyship and Sentinel are Cadillacs, then American Blimp's Lightship is a Honda Civic, simpler and

THE *MACON*'S LAST RESTING PLACE

In June 1990, deep-towed, remotely operated cameras photographed the remains of the U.S.S. *Macon* in 1,500 feet of water just south of Point Sur, California. Apart from the discovery in 1951 of a mangled ten-foot section of one of the ship's big wooden propellers (above) on a lonely beach on Santa Rosa Island (almost 200 miles south of the crash site), this was the first glimpse of the last American rigid airship since its loss on February 12, 1935. Fifty-five years after the crash little could be seen of the ship itself—the framework had collapsed—but in the flattened control car the cameras glimpsed chart tables, chairs and a lone lead pencil. The most vivid reminders of what the *Macon* was and might have been were the skeletons of three of her four Sparrowhawk fighters (right), whose heavily silted cockpits now sometimes serve as lairs for the Pacific thorny-head (below).

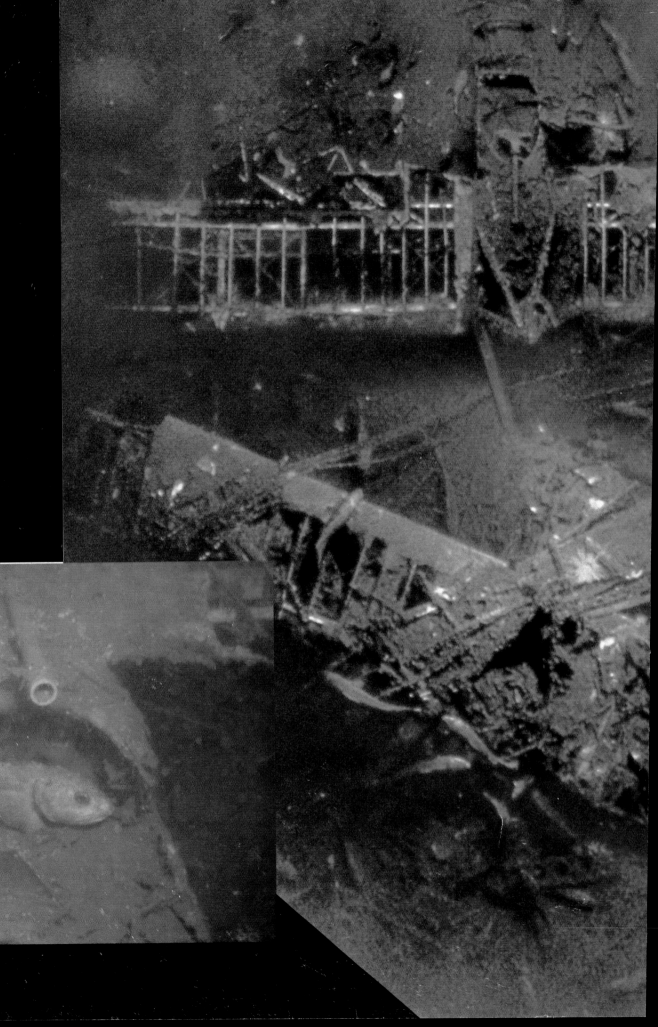

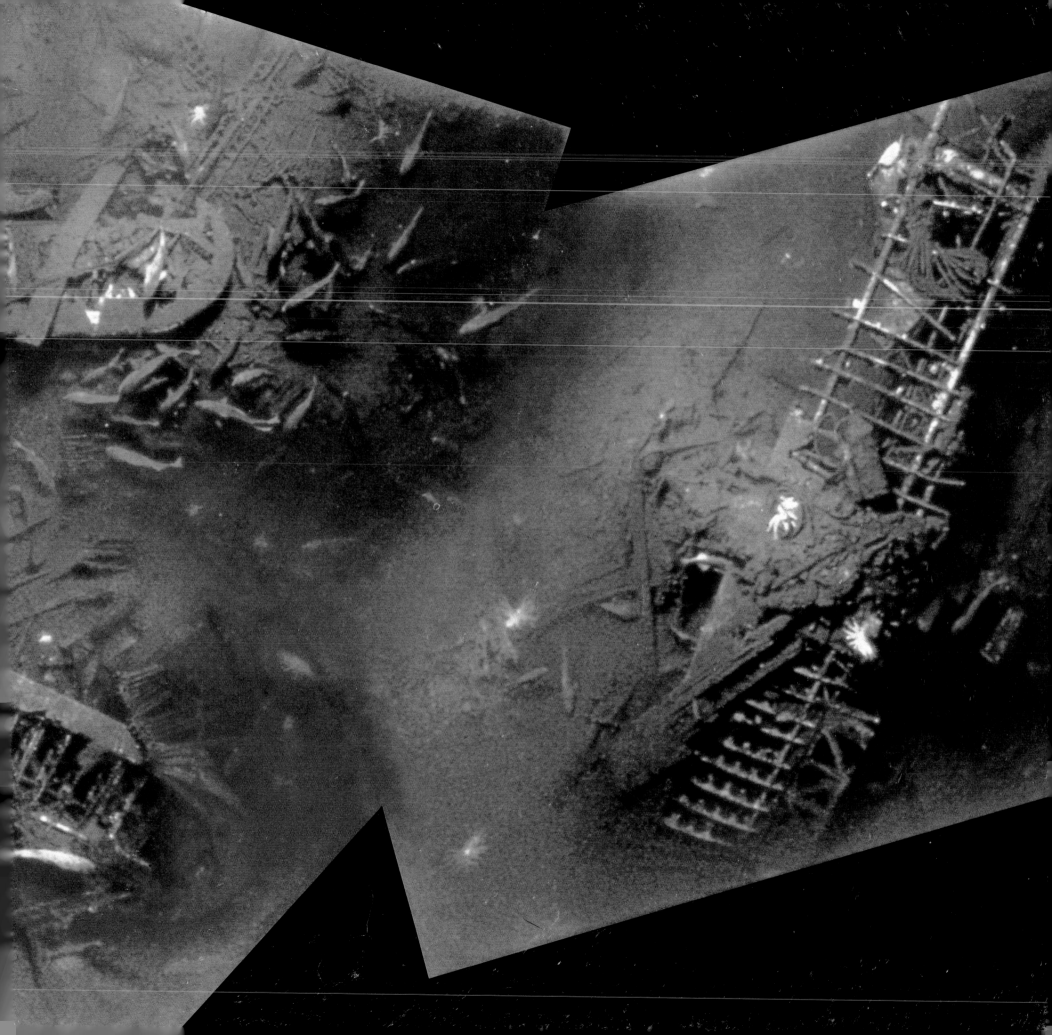

(Above) The Westdeutsche Luftwerbung (WDL) blimp is 196.5 feet long and has a 254,000-cubic-foot gas capacity. (Below) The British-designed Skyship 600 employs ducted propellers that can swivel downward to provide extra thrust during takeoff and landing.

cheaper to construct and less expensive to operate. Part of the saving comes from the fact that these small blimps occupy roughly one-quarter of the volume of the much larger Skyships. (The A-60 Plus has a gas capacity of 68,000 cubic feet.) American Blimp's Jim Thiele, the man behind the Lightship, set out to build a small practical pressure ship for mainly commercial applications. His major innovation was to light his ship from inside—hence the name Lightship. He achieved this by putting a light source inside a transparent gasbag within a translucent envelope. At night the airship becomes a flying lightbulb, dramatically backlighting its advertising message.

Right now the future of airships promises to be a continuation of the post-World War II story. For the most part blimps will carry television cameras and advertising messages and give paying passengers short-hop sight-seeing rides. Other police forces around the world may soon join Tokyo and Seoul in keeping an airship on hand for aerial surveillance, primarily for use during special events. Coast guards and navies may finally decide they do need airships. The British defense ministry recently purchased a Skyship 600 for experimental use, while the United States Coast Guard is considering using blimps for drug surveillance off the Florida coast.

The greatest untapped potential for the airship continues to be its use in remote and inaccessible areas for transport and heavy-lifting. Recently the largest hot-air blimp ever built helped scientists study the rain forest canopy in French Guiana. They used the blimp to transport an inflated raft and a scientific team to a treetop location for extended biological research. Siberia, Alaska and the Canadian Arctic look like natural environments for airship operation, as do inaccessible parts of Africa and South America.

This remotely controlled scale-model was too small to carry even a pilot, but it proved the basic soundness of the Zeppelin NT design. A full-size prototype has yet to be built.

One of the more intriguing recent developments has occurred in Friedrichshafen, where the long-dormant Zeppelin Company has announced plans to build its first airship since the *LZ 130*. The so-called Zeppelin NT (New Technology) combines rigid and nonrigid technology in an unusual hybrid. As with a purebred pressure airship, in the NT, internal pressure maintains the envelope's shape by means of a ballonet—an air balloon inside the hull that expands or contracts to compensate for changing helium pressure. The rigid frame, a series of triangular "rings" attached by three longitudinal girders running the length of the ship, not only adds strength, but can bear all the load in the event of an emergency deflation of one of the three helium-filled cells. It also allows the three vectored-thrust propellers to be mounted away from the control cabin, making for a much quieter ride. The passenger cabin will be able to accommodate up to twelve people or the equivalent payload of scientific equipment. Its

designers claim that, thanks to its vectored propellers and a highly automated mooring system, the NT will need a ground crew of only three, remarkable for an airship of a quarter million cubic feet of gas capacity. A prototype is scheduled to make its first flight in 1997. If this proves successful, there are plans for a larger version of a one million cubic feet.

The story of the dirigible, and above all the rigid airship, has been as much one of what-ifs and might-have-beens as it has of ships built and successfully flown. Had World War I lasted a little longer, the Germans might have built and flown the *L 100*, the size of the *Graf Zeppelin*, as early as 1919. And what if the Allies had been more lenient in their peace terms, allowing the Zeppelin Company to pursue its postwar plans for passenger airship construction? Eckener's "ideal transatlantic airship" might have landed at Lakehurst far sooner, and his dream of an airship fleet might actually have become reality. It was not until the early 1950s, after all, that

airplanes could economically and reliably transport passengers nonstop across the Atlantic. Or imagine the scenario if, in the 1920s, the British had pooled their expertise and built one top-notch prototype passenger ship instead of two flawed craft. Lord Thomson's vision of a fleet of airships linking the far-flung capitals of the British Empire might then have become a reality. And what if the *Akron* and *Macon* had survived their early years? They might well have led to a series of U.S. Navy giants patrolling the far reaches of the Pacific.

Will a rigid airship ever fly again? It seems unlikely. Yet airship enthusiasts—and even more hardheaded airship builders and operators—won't let go of that romantic dream. Bruce Renny, the marketing director of Virgin Lightships, which operates a fleet of four Lightships, has looked into the possibility of a *Hindenburg*-sized rigid airship. Such a ship would be very expensive to build and operate—Renny estimates annual operating costs alone at $1.5 million. But imagine the advertising impact of holding the exclusive rights to put your company's name on an airship the size of the *Hindenburg*—or even bigger. According to a study performed by Donald Woodward and F. Marc Piolenc of the San Diego-based Association of Balloon and Airship Constructors, the largest rigid airship that could fit into Hangar No. 1 at Moffett Field, the former home of

the *Macon*, would be 160 feet in diameter and 975 feet long, with a total capacity of 14.6 million cubic feet.

More likely of realization is Jim Thiele's dream of reenacting the *Graf Zeppelin*'s world flight of 1929—although not in a rigid airship. Thiele envisions finding corporate sponsors to back a pressure ship that could carry thirty to forty passengers and have sufficient range to travel nonstop across the Pacific. This ship would circle the earth to galvanize public support for some great cause—the fight against AIDS perhaps, or the pursuit of world peace. One imagines Hugo Eckener smiling at the thought. The zeppelin may have been conceived as a weapon of war, but Eckener always believed his vast silver-gray skyfish was meant to be a vehicle of peace and co-operation between people and nations.

ON SATURDAY, JULY 9, 1988, A GROUP OF PERHAPS TWO HUNDRED elderly men (and a few women) sat eating a delicious luncheon in the otherwise deserted dining hall on the grounds of Zeppelin Metallwerke in Friedrichshafen, the former location of the Luftschiffbau Zeppelin. (The main company that bears the Zeppelin name today manufactures metal products ranging from aluminum containers to radio antennas.) Seated at one of the

(Opposite) The gates of Zeppelin-Metallwerke in Friedrichshafen, which now occupies the grounds where the Zeppelin Company's big building sheds once stood and where the giant rigids, the *Graf Zeppelin*, the *Hindenburg* and the *Graf Zeppelin II*, were built. (Below) On May 7, 1987, the fiftieth anniversary of the *Hindenburg* disaster, four survivors stand at the Friedrichshafen monument memorializing their fallen comrades: (left to right) Hans König, Werner Franz, Richard Kollmer and Xavier Maier. (Right) Rigid airship veterans mark the count's 152nd birthday at the Luftschiffbau Zeppelin reunion in July 1990.

tables, a much younger man—thirty-eight years of age, to be precise—chatted amiably with his companions. Count Albrecht von Brandenstein-Zeppelin knew everyone in the room by name. As the great-grandson of the inventor of the rigid airship, it fell to him to host this annual reunion of the surviving employees of the old Zeppelin Company, a tradition begun by his late father, Alexander, a few years after the end of World War II. Because of the significance of the anniversary—Count Ferdinand von Zeppelin's 150th birthday had occurred the day before—the turnout was unusually high.

The men at the count's table formed a rather special subgroup within this much larger gathering. They were all surviving crew members of the last three German rigid airships. They had counted many hours flying on the *Graf Zeppelin*, the *Hindenburg* and the *Graf Zeppelin II*. They had jolted up the Rhone into the teeth of a mistral, passed through tropical storms and North Atlantic squalls, floated silently over Rio de Janeiro by moonlight. A few of them had vivid memories of the *Hindenburg*'s last flight: Werner Franz, the mess boy saved by a timely shower of ballast water; Richard Kollmer, one of the four men in the lower fin who, though closest to the origin of the fire, escaped with minor injuries or none at all; Eugen Bentele, on duty in the forward port engine car during the final approach, who was thrown free when the burning ship hit. He regained consciousness in time to run to safety without even singeing his uniform.

Since the 1988 reunion, several members of that elite brotherhood have died. As of this writing, fewer than twenty of those who flew on the giant German airships remain. One of the three men who survived the fiery crash of the *R 101* is still alive. And a handful of veterans of the *Macon* can still talk about their ill-starred aircraft, arguably the most technically advanced rigid airship that ever flew.

None of the surviving zeppeliners met the old count himself, but they all have respectful memories of the generation that carried on after him, of von Schiller, Wittemann, Sammt, Pruss, Lehmann and Eckener. Hugo Eckener in particular lives on as something of an icon, the stern but fair leader, the weather-deciphering genius, the ultimate airshipman.

When the few remaining zeppelin men are gone, and it won't be much longer now, the last living record of the age of the giant airships will have perished. Then there will be no one to recall just how placidly the *Hindenburg* rode through a roiling, angry storm, how Eckener's eyes blazed and his voice barked when a crewman had let him down, what it felt like to rule the skies in the largest flying craft the world has ever known.

ACKNOWLEDGEMENTS

AN ILLUSTRATED HISTORY IS A COMPLEX ENTERPRISE. WHEN THE SUBJECT involves several countries, a timespan of more than two hundred years, an epic cast of characters and a dizzying range of technical details, it becomes more complicated still. This book is as complete and accurate as it is because of the help of large number of individuals, many of them experts in particular aspects of the history of lighter-than-air flight, who willingly contributed their time and expertise to it. I would like to thank them here.

Our historical consultants, Dennis Kromm, John Provan and Henry Cord Meyer vetted both the text and captions and caught many errors of fact or emphasis. As well, Dennis and John spent countless hours providing factual and moral support by fax and phone, lent freely from their private archives and acted as expert picture consultants. John also made numerous translations from the German and proved a warm host and able guide during my research trip to Germany. (John's wife, Helga Kueppers, deserves special mention here for her generous hospitality and unflagging sense of humor.)

Count Albrecht von Brandenstein-Zeppelin, the inventor's great-grandson, welcomed me in his home and family archive.

Kent O'Grady read parts of the text and offered helpful suggestions, as did Don Woodward, editor of *Aerostation* magazine. A special thanks to Don for his unstinting advice on a legion of historical, pictorial and technical questions.

Manfred Bauer helped flesh out the zeppelin career of his father, Captain Heinrich Bauer.

Eugen Bentele, Howard Coulter, Norbert Heiss, Richard Kollmer and George Watson graciously shared their memories of their days flying on rigid airships.

Barry Countryman, author of *R 100 in Canada*, opened his voluminous airship library to me, providing access to many books that would otherwise have been difficult or impossible to procure.

Henry Jay Applegate generously led me on a fascinating tour of the Lakehurst air station and vicinity.

William Althoff, author of *Sky Ships*, shared valuable primary source material relating to the *Hindenburg* story.

Crew chief Paul Adams and pilot Alan Burrows of Virgin Lightships arranged for an unforgettable blimp flight over Berlin.

Keith Fleming and Denis Weil skillfully translated published reminiscences of *Hindenburg* survivors.

J. Gordon Vaeth, author of *Graf Zeppelin* and *Blimps and U-Boats*, helped bring Hugo Eckener and Charles Rosendahl to life and provided much valuable advice and information.

Madison Press Books and Rick Archbold would like to thank the following for providing important help with either text or pictures: Michael Allen, University of Toronto Department of Astronomy; Henry Jay Applegate; Edna Barker; Jud Brandreth, Westinghouse Airships, Inc.; Eric Brothers, The Lighter-Than-Air Society; Dennis Burchmore, Airship Heritage Trust; Barry Countryman; James F. Danner; Lloyd Davis; Martin Dowding; Dr. James Ellern, University of Southern California, Department of Chemistry; Jarvis Frith, Airship Heritage Trust; Nan Froman; Group Captain Peter Garth, Airship Heritage Trust; Roger Gilruth; Albert Hunt, Airship Heritage Trust; Charles Jacobs; Frau E. Koetter, Zeppelin Museum, Zeppelinheim; Robert Kopitzke, The Rosendahl Collection; Sir Peter G. Masefield, author of *To Ride the Storm*; Dr. Wolfgang Meighörner-Schardt, Luftschiffbau Zeppelin GmbH, Friedrichshafen and Zeppelin-Museum Friedrichshafen; Dr. Gertrude Nobile; Kevin Pace, Navy Lakehurst Historical Society; Bruce Renny, Virgin Lightships; Eric Sauder; John Shackelton, Moffett Field Naval Air Station; James Shock; David Simmons, Ohio Historical Society; Werner Strumann; Tara the Cat; Jim Thiele, American Blimp Corporation; Richard Van Treuren; Hepburn Walker, Jr.; Gordon S. Wiley; Mickey Wittman and Edward Ogden, Goodyear Tire and Rubber Company.

Dennis Kromm, Henry Cord Meyer and John Provan would like to thank Dr. Douglas H. Robinson, dean of American airship historians. His scholarship, dedication and high standards of historical accuracy have been our inspiration.

PHOTOGRAPH AND ILLUSTRATION CREDITS

Every effort has been made to correctly attribute all material reproduced in this book. If any errors have unwittingly occurred, we will be happy to correct them in future editions.

The passage on page 1 is by the anonymous author of *Even the Birds*, copyright 1934, U.S. Naval Institute.

Front cover painting by Ken Marschall
Back cover paintings by Ken Marschall

Endpapers Bilderdienst Süddeutscher Verlag
1   Bildarchiv Preussischer Kulturbesitz
2–3 Painting by Ken Marschall
5   Collection of Dennis Kromm
6–7 Ullstein Bilderdienst
8   John Provan: Luftschiff Zeppelin Collection
9   Painting by Ken Marschall, Collection of Dennis Kromm

CHAPTER ONE

10 Courtesy Minnesota Historical Society
11 (Left) Library of Congress
    (Top right) Library of Congress
    (Middle right) Courtesy Minnesota Historical Society
    (Bottom right) Library of Congress
12 The Bridgeman Art Library
13 (Top) Musée de l'Air, Paris
    (Bottom left, middle and right) Mary Evans Picture Library
14 Mary Evans Picture Library
16 Mary Evans Picture Library
17 The Hulton Deutsch Collection
18 Bildarchiv Preussischer Kulturbesitz
19 (Top) John Provan: Luftschiff Zeppelin Collection
    (Bottom) The LTA Society Collection, University of Akron Archives
20 (Top, middle and bottom left) The Hulton Deutsch Collection
    (Right) Mary Evans Picture Library
21 Mary Evans Picture Library
22 Tourist Information Office, Friedrichshafen
    (Inset) The LTA Society Collection, University of Akron Archives
23 (Top and bottom left) Luftschiffbau Zeppelin GmbH
    (Right) The LTA Society Collection, University of Akron Archives
24 Mary Evans Picture Library
25 Illustration by Jack McMaster
26–27 Luftschiffbau Zeppelin GmbH
28 Zeno Diemer, *Aufsteig des LZ 1908 in der Buch von Manzell bei Friedrichshafen*. Zeppelin-Museum Friedrichshafen
29 (Left) The LTA Society Collection, University of Akron Archives
    (Right) Luftschiffbau Zeppelin GmbH
30 (Parseval airship) Mary Evans Picture Library
    (August von Parseval portrait) Ullstein Bilderdienst
    (All others) Bettmann
31 Mary Evans Picture Library
32 (Top and bottom left) Luftschiffbau Zeppelin GmbH
    (Top middle) John Provan: Luftschiff Zeppelin Collection
    (Top right) Bilderdienst Süddeutscher Verlag
    (Bottom right) Bettmann
33 Bilderdienst Süddeutscher Verlag
34 (Top) Bildarchiv Preussischer Kulturbesitz
    (Bottom left) Ullstein Bilderdienst
    (Bottom right) Luftschiffbau Zeppelin GmbH
35 (Top) Ullstein Bilderdienst
    (Middle) Collection of Dr. Douglas Robinson
    (Bottom) Bildarchiv Preussischer Kulturbesitz

CHAPTER TWO

36–37 Zeno Diemer, *Luftschiff über Fridrichshaven um 1915/18*. Zeppelin-Museum Friedrichshafen
37 Marine-Luftschiffer-Kameradschaft
38 Luftschiffbau Zeppelin GmbH
39 Bilderdienst Süddeutscher Verlag
40 (Paper seal) Collection of Charles Jacobs
    (Match box and cartoon) John Provan: Luftschiff Zeppelin Collection
41 Mary Evans Picture Library
42–43 Bildarchiv Preussischer Kulturbesitz
43 (Top) Bildarchiv Preussischer Kulturbesitz
    (Bottom left) John Provan: Luftschiff Zeppelin Collection
    (Bottom middle and right) The Robert Hunt Library
44 (Left) Mary Evans Picture Library
    (Right) John Provan: Luftschiff Zeppelin Collection
45 (Left) Colonel Richard Gimbel Aeronautical History Collection, USAF Academy Library
    (Top and bottom right) The Robert Hunt Library
46 (All) Luftschiffbau Zeppelin GmbH
47 (Top) Imperial War Museum
    (Bottom) Mary Evans Picture Library
48 (Airship) Bilderdienst Süddeutscher Verlag
    (Portrait of Johann Schütte) Ullstein Bilderdienst
49 (All) Mary Evans Picture Library
50–51 The Hulton Deutsch Collection
51 (Insets left and right) Luftschiffbau Zeppelin GmbH
52 (All) Imperial War Museum
52–53 Imperial War Museum
54 Luftschiffbau Zeppelin GmbH
55 Luftschiffbau Zeppelin GmbH

CHAPTER THREE

56–57 Bilderdienst Süddeutscher Verlag
58 John Provan: Luftschiff Zeppelin Collection
59 Collection of Dr. Douglas Robinson
    (Inset) Collection of Charles Jacobs
60–61 Imperial War Museum
61 U.S. Naval Historical Center

BIBLIOGRAPHY

Adelt, Leonhard. "The Last Trip of the *Hindenburg*," *Reader's Digest*, November 1937.

Althoff, William F. *Sky Ships: A History of the Airship in the United States Navy*. New York: Orion Books, 1990.

Amundsen, Roald, and Lincoln Ellsworth. *First Crossing of the Polar Sea*. New York: George H. Doran Company, 1927.

Bentele, Eugen. *The Story of a Zeppelin Mechanic: My Flights, 1931-1938*. Friedrichshafen, Germany: Zeppelin-Museum, 1992.

Botting, Douglas, and the editors of Time-Life Books. *The Giant Airships*. Alexandria, Virginia: Time-Life Books, 1981.

Brooks, Peter W. *Zeppelin: Rigid Airships, 1893-1940*. London: Putnam Aeronautical Books, 1992.

Buttlar-Brandenfels, Treusch von. *Zeppelins over England*. New York: Harcourt, Brace & Company, 1932.

Countryman, Barry. *R 100 in Canada*. Erin, Ontario: The Boston Mills Press, 1982.

Deighton, Len, and Arnold Schwartzman. *Airshipwreck*. New York: Holt, Rinehart & Winston, 1978.

Deutsche Zeppelin-Reederei. *Airship Voyages Made Easy*, n.d.

Dick, Harold G., with Douglas H. Robinson. *The Golden Age of the Great Passenger Airships: Graf Zeppelin & Hindenburg*. Washington, D.C.: Smithsonian Institution Press, 1985.

Eckener, Hugo. *Count Zeppelin: The Man and His Work*. Translated by Leigh Farnell. London: Massie Publishing Company, 1938.

———. *My Zeppelins*. Translated by Douglas H. Robinson. London: Putnam & Company, 1958.

The Editors of American Heritage Magazine. *The American Heritage History of Flight*. New York: American Heritage Publishing Company, 1962.

Goldsmith, Margaret. *Zeppelin: A Biography*. New York: William Morrow & Company, 1931.

Higham, Robin. *The British Rigid Airship, 1908-1931*. London: G. T. Foulis & Company, Ltd., 1961.

Hinrichs, Hans. "My *Hindenburg* Log," *Modern Brewer*, June 1936.

Hoehling, A. A. *Who Destroyed the Hindenburg?* Boston: Little, Brown & Company, 1962.

"Honors to Dr. Hugo Eckener: The First Airship Flight around the World." *The National Geographic Magazine*, June 1930.

Hook, Thom. *Shenandoah Saga*. Annapolis, Maryland: Air Show Publishers, 1973.

———. *Sky Ship: The Akron Era*. Annapolis, Maryland: Air Show Publishers, 1976.

Kromm, Dennis. "Homecoming." Article about *Hindenburg* last-flight passenger Burtis J. Dolan, published in the COMPEX 1987 directory.

Leasor, James. *The Millionth Chance: The Story of the R.101*. New York: Reynal & Company, 1957.

Lehmann, Ernst A. *Zeppelin: The Story of Lighter-than-air Craft*. New York: Longmans, Green & Company, 1937.

Lehmann, Ernst A., and Howard Mingos. *The Zeppelins: The Development of the Airship, with the Story of the Zeppelin Air Raids in the World War*. New York: J. H. Sears & Company, 1927.

Lochner, Louis P. "Aboard the Airship *Hindenburg*: Louis P. Lochner's Diary of Its Maiden Flight to the United States." *Wisconsin Magazine of History* 49, no. 2, Winter 1965-66.

Maitland, E. M. *The Log of H.M.A. R 34*. London: Hodder & Stoughton, 1920.

Marben, Rolf. *Zeppelin Adventures*. London: John Hamilton, Ltd., 1931.

Masefield, Sir Peter G. *To Ride the Storm: The Story of the Airship R.101*. London: William Kimber & Company, Ltd., 1982.

Mather, Margaret G. "I Was on the *Hindenburg*." *Harper's*, November 1937.

Meager, George. *My Airship Flights: 1915-1930*. London: William Kimber & Company, Ltd., 1970.

Medem, W.E. von. *Kabinenjunge Werner Franz vom Luftschiff Hindenburg*. Berlin: Franz Schneider Verlag, 1938.

Meyer, Henry Cord. *Airshipmen, Businessmen and Politics, 1890-1940*. Washington, D.C.: Smithsonian Institution Press, 1991.

Miller, Webb. "Two 27-Hour Days." In *I Found No Peace: The Journal of a Foreign Correspondent*. New York: Simon & Schuster, 1936.

Mooney, Michael. *The Hindenburg*. New York: Dodd, Mead & Company, 1972.

Nielsen, Thor. *The Zeppelin Story*. London: Allan Wingate Ltd., 1955.

Nobile, Umberto. *My Five Years with Soviet Airships*. Akron, Ohio: The Lighter-Than-Air Society, 1987.

———. *My Polar Flights: An Account of the Voyages of Airships Italia & Norge*. New York: G. P. Putnam's Sons, 1961.

———. *With Italia to the Pole*. London: George Allen & Unwin, 1930.

Payne, Lee. *Lighter than Air: An Illustrated History of the Airship*. New York: Orion Books, 1991.

Provan, John. "The German Airship in World War One." Privately published thesis.

———. "Count Zeppelin: A System Builder. The Zeppelin Company and its Subsidiaries." Privately published monograph.

———. "Clara Adams." Unpublished pamphlet.

———. "Rhein-Main." Unpublished pamphlet.

Rimell, Raymond Laurence. *Zeppelin! A Battle for Air Supremacy in World War I*. London: Conway Maritime Press, Ltd., 1984.

Robinson, Douglas H. *Giants in the Sky: A History of the Rigid Airship*. Seattle: University of Washington Press, 1973.

———. *The LZ 129 Hindenburg*. Famous Aircraft Series. Dallas, Texas: Morgan Aviation Books, 1964.

———. *The Zeppelin in Combat: A History of the German Naval Airship Division, 1912-1918*. Sun Valley, California: John W. Caler Company, 1966.

———. "*Hindenburg* Retrospect," *American Aviation Historical Society Journal*, Spring 1960.

Rosendahl, Charles. *Up Ship*. New York: Dodd, Mead & Company, 1931.

———. *What About the Airship? The Challenge to the United States*. New York: Charles Scribner's Sons, 1938.

Sammt, Albert. *Mein Leben für den Zeppelin*. Verlag Pestalozzi Kinderdorf Wahlwies, n.d.

Santos-Dumont, Alberto. *My Air-Ships: The Story of My Life*. New York: Dover Publications, 1973.

Schiller, Hans von. *Zeppelin: Wegbereiter des Weltluftverkehrs*. Bad Godesberg, Germany: Kirschbaum Verlag, 1967.

Shute, Nevil. *Slide Rule*. New York: William Morrow & Company, 1954.

Smith, Richard K. *The Airships Akron & Macon*. Annapolis, Maryland: United States Naval Institute, 1965.

Toland, John. *The Great Dirigibles: Their Triumphs and Disasters*. New York: Dover Publications, 1972.

Vaeth, J. Gordon. *Blimps & U-Boats: U.S. Navy Airships in the Battle of the Atlantic*. Annapolis, Maryland: United States Naval Institute, 1992.

———. *Graf Zeppelin: The Adventures of an Aerial Globetrotter*. New York: Harper & Brothers, 1958.

———. "What Happened to the *Hindenburg*?" *Weatherwise*, December 1990.

Van Orman, Ward T. *Wizard of the Winds*. St. Cloud, Minnesota: North Star Press, 1978.

Ventry, Lord, and Eugène M. Kolesnik. *Jane's Pocket Book of Airships*. Macmillan Publishing Company, 1977.

Wellman, Walter. *The Aerial Age*. New York: A. R. Keller & Company, 1911.

Wiegand, Karl H. von, and Lady Drummond Hay. *The First Trans-Oceanic Voyage of a Commercial Air-Liner*. King Features Syndicate, 1928.

NEWSPAPERS AND MAGAZINES

All issues of *Buoyant Flight*, published by The Lighter-Than-Air Society (1436 Triplett Blvd., Akron, Ohio 44306, U.S.A.) were an invaluable resource.

LIGHTER-THAN-AIR ORGANIZATIONS

The Airship Association, 6 Kings Road, Cheriton, Folkestone, Kent, CT20 3LG England

Airship Heritage Trust (formerly Friends of the Cardington Airship Station/FOCAS), Windsor Loft, 75 Albany Road, Old Windsor, Berkshire, SL4 2QD England

Arbeitsgemeinschaft Zeppelinpost, Postfach 42, 65598 Dornburg, Germany

Association of Balloon and Airship Constructors, P.O. Box 90864, San Diego, California 92169, U.S.A.

British Balloon and Airship Club, 7 Llewellyn Road, Penllergaer, Swansea SA4 1BB, England

Freundeskreis Luftschiffbau Schütte-Lanz, Harmsweg 2, 23758 Oldenburg, Germany

Freundeskreis zur Förderung des Zeppelin Museum, Postfach 1448, 88004 Friedrichshafen, Germany

Lighter-Than-Air Institute, P.O. Box 51-182, Auckland 6, New Zealand

Lighter-Than-Air Society, 1436 Triplett Blvd., Akron, Ohio 44306, U.S.A.

Marine-Luftschiffer-Kameradschaft, Ernst Kabel Stieg 5a, 22087 Hamburg, Germany

Moffett Field Historical Society, P.O. Box 16, Moffett Field, California 94035-0016, U.S.A.

Naval Airship Association, 2547 Hyde Park Rd., Jacksonville, Florida 32210, U.S.A.

Navy Lakehurst Historical Society, P.O. Box 328, Lakehurst, New Jersey 08733, U.S.A.

Zeppelin Collectors Club, P.O. Box A3843, Chicago, Illinois 60690-3843, U.S.A.

Zeppelin-Kameradschaft Zeppelinheim, e.V., Kapitän-Lehmann-Strasse 2, 63263 Neu-Isenburg/Zeppelinheim, Germany

Zeppelin-Gruppe Tondern, Kelkheimer Str. 29a, 65779 Kelkheim, Germany

MUSEUMS

Albert Sammt Zeppelin Museum, 97996 Niederstetten, Germany

Deutsches Museum, Museumsinsel 1, 80538 Munich, Germany

Experimental Aircraft Association Museum, 3000 Poberezny Rd., Wittman Field, Oshkosh, Wisconsin 54903, U.S.A.

Imperial War Museum, Lambeth Road, London SE1 6HZ, England

Luftfahrthistorische Sammlung, Frankfurt International Airport, 60547 Frankfurt, Germany

Luftschiffhafen Potsdam Museum, LBS, Luftschiffhafen 1, 14471 Potsdam, Germany

Luftschiffhafen Tønder Museum, Kongevejen 55, 6270 Tønder, Denmark

Marine Luftschiff Museum, Oberweg 65, 27637 Nordholz, Germany

Musée de l'Air et de l'Espace, Aéroport du Bourget, BP 173, Le Bourget 93352, France

Museum of Flight, East Fortune Airfield, North Berwick, EH39 5LF, Scotland

Museum of the History of Italian Military Aviation, Aeroporto di Vigna di Valle, 00062 Vigna di Valle, Italy

National Air and Space Museum, Smithsonian Institution, 7th St. & Independence Ave. SW., Washington, D.C. 20560, U.S.A.

National Museum of Naval Aviation, 1750 Radford Blvd., Pensacola, Florida 32508-5402, U.S.A.

San Diego Aerospace Museum, 2001 Pan American Plaza, Balboa Park, San Diego, California 92101, U.S.A.

Science Museum, Exhibition Road, South Kensington, London SW7 5NH, England

Swiss Transport Museum, Verkehrshaus der Schweiz, Lido Str. 5 CH-6006 Luzern, Switzerland

The World of Rubber, 1144 East Market St., Akron, Ohio 44316, U.S.A.

World War II Airship Museum, 4000 Blimp Blvd., Tillamook, Oregon 97141, U.S.A.

Zeppelin Museum, Kapitän-Lehmann-Str. 2, 63263 Neu-Isenburg, Germany

Zeppelin-Museum Friedrichshafen, Adenauerplatz 1, 88045 Friedrichshafen, Germany.

Zeppelin-Museum Heinz Urban, Schloßplatz 8, 88709 Meersburg, Germany

INDEX

DESIGN, TYPOGRAPHY AND ART DIRECTION: Gordon Sibley Design Inc.

EDITORIAL DIRECTOR: Hugh M. Brewster

PROJECT EDITOR: Mireille Majoor

COPY EDITOR: Shelley Tanaka

PRODUCTION DIRECTOR: Susan Barrable

PRODUCTION CO-ORDINATOR: Donna Chong

ORIGINAL PAINTINGS: Wes Lowe, Ken Marschall

MAPS AND DIAGRAMS: Donna Gordon, Jack McMaster

COLOR SEPARATION: Colour Technologies

PRINTING AND BINDING: Sfera/Garzanti

HINDENBURG: AN ILLUSTRATED HISTORY
was produced by Madison Press Books
under the direction of Albert E. Cummings